John Boyko

INTO THE
HURRICANE
ATTACKING SOCIALISM
AND THE CCF

J. GORDON SHILLINGFORD
PUBLISHING INC

INTO THE
HURRICANE

ATTACKING SOCIALISM
AND THE CCF

Into the Hurricane: Attacking Socialism and the CCF
First published 2006 by
J. Gordon Shillingford Publishing Inc.
©2006 John Boyko

Cover design by Doowah Design Inc.
Interior design by Relish Design Studio Ltd.
Author photo by Simon Spivey
Printed and bound in Canada

We acknowledge the financial support of the Manitoba Arts Council,
The Canada Council for the Arts and the Government of Canada through
the Book Publishing Industry Development Program (BPIDP) for our
publishing program.

Library and Archives Canada Cataloguing in Publication

Boyko, John, 1957-
            Into the hurricane: attacking socialism and the CCF / John Boyko.

Includes bibliographical references and index.
ISBN 1-897289-09-X

1. Co-operative Commonwealth Federation. 2. Socialism-Canada.
3. Canada-Politics and government-20th century. I. Title.

JL197.N4B69 2006   324.27107   C2006-903946-1

J. Gordon Shillingford Publishing
P.O. Box 86, RPO Corydon Avenue, Winnipeg, MB Canada R3M 3S3

ACKNOWLEDGEMENTS

I would like to thank Jim Struthers and Jim Driscoll of Trent University and Laurel Sefton MacDowell of York University, who read early versions of the manuscript and made many helpful suggestions. A special thank you is owed to Joan Sangster of Trent University whose help throughout the research and writing process was invaluable.

Gordon Shillingford and his staff were professional in their final polishing and preparation of the manuscript and the good people at the Trent University Library in Peterborough and the National Library and Archives in Ottawa were patient and exceptionally helpful.

Most importantly, over the years Sue Boyko has seen me through many projects and her support and encouragement with this one was absolute. This book is dedicated to Sue.

TABLE OF CONTENTS

INTRODUCTION:
A STORM BORN OF FEAR

New ideas are always ruthlessly attacked by those with the most to lose.

In 2004, the Canadian Broadcasting Corporation undertook a process to determine who should be lauded as the "Greatest Canadian." The process had more to do with pop culture and television ratings than intellectual debate, but it was nonetheless illuminating to see Tommy Douglas declared the Greatest Canadian. Douglas was touted on the state-owned television network as the father of medicare who stayed true to his socialist roots. It was fascinating to see that medicare, the most socialist of ideas, had by 2004 become so entwined into the fabric of Canada's political culture that its most important proponent had reached an iconic status among the ordinary Canadians who participated in the CBC selection process.

One was left wondering if medicare's place in the Canadian ethos and Douglas' place in Canada's collective popular memory was such that the terror that socialist ideas had caused only decades before had somehow been forgotten. What had happened to the idea that the Cooperative Commonwealth Federation, the political party in which Tommy Douglas had risen to prominence, needed to be destroyed because its socialist ideas would wreck all that was great about Canada? Was the CBC's *The Greatest Canadian* exercise an indication that an ideological shift had silently and insidiously occurred and that socialism and those who promoted it were no longer to be attacked as treasonous, anti-Christian demagogues but, rather, promoted as heroes?

Ideology has always played an important role in delineating the debates that have shaped Canada's development. Ideologies have power in that they provide values that influence political and economic policy decisions while legitimizing social beliefs, structures, and relationships. They provide strategies and tactics to improve society for everyone's best interest or to deceive in order to perpetuate or win dominance over others.[1]

For the first half century of Canada's development, the young nation's party system was dominated by the ideas inherent in liberal democracy and industrial capitalism. That is, Canadians generally voted for political parties that celebrated John Locke's notions of political freedom and individual self-determination as expressed through the power of the ballot while living comfortably with Thomas Hobbes' suspicions of that freedom as seen in the constitutional monarchy and appointed Senate. So too, Canadians generally endorsed parties that supported notions of opportunity for all and prosperity for the country as tied to an adherence to the economic theories of Adam Smith, while accepting that a player in the competitive marketplace would be the very visible hand of the federal government establishing tariffs, enforcing regulations, and offering loans and other support to particular industries and regions. Seymour Lipset, an American sociologist, argued that these ideas were the natural manifestations of a society that was predominantly traditional, hierarchical, and elitist. It was a society where deference to authority was the norm.[2]

Contrary ideas were raised by various political, labour, and societal groups and were acted upon, perhaps most explicitly, on the streets of Winnipeg in 1919. However, alternative ideas seemed to be lost in the overwhelming adherence to the security, optimism, and hope offered by Canada's dominant ideology. As political theorist C.B. Macpherson has suggested, Canada's dominant ideology came to justify the relationships between societal groups and between individuals with respect to the protection of private property, while also reflecting society's most cherished values, including, first and foremost, freedom. These relationships and values were linked through ideas regarding the importance of duty, family, tradition, competitive individualism, and anti-statism. The ideologically based values and relationships came to be accepted by most as essential to the country's well-being and hope for the future. It can thus be argued that, at the country's birth and in its early years, Canada's dominant ideology was so powerful as to define not just the views of competing political parties, or the structures of its government and economy, but the nature of its social fabric.[3]

3

Just over sixty years after its creation, the country fell into the worst economic crisis of its history. Before the ravages of that experience were over, Canada entered its most devastating war. Many people came to question Canada's guiding ideology in the wake of the enormous economic, political, and social prices exacted by the Depression and the Second World War: If the economy was broken, then why retain faith in capitalism? If conscription could be imposed and companies and workers dictated to by the state, then what had happened to liberal democracy? As Leon Fink noted with respect to the similar American situation, there appeared to be a "disparity between national ideological expectations and material realities."[4] Maybe the populists and radicals had something valuable to say after all.

Among the voices in the wilderness were those that, in 1932, came together in Calgary to create the Cooperative Commonwealth Federation. It began as a loose and uneasy coalition of farmers, workers, and eastern social-democratic intellectuals. Its founding document, the Regina Manifesto, was an amalgam of Social Gospel dreams, British Fabian ideas, Prairie populist sentiment, labourite beliefs, and democratic socialist plans. It expressed the optimism that a society could be created that was based not on the industrial capitalist notion of perpetual inequality but, rather, upon equity, fairness, and community. Gradual, negotiated, democratic change was seen as the means to create the new society. The state, through public ownership and other means, would play an active and powerful role in such a society. The current economic system was the enemy of "the people" —the farmers, industrial workers, and general middle class—and it needed to be destroyed in order to initiate the process of creating the new society. The Regina Manifesto was blunt in this regard, stating, "No CCF government will rest content until it has eradicated capitalism."[5]

The CCF's founding leader was a slight, bearded, Methodist minister named James Shaver Woodsworth. His political experience as a Labour Member of Parliament, his activist past as a leader of the Winnipeg General Strike, his soft-spoken charisma, and the respect he earned from political friends and foes, was indispensable to the party's early years. He has been called a saint, a prophet, and a giant. While chairing a strategy planning meeting in March 1940, Woodsworth suffered a stroke and fell onto the shoulder of M.J. Coldwell. Major James Coldwell assumed the leadership of the party that day, although his leadership was not made official until

Woodsworth's death two years later. Coldwell shared Woodsworth's Winnipeg upbringing and his work ethic, but not his charisma; his determination, but not his passion. People worked for Woodsworth but with Coldwell. His leadership saw the CCF through the rise and fall of the party through the tumultuous 1940s.

The CCF was not Canada's first or only left-wing or socialist party, but it was the most successful in terms of membership, influence, and electoral success. It offered something the traditional Liberal and Conservative parties did not and could not. Despite the catastrophic effects of the Depression and the war, the Liberals and Conservatives were doing as they had always done: simply offering voters different shadings of the same option. Their policies were similar because they did not challenge the ideological base upon which they both rested, namely a basic acceptance of capitalism.[6] The Regina Manifesto, with its pledge to destroy capitalism, was different. The CCF offered not just a change in policies but a change in the economic foundation of the country.

As the CCF began to make political noise, however, the traditional parties reacted as they often do in such circumstances and brokered new initiatives to try to reduce the volume. Prime Minister William Lyon Mackenzie King's cynical use of brokerage politics is revealed in a 1943 diary note regarding his pride in a speech he had made regarding future legislation. He wrote, "I have succeeded in making declarations that will improve the lot of…farmers and working people… I think I have cut the ground in large part from the CCF."[7] King had used his wiles to end the Progressive Party challenge, and the CCF appeared to be headed toward a similar fate.

In this way, the CCF influenced policy initiatives, but it seemed unable to persuade the traditional parties or enough votes to question their ideological foundations. Accordingly, as voters alternated between electing Liberal and Conservative governments, little fundamentally changed. As social scientist Walter Young has noted of this pattern, using a contemporary analogy, "You can switch your allegiance from the Argos to the Rough Riders and not question your faith in football."[8] In other words, despite CCF influence in social policy, those who voted for Liberal or Progressive Conservative candidates and, more importantly, the businesses, newspapers, and organizations that supported the parties, had not questioned their faith in Canada's dominant ideology.

The CCF struggled to avoid the fate of the short-lived Progressive Party, however, and continued to offer something more profound and uncommon in that it tried to persuade people to question well-worn ideological assumptions. Slowly, that offer seemed to become worthy of consideration by more Canadians, and to prove resistant to the time-honoured tactics of the Liberals and Conservatives. In its first two federal elections, in 1935 and 1940, the CCF had won only 7 and 8 seats, with 8.7% and 8.5% of the popular vote respectively. However, from 1943 to 1945, the CCF enjoyed several smaller victories: a CCF candidate defeated former Prime Minister Arthur Meighen in an Ontario by-election; it formed the government in Saskatchewan; it won 43 seats and formed the official opposition in Ontario; and, in the first nationally conducted popularity poll assessing support for political parties, it found itself standing first. In the 1945 federal election, the party moved from 8 to 28 seats and to 15.6% of the popular vote. It appeared that the 816,259 Canadians who voted for the CCF were questioning their faith in the country's dominant ideology and in the traditional parties that supported it. They were, perhaps, indicating by their votes a willingness to consider a restructuring of their country according to new core beliefs. Canada had reached an ideological turning point.

However, a turn would not be made. In the 1949 federal election, the CCF dropped to 13.4% of the popular vote and only 13 seats. In the 1953 election, due to strong support in a few urban ridings, the party appeared to rebound, winning 23 seats; but its popular vote revealed a party in decline as it fell to 11.3%. In the last election the party contested, in 1958, it was reduced to an 8-seat rump and only 9.5% of the popular vote (see appendix 1). In the late 1950s, a process began that led to the party's end and phoenix-like resurrection, first as the New Party; then, in 1961, as the New Democratic Party.

The CCF had failed to become a major electoral choice for Canadians. That failure can be interpreted in many ways. One of those ways is as the outcome of an ideological debate between those who wished to maintain the ideological status quo and those who were attempting to present a new option. While the debate was played out over the 28 years of the party's existence, the spike in the party's electoral support suggests that the period from 1943 to 1949 was a critical juncture. The party gained momentum, then lost it. The CCF's national secretary, David Lewis, acknowledged that fact in his memoirs, observing, "The CCF advance was not only arrested, it was pushed back, and the party never regained the momentum it enjoyed in the early war years."[9] To understand that pivotal time one must first see that the ideological debate did not happen in a vacuum but rather was part of a larger struggle that was taking place in many countries.

The socialist alternative had begun in most countries with Karl Marx's interpretation of industrial capitalism and had been developed through the work of the International Working Men's Association in 1864 and, more importantly, the Second International in 1889. It was at the Second International that German socialist Eduard Bernstein had proposed, to the consternation of revolutionary socialists, that ideological goals could be met through elected governments gradually enacting socialist policies. While his revisionism was defeated at the conference, many socialist parties developed by adapting themselves to that idea and to their particular circumstances. Significant strides were made through revisionist democratic socialism in France, Germany, New Zealand, and Australia. To place the Canadian debate in an international context, it is instructive to glance briefly at related events in Great Britain and the United States. They are significant because they have been influential in terms of their historical, cultural, and economic ties to Canada and because one presents a case where socialism succeeded and the other where it failed.

Socialist discourse and the creation of socialist organizations in the United States began in the late 1800s. The Socialist Labor Party was created in New York City in 1877, and 20 years later, Eugene Debs created the Social Democracy Party of America. In 1901, the two parties combined to form the Socialist Party of America. At its peak, the party won 6% of the popular vote in the 1912 presidential election with Debs as its flag-bearer. Although the party did not officially dissolve until 1964, it had ceased to be of political importance, ironically, just as the Depression began to destroy the American economy in the early 1930s.

There is substantial scholarship addressing the failure of socialism in America, beginning with the seminal work by German economist and social activist Werner Sombart in 1905. He wrote that there was something unique about the United States that had led it to become the only industrialized country in the world that had not seen the rise of a credible socialist party. In his examination of the reasons for this uniqueness, he introduced the idea of American exceptionalism, which has informed the scholarship regarding American socialism ever since.

The scholarship has addressed three overlapping factors regarding that exceptionalism. First is the idea, as seen in the Declaration of Independence and the Constitution, that America was born of a desire to limit the size and scope of government. This visceral suspicion of the state was further seen in the celebration of rugged individualism in popular culture. The idea was supported by churches that rejected state influence in religious matters. Thus, in political, cultural, and spiritual realms, Americans were taught that the collectivist, statist ideas that seemed to be at the heart of socialism were to be rejected as anti-Christian and anti-American.

The effects of race, class, and gender have also been questioned with respect to the creation and perpetuation of American exceptionalism. It has been posited that American social democrats failed to win the hearts of Americans because its leaders embraced and acted according to early-20th-century racism and nativism. Their efforts were further compromised by the weakness or failure of organized labour organizations that were supportive of, or at least sympathetic to, social-democratic ideas and the success of others, such as the American Federation of Labor, that opposed those ideas in their promotion of the Gomperist notion of accommodating capitalists and the capitalist system. Further, though the Socialist Party of America had many women supporters and passed motions that spoke to the equality of the sexes, it did little to promote suffrage or other issues important to women, and thus missed an opportunity to win the support of half the population.

A third factor that has been a theme in much of the scholarship involves the significance of the American political structure. The evolution of the American two-party system and the emphasis placed on the election of a president denies third parties the ability to enjoy electoral success. The system has allowed the two mainstream parties to successfully play brokerage politics while ensuring that the ideological ideas of the elite remain predominant in both parties and in the country.

Beyond these ideas, one must acknowledge the importance of actions that were undertaken to crush the Socialist Party of America and its leaders. The church and organized labour played roles in these actions, but the government was the primary force and acted ruthlessly. In 1917, the Espionage and Sedition Acts allowed the banning of socialist party newspapers, the raiding of offices, the breaking up of meetings, and the arrest of party leaders. Eugene Debs served ten years in prison. The Socialist Party was demoralized, and any social-democratic ideas still palatable to the American electorate were snapped up by the Democratic Party.

Great Britain's experience with the socialist alternative has been quite different. The British Labour Party achieved its first electoral success with the formation of a minority government in January 1924. The party would be in and out of power throughout the twentieth century, and its influence was seen in the elimination of the Liberal Party and in the transformation of Great Britain into a society that reflected social-democratic values. Even the advent of Thatcherism in the 1980s and Tony Blair's Third Way in the 1990s did not completely eliminate all that the Labour Party and its influence had wrought.

The socialist alternative successfully presented by the British Labour Party to the electorate in that first victory came from many strands and from a long history. Scholarship addressing that success was most prolific following the failures of the Labour Party in the early 1930s and late 1970s. Much of that scholarship has been written from a leftist and Marxist perspective and has tended to see the march toward a socialist society as a struggle for the ideal and a fight against the forces of elitism, oppression, and greed.[10] Important in the scholarship is the idea that Britain, as the birthplace of the Industrial Revolution, and due to a number of other factors, has possessed a working-class consciousness for a long time. British historian E.P. Thompson, in his seminal work, *The Making of the English Working Class*, argued that this class-consciousness was present in the early guilds and translated easily into the organized labour movement of the late 19th century and that the Labour Party grew from these roots.

This class-consciousness allowed early socialist groups, such as the Independent Labour Party, to legitimately claim to be the voice of the working class, replacing the Liberal/Labour coalitions of the day. The British Labour Party proved to be skilful in organizing the labour vote by doing what its American and Canadian counterparts did not: allowing workers to join the party as individuals rather than inviting unions to join as entities. The power of the link between organized labour, working people, and the Labour Party was reflected in the fact that, by 1915, the party boasted 2.1 million members, of which only 33,000 were not also union members.[11]

There is a consensus in the scholarship that the party was helped by the broadening of the franchise in the late 1800s, which had extended the vote to more and more working people, and that the British parliamentary system allowed for the success of individual Labour candidates and the eventual formation of the minority Labour government. Further, the party was helped by its support of Irish Home Rule, which led Irish voters to its ranks as nationalists, union members, and grateful Catholics. The Catholic Church did not seek to persuade its adherents to see the socialism of the Labour Party as anti-Christian, as happened in Canada and the United States. Important, too, is the fact that, though there were many people and groups that argued vehemently against the party and its increasingly popular ideas, there was not the same organized movement against the party and its leaders as was seen in Canada and the United States.

In Canada, despite the CCF's relatively short history, a great deal of scholarship has been devoted to the party and its demise. Much of the work has been celebratory and biographical. The careers of the party's leaders have been addressed, some of whom made valuable contributions with their memoirs and musings. The celebratory and biographical works are similar in that, to varying degrees, the efforts of the party's leaders and workers are applauded, the party's ideological views defended, and its failure to excite more of the electorate bemoaned. All praise the influence that the party managed to exert in bringing working-class issues to the fore and social legislation to fruition. These conclusions have been supported by scholars such as Gad Horowitz, Alan Cairns, and Jack Granatstein, all of whom acknowledged the influence of the CCF on Canadian political and social development. This work is important and interesting, but scholarship more relevant to this study has attempted to answer two fundamental questions regarding the party's failure to excite more voters.

The first question pondered barriers to party growth and asked whether the party failed because of a lack of a class-consciousness in Canada or because it failed to sufficiently engage the people of that class so that they would support the party. Complex questions regarding class and class-consciousness have been addressed by a number of labour and Marxist scholars and are still the source of much debate. Among those whose work specifically addresses the CCF, there appears to be a general consensus that a working-class identity existed and that there were instances of class-consciousness. The first scholars to seriously examine the party argued that to be of the working class in Canada did not only mean to be an urban worker, but also a rural farmer, as class was based more upon one's social location and relationship to economic power and influence than to one's particular occupation.[12] Seymour Lipset was influential in this area of investigation through his examination of the rise of the cooperative and progressive movements and the strength of the Social Gospel movement. He concluded that class-consciousness existed among Canadian workers and farmers and that it was present long before the CCF or other socialist groups came on the scene to attempt to deal with the oppression and exploitation that those of the working class already understood.[13] More recently, historian Peter Campbell added important points to the discussion, arguing that a class-consciousness existed and that the people of, and leaders from, that class enjoyed agency and influence as seen in societal groups, the cooperative movement, organized labour, and various avenues of political participation.[14]

Theories as to why the party was unable to win substantial and sustained support among those of the Canadian working class are rich and varied. One answer relies on French sociologist Émile Durkheim's thesis that, perhaps counterintuitively, poverty does not inspire increased political activity. Rather, poverty restrains one from acting, while wealth leads one to a belief that prosperity is gained through one's own effort and, in turn, to a feeling of empowerment and political daring. This thesis has been used by Lipset, Michael Mann, and others who have pondered the CCF's waxing and waning popularity.[15]

Another answer explored the degree to which the party failed to adequately address the diversity within the working class. For some, the answer lay in its simplistic conception of unity within the working class and its underestimation of the power of the traditional parties to keep class from becoming an important factor in Canadian political debate. Political scientists Janine Brodie and Jane Jensen were important in making these points, in a more contemporary study, arguing that parties are not just mirrors of public opinion, but that they actively seek to control and exploit cleavages in society. The traditional parties kept the cleavages of region, ethnicity, and language in the public domain, while keeping class from becoming part of the public discourse.[16]

Further to the presumed unity of the working class, it has been argued that in the 1930s and 1940s most unions still based membership on criteria that tended to fracture the working class according to race, ethnicity, and gender. In attempting to rally working-class people to act as one, the party failed to appreciate the degree to which unions were often agents of disunity within that class. This diversity was present, too, in farm organizations, and in both city and country households, where traditional roles for women were the norm. In failing to properly adjust to working-class diversity, the party failed to become a voice for that class.[17]

Meanwhile, others have offered a materialist argument: that it was wrong to consider farmers as part of the working class, as they were more interested in immediate economic conditions and were petit-bourgeois land owners with an interest in populism, yet with no dedication to socialism. The CCF, it follows, wasted time, effort, and money in trying to win working-class electoral support as it based its efforts on the false premise that workers and farmers were united in one class and seeking the same goals.[18]

Also important has been the argument that the CCF erred in ignoring its own principles by not pressing the federal and provincial governments for more far-reaching labour and working-class legislation. In its frustrating attempt to win support from union leaders, the CCF did not exert enough energy to address the problems of non-union workers. Furthermore, others point out that, when the party backed away from its goal of eradicating capitalism, it failed to live up to its social-democratic principles by not promoting greater worker participation in factory ownership or management, dropping, as well, its earlier commitment to collective public ownership.[19]

The scholarship examining communism and labour in Canada offers another part of the answer, suggesting that the CCF was in a ruthless battle for the allegiance of the working class. In 1929, before the CCF was created, the Communist Party of Canada had set a goal to establish communist labour cells in factories across the country, and its success in doing so was reflected in its generally accepted claim that, by 1933, it played a role in 75% of Canadian strikes.[20] Despite heroic efforts by many CCF leaders and workers, by 1945 the Communists had a strong base in many unions. Communists were able to forward union funds to Communist Party candidates, causes, and publicity, and to support the publication of the communist *Canadian Tribune*, while at the same time acting against the CCF.[21] Meanwhile, many Canadian unions were affiliates of American organizations, which were dominated by Gomperist ideas that rejected socialism as a political option for dealing with working-class issues, while some were international institutions that forbade participation in politics altogether.

The second fundamental question posed by the scholarship is whether the CCF fatuously or guilefully abandoned the socialist ideological principles upon which it was based. Two schools of thought regarding the question have evolved. One speaks of betrayal and argues that the CCF unwisely abandoned its principles and followers as it ceased to be a movement and became a party. The other speaks of pragmatism and contends that the CCF, quite shrewdly, adjusted its ideological stance to meet changing circumstances. Both schools of thought owe a debt to the work of German sociologist Robert Michels, who postulated the iron law of oligarchy: all parties begin as movements but organize themselves to become political parties to win electoral success in order to bring their policies to practice. The transformation from movement to party to power, he wrote, involves a professional oligarchy taking control to dominate its development.[22]

The betrayal school was pioneered by sociologist Leo Zakuta, who argued that the CCF began as a principled protest movement, turned into a major party, and then ended in failure as a minor party. He contended that the desire for political power led leaders to forsake key socialist principles, the most important of which were pacifism and the eradication of capitalism. The desire for electoral gain and respectability also led to an abandonment of a grassroots organization and to the creation of a more centrally organized structure run by paid, professional bureaucrats. In a memorable phrase that hinted at the work of CCF National Secretary David Lewis and first federal party leader J.S. Woodsworth, Zakuta wrote that the changes turned "rebels into reformers and prophets into politicians."[23]

Another important voice in this school is that of social scientist Walter Young, who agreed with Michels' thesis and with Zakuta's conclusions that the CCF became the kind of institutional party it had been created to fight. Young wrote that the CCF diluted the ideology the party had been created to offer: a radical, alternative guide to building a better Canada. The only quarter Young allowed is that, while the CCF failed as a party, it succeeded as a movement.[24]

The pragmatic school offered a different answer to the question of the party's failure, echoing many of the same points and using similar evidence, but adding valuable detail to the analysis examining the party's organization and structure. Rather than criticizing the party for too quickly abandoning the grassroots structure of a movement and adopting the centralized structure of a party, scholars of this school contend that the CCF erred and ultimately failed because it did not make the shift sooner or more efficiently. Gerald Caplan and Alan Whitehorn have written that, rather than strictly adhering to the ideas and rhetoric of the Regina Manifesto, as the betrayal school contends the party should have done, the party did irreparable political harm to itself and its cause by not distancing itself from that document or, at least, bringing clarity to the more extreme statements in it. The party thereby failed to ease the fears of those who worried about the party's ideological novelty, while also failing to adequately articulate the principles for which it stood. This ideological confusion, it is argued, could have been addressed, but it was coupled with the absence of an efficient, centralized, professional, and adequately funded organization, rendering it impossible for the party to maneuver.

Political historian Dan Azoulay is of this school. His 1997 book, *Keeping the Dream Alive: The Survival of the Ontario CCF/NDP, 1950-1963*, is the most recent major scholarly work on the CCF. He focused only on Ontario, but he brought important ideas to the broader debate. Azoulay criticized the methods and conclusions of Zakuta and Young of the "betrayal" school and argued that it is people at the local level that make or break political parties, rather than the party principles and ideas to which scholars traditionally address themselves. If properly organized at that level and by those people, he wrote, adversities can be overcome. He contended, as others had mentioned with respect to the national party, that the greatest problems the Ontario CCF/NDP faced were the degree to which the Cold War rendered all dissent and left-wing ideas suspect; the long post-war prosperity coupled with the conformist, relaxed mood of the 1950s that left most Canadians unwilling to seek substantive change; and, specific to Ontario, the political acumen of premiers Leslie Frost and John Robarts. Given these factors and the resultant decline in CCF electoral support, membership, and money, the party leadership had to decide whether to fade away or organize to fight. The party chose to fight and to organize itself back into significance. This reaction was not the failure of a doomed movement, Azoulay argues, but the action of a vibrant party.

Azoulay found that, throughout the organizing process, the party did not compromise its ideological principles. Rather, the moderation of the radical wording of the Regina Manifesto was essential given the times and challenges. Its revised guiding policy document, the 1956 Winnipeg Declaration, proved to be a valuable gift for the Ontario CCF, allowing it to undertake a new wave of education with a message more clearly in line with the society of the day. He argues that the CCF was consistent in its goals and strategy and that other, more critical, analysts were concerning themselves too much with tactics.[25]

The notion that is common to the answers offered to the two fundamental questions and, consequently, to all of the scholarship addressing the demise of the CCF, is that the party's downfall was due primarily to actions that it took or failed to take. The party's collapse was thus its own fault. Missing in this conclusion and analysis is a substantive assessment of the actions of those who had undertaken to destroy the party. There has been inadequate analysis of those diverse but related actions that, when taken together, formed a well-financed, carefully organized, multi-layered, and sustained anti-socialist/anti-CCF movement that played a significant role in the party's destruction, especially in the critical years from 1943 to 1949. A helpful metaphor is to consider the CCF as a new tent being erected on the Canadian political landscape. One can see the existing scholarship as concerning itself primarily with arguments regarding the party's contemplation of the tent's location, the positioning of the poles, the wording of the instructions, and who was to be invited to participate in the task. Meanwhile, it affords inadequate attention to the notion that the tent was being erected in a hurricane. Let us consider the hurricane.

It must be noted that the scholarship is not silent on the matter of anti-socialist/anti-CCF activities. However, while most examinations of the CCF mention it, only three afford it more than a cursory investigation. In *The Anatomy of a Party: The National CCF, 1932-1961*, Young wrote, "In 1943, when the Gallup Poll showed CCF strength increasing, the most extensive and most vicious propaganda campaign ever directed against a single political party in Canadian history was mounted."[26] He went on to briefly explain some of the aspects of that campaign, but then ignored it in his conclusion when summing up the reasons for the party's failure. In *The Dilemma of Canadian Socialism: The CCF in Ontario*, Caplan devoted attention to the anti-CCF movement, but the analysis is limited by its focus on only one province and, further, by his emphasis on the party's inability to organize itself to respond. Finally, the anti-CCF activities of the Communist Party and of newspapers are sprinkled throughout David Lewis' *The Good Fight: Political Memoirs, 1909-1958*, with more substantive attention afforded the actions of those acting on behalf of big business and Premier George Drew of Ontario. Lewis quoted a 1943 article in which he had written, "The signs point to a concentrated campaign against the CCF more intensive than Canada has ever known."[27] While Young, Caplan, and Lewis considered anti-CCF activities more seriously than did others, even they afforded those activities inadequate consideration, since the anti-CCF movement was, after all, tangential to their theses and analyses.

To theoretically frame an analysis of the anti-socialist/anti-CCF campaign it is helpful to consider the work of Italian Marxist Antonio Gramsci. Although he wrote his influential essays in the 1920s and 1930s, Gramsci's ideas rose to prominence during the "Crisis of Marxism" of the 1970s, when many scholars were seeking to understand whether Marxism was incomplete, incorrect, or irrelevant.[28]

Gramsci's ideas invite one seeking to understand the Canadian ideological debate of the 1940s, and the anti-socialism/anti-CCF campaign that was a part of it, to look at the arena in which that debate occurred. That arena is suggested by Gramsci's conception that the state is more complex than the traditional Marxist metaphor of base/superstructure. Gramsci contended that the state consists of separate but interconnected political and civil societies, with power resting in the political state and exerted through various means of coercion and consent. However, power is obtained and maintained through struggles for leadership and control in the civil society. That leadership and control is won when a consensus with respect to societal goals and ideas is formed and coercion becomes unnecessary. When this consensus is obtained, the subaltern class becomes complicit in its own oppression through its support of the ideas at the core of its own exploitation.

In the attempt to obtain and retain hegemonic control, societal change is not only a class struggle but also a struggle involving political ideas and ideology. Similarly, winning and maintaining hegemonic control is more complex than an economic struggle between classes or between capital and labour. The successful group is the one that creates political and ideological alliances that involve all classes and skillfully manages the levers of coercion, consensus, and control. Hegemony becomes a fluid, dynamic, and "lived" process. In making their rule, and the systems by which they rule, legitimate in the eyes of the subaltern group, the ruling class can discuss and "sell" the ideological ideas that are at the heart of their dominance while, at the same time, attending to some of the immediate materialist needs of that subaltern group, confident that no serious questions will arise regarding the political and economic system that created such needs in the first place. As English cultural theorist Terry Eagleton argues, "successful ideologies are often thought to render their beliefs natural and self-evident—to identify them with the 'common sense' of a society so that nobody could imagine how they might ever be different."[29]

Essential to this study, then, is Gramsci's contention that the creation and maintenance of the hegemonic moment allows those of the dominant group to attack those who threaten its dominance while retaining the allegiance of the dominated. Referring to the Italian situation, Gramsci contends, "These forces took power and united in the modern Italian State, in a struggle against specific other forces and helped by specific auxiliaries or allies."[30] Thus, we can see that it is important to understand how and where the dominant group acts to win and preserve hegemony, as it seeks alliances and organizes attacks on opposing ideas and groups when those ideas and groups contradict or question the dominant ideology. Gramsci leads one to explore the areas of civil society where the struggle for hegemonic control has occurred and also to explore the individuals and groups that led it.

Gramsci's ideas suggest that one way to consider the political debate of the 1940s might be to assume that, since the late 19th century, a dominant group had manipulated a hegemonic control of Canada, and the significant and growing popularity of the CCF presented a challenge to that hegemony that needed to be addressed. Such an assumption might suggest that the anti-socialist/anti-CCF campaign was an attempt by those with power to maintain hegemonic control.

By this suggestion, one who is interested in the electoral failure of the CCF might be led to address a gap in the current scholarship addressing the party's demise. One might be led away from examinations of squabbles in parliament, discussions regarding the party's internal organizational challenges and its petty failings, and away from a consideration of its ideological consistency or its inability to attract a broad working-class allegiance. Rather, one might be inspired to investigate the ideological fight that was taking place for the hearts and minds of Canadians and to identify the dominant class, and those speaking for it, who were acting to rid Canada of socialism and the CCF.

To that end, this study will examine actions taken by business leaders, who acted on their own and through others; by the newspapers that reflected on and participated in the struggle; by the various political parties; and by the

Catholic Church and those who brought religion to the debate. This study will examine the many avenues through which the anti-socialist/anti-CCF messages, words, and images were presented to Canadians. Those avenues included sermons and speeches at clubs and political meetings. They also included newspaper articles, advertisements, cartoons and editorials, business newsletters, books, pamphlets, letters to employees, and pay-packet inserts. Canadians met the campaign at home, at church, at work, and at their leisure. It will be demonstrated that the campaign's power was based on the fact that, through its many facets, the campaign's messages, words, and images were consistent and pervasive; that its communicators enjoyed status in the civil society; and that the CCF was unable to adequately respond.

A great amount of scholarship exists, beyond that noted above, and is helpful in undertaking such a study. More important, however, are the primary sources that are available and, again, there is much to be examined. The CCF papers are rich and invaluable in their discussion of the attacks made against the party and the party's reaction to those attacks. The papers of those who played important roles in the campaign, such as Gladstone Murray, George Drew, Harry Robbins, and the Canadian Chamber of Commerce, are also enlightening, offering insight into the ideas that motivated the actions taken against the party and the strategies used to carry them out. Newspapers afford an appreciation of the images, diction, tone, and emotion of the day.

Archival research, therefore, was essential in shaping this study. Important in the CCF papers are the letters among party leaders and to and from rank-and-file members. They reveal that, beginning in 1943, the party recognized both the increased ferocity of the fight in which it was engaged and the ideological nature of that fight. The letters, meeting minutes, and party communications to members and to the public also show the degree to which the campaign put the party on the defensive at the very time that it had attained the peak of its popularity and efficacy. The papers reveal the extent to which its actions and pronouncements became reactive. One could argue that this reactive, defensive posture affected organization, fund raising, membership, and electoral support as the party became increasingly shaped by the anti-CCF forces arrayed against it.

The CCF papers, as well as those of its opponents, also afford insight into the planning, financing, and execution of the anti-socialist/anti-CCF campaign. They allow an understanding of the connections between the groups and individuals of the campaign and the extent to which the actions of some were noted by, and affected the subsequent actions of, others. In this way, the papers remind one of Gramsci's suggestion that the connections between those of the dominant class acting against a counter-hegemonic challenge are often personal and professional, but the more essential link is the belief in, and the defence of, an ideology. It is instructive that nowhere in any of the papers of those involved in the campaign is there doubt expressed or debate recorded regarding the correctness of the ideas being defended, or the necessity of the fight.

This study will begin with a look at the Canadian business community's part in the anti-socialist/anti-CCF campaign. This will be done through exploring the actions taken by the insurance industry, the Canadian Chamber of Commerce, and certain newspapers, as case studies. It will then move to consider the actions of Gladstone Murray of the CBC and former ad-man Burdick Trestrail, who led campaigns on behalf of business leaders. Actions taken by church leaders and those using religion, and Christianity in particular, as a platform for their actions, as well as the activities of the Progressive Conservative Party, which was an active participant in the campaign, will be explored. Finally, this study will explore the attacks from the ideological left as seen primarily through the actions of the Communist Party of Canada, using its ties with, and goals for, organized labour, while welcoming the cynical cooperation of both the Liberal and Progressive Conservative Parties to sow confusion and break the CCF. These investigations lead to a conclusion that the CCF's failure must be understood as part of an ideological struggle that climaxed in the 1940s with a web of people, parties, groups, businesses, and institutions combating an idea and a party which was seen as threatening all that they believed was necessary for Canada and Canadians to evolve and succeed.

It should be noted at the outset that this study avoids an analysis of the ideology that the CCF was promoting and defending, not because this ideology was unimportant, but because the emphasis is on a social and intellectual dissection of the anti-socialist/anti-CCF campaign. This study is concerned with what those on the right and left were doing and saying in their attacks on the party and its guiding ideology. It will concentrate on the fight initiated in the civil society to crush democratic socialism and the party that was bringing it to the Canadian people. It will explore the attempt to destroy a party and ideology that, in an ironic turn, would come to be celebrated in 2004 with one of its own being selected as the Greatest Canadian in our history for the degree to which the democratic socialist values his party and policies had espoused had become core Canadian values. In short, it will examine the hurricane.

BIG BUSINESS ATTACKS SOCIALISM AND THE CCF

I n 1944 a book entitled *The Road to Serfdom*, by University of London Economics Professor Friedrich von Hayek, became a North American sensation. Beyond the book's sales, which propelled it to bestseller lists, Hayek's ideas were guaranteed even wider circulation when the book was reprinted in a 20-page condensed form in the April 1945 edition of *Reader's Digest*. It was also a Book-of-the-Month selection, which meant that reprints of the *Reader's Digest* version cost only $18 per thousand.

The Road to Serfdom found its audience when the Second World War was still raging, with chilling telegrams bearing the horrible news of fallen family members being received with increasing frequency. It was read by people who were also reading accounts of the Holocaust, of the horrors of Stalinism, and of the growing tension between leaders at international conferences. The book argued that the lesson to derive from Stalin, Mussolini, and Hitler was that the power of the state must be curtailed: a powerful state leads to the totalitarian control of society and the end of the political and economic freedoms offered by liberal democracy and industrial capitalism. Societies based on these ideas must protect themselves by resisting attempts to locate more power in the state through the imposition of economic planning. The *Reader's Digest* version's second-last paragraph stated,

> It is not those who cry for more "planning" who show the necessary courage, nor those who preach a "New Order,"

which is no more than a continuation of the tendencies of the past 40 years, and who can think of nothing better than to imitate Hitler. It is, indeed, those who cry loudest for a planned economy who are most completely under the sway of the ideas which have created this war and most of the evils from which we suffer.[1]

Despite the book's enormous popularity, not everyone was impressed. April's *Harper's* magazine, for example, ran a highly critical article by C. Hartley Gratten, entitled "Hayek's Hayride," which criticized the book's sweeping assumptions and generalizations which, it contended, flew in the face of established economic and political theories. It argued that Hayek's thesis was, in fact, dangerous as it proposed to do away with all government regulatory power, thus granting a gift to what would become the unchecked power of monopolistic business. Gratten cited respected American economists Charles Marriam and Louis Wirth as having written similarly scathing reviews of the book. Even more convincingly, Gratten quoted Hayek himself, who had said in an interview that he wished he had taken greater care in his writing to point out that he did not really oppose all government intervention in the economy.[2]

Despite these criticisms of Hayek's work and his own clarification of it, many Canadian business leaders found in Hayek's book valuable ammunition to support their ideological beliefs while attacking those of the CCF. Business leaders who had not understood the opportunity Hayek offered were helped to see it by the Canadian Chamber of Commerce, which, the previous year, had struck a committee to promote capitalism and fight the CCF. In 1944, the committee had published and distributed 100,000 copies of articles such as "Canada's Future Belongs to Free Canadians", "The Principles of Post-War Progress," and "Who Gets the Money and How Much?" It had also copied and distributed the *Reader's Digest* condensed version of *The Road to Serfdom* to local Chambers of Commerce and, through them, to business people across the country.[3]

Some business leaders either took the Chamber's lead or acted on their own in using Hayek's ideas and language. An example can be made of Lyman House Limited, a Montreal wholesale drug company. Shortly before the 1945 federal election, Lyman House employees found a notice in their pay-packets from company President J.H. Andrews. The notice, addressed to all employees and reminding them that June 11 was election day, said,

> Some of you may have listened to the recent propaganda in favour of the CCF party. I have made a study of this Party for the past five years. My findings are that should the CCF win this election, Canada will face the same perils as did Germany under the National Socialist Party that installed Hitler to power. The CCF program is to merge the railroads, banks, insurance companies... You may vote CCF against my advice as this is your privilege. I cannot, however, accept the responsibility of maintaining employment for you and the other members of our organization for any length of time under a CCF controlled government. [4]

To help his employees to exercise their franchise as he believed they should, Mr. Andrews helpfully included with every notice a copy of the condensed version of *The Road to Serfdom.* Andrews wrote, "The article was written by an internationally known economist. Canada faces the same problems under the CCF as Central Europe faced during the rise of Fascism. The fundamental truths brought to light in this booklet should convince you that Canada needs no CCF or Socialistic Government."[5]

The power of the direct anti-socialist/anti-CCF activities undertaken by business leaders such as Andrews in defence of the ideas articulated by Hayek was recognized by the CCF leadership of the time. In a December 9, 1945 *New Commonwealth* article, ominously entitled "The Ranks Are Closing—Big Interests Marshal Forces," David Lewis had observed, "The signs point to a concentrated campaign against the CCF more intensive than Canada has ever known."[6] Nine years later, A.G. Shultz, the United Automobile, Aircraft, and Agricultural Implement Workers of America (UAW-CIO) Director of Political Action, wrote to the CCF national office, expressing his opinion as to why the party failed to do well in that year's Ontario by-elections. He wrote, "Number one with me, of course, is the day-to-day campaign by big business through press, etc. to discredit the trade unions and the CCF and build up a prestige for the free enterprise of big business."[7]

The Canadian business community was active and influential in promoting liberal-democratic and industrial capitalist ideas, while attacking socialism in general and the CCF in particular as threats to the most basic ideals of Canadian society. It located this debate in the places people earned their livings, made personal financial decisions, and gleaned their news of the day. It focused the debate on a fight between all that was good about living in Canada and all that was evil in enemy regimes, between a hope for a better future and a fear of that foreign evil visiting Canada. It created the discursive terrain for the debate and, in doing so, played fast and loose with facts, which created fear and confusion and reduced the effectiveness of the CCF's responses.

This chapter will not attempt to look at the actions of all companies or business sectors, but will examine as case studies the insurance industry, the Canadian Chamber of Commerce, and significant newspapers. The insurance industry is ideally suited as a case study since it quite legitimately felt itself threatened by the CCF and because it acted to defend itself by directly engaging the party over a number of years and in a number of ways. The Canadian Chamber of Commerce also makes a good case study because it took direct action against the party, and through its actions, one can extrapolate the opinions and actions of many Canadian business leaders inasmuch as it was an organization to which nearly all Canadian businesses belonged. Newspapers are useful as sources, for many of them were big businesses themselves; moreover, they were employed by business leaders in their ideological battles. Newspaper articles, editorials, cartoons, and advertisements thus help to reveal the ideas, language, and images of the fight.

The Insurance Industry

Calgary's Bill Irvine was a soft-spoken man who, along with J.S. Woodsworth, was elected to parliament in 1921 as a Labour candidate prior to the creation of the CCF. On February 12, 1934, Irvine, then a CCF Member of Parliament, stood to make a motion in the House of Commons, stating, "In the opinion of this House the Government should give immediate consideration to the advisability of nationalizing life insurance."[8] The motion did not carry, but it served notice to Canadians that the CCF was serious about moving forward with the Regina Manifesto's promise to take action regarding the insurance industry.[9]

Nearly ten years later, on December 9, 1943, *The Globe and Mail*, without revealing its sources, ran an article that claimed the CCF was about to begin an investigation of the insurance industry.[10] The article was correct. In January 1943, Ontario CCF MLA William Dennison had written to CCF National Research Director Dr. Stuart Jamieson asking for research regarding the effect on rates and coverage for fire insurance if it were socialized. The notion of creating a scheme whereby municipalities could self-insure was also being investigated by the party.[11]

Days after *The Globe and Mail* article scooped the party, the CCF's new National Research Director, Lloyd Shaw, made a presentation to party supporters at Halifax's Lord Nelson Hotel. He stated that the main case against the insurance companies rested first on the CCF belief that they were at the centre of Canadian economic monopolies through interlocking directorships; and second, that insurance consumers were ill-served, as too much money was wasted by insurance companies through competition and through the use of sales agents, which cost insurance holders in increased premiums while the agents themselves made poor salaries. Finally, Shaw argued that the companies derived unfair profits through the perpetuation of premiums that they knew were too high and on benefits on claims and investments that they knew were too low.[12]

Insurance companies saw Shaw's speech as a declaration of war. They were quickly joined by many newspapers that had already shown their allegiance to business and their enmity toward the CCF. On December 22, 1943, *The Globe and Mail* published an article entitled "Prestige of Life Insurance Industry in Canada All Over World Has Been Pride of Canadians: Forges Forward in Face of World Free Trade." The article derided the CCF for asking for an investigation of insurance companies on the grounds that the government already regulated them, noting that they were forced by strict laws and regulations to have their books open for government inspection at all times. The interlocking directorship argument was called a canard, for companies that sought to serve their customers and shareholders must always seek information and cooperation with other businesses, and interlocking directorships were the best way to accomplish that goal. Regarding the CCF's second criticism, the article argued that the law stated that 90% of profits had to be returned to shareholders. The article concluded with a prediction of the consequences of insurance nationalization, contending, "Many would soon be without insurance under such a plan unless the CCF proposes in the event of securing power to insure everybody willy-nilly and to take their premiums out of taxation."[13]

Joining *The Globe and Mail* in its defense of the insurance industry and, as always, showing vigour in its criticism of the CCF, the *Ottawa Post* ran an editorial on December 22 that attacked the CCF for failing to complete its research before lashing out at insurance companies. The editorial ignored the fact, or perhaps chose not to check, that the party had been conducting research of that nature for nearly a decade. The editorial concluded, "The dangerous thing about this CCF attack—and revealing of the party's mood and methods—is that the insurance companies are condemned without trial."[14]

The *Winnipeg Free Press* was another newspaper that seldom missed an opportunity to vilify the CCF. A December 1943 editorial began by questioning the temerity of CCF leaders in criticizing the probity of the insurance industry, singling out CCF federal leader M.J. Coldwell. It concluded:

> Our quarrel with the CCF and Mr. Coldwell is not only that we believe the implementation of their programme would be a disaster to Canada. It is based also on the conviction that they are indulging in wholesale debauchery of the electorate… If the Canadian people want to vote for the CCF programme that is their right which they will exercise or not in due time as they please. But when they vote for it, we hope that it will be clear to them that they are not voting for a Santa Claus who will come climbing down the chimney on Christmas Eve and fill their stockings with presents they don't have to pay for.[15]

Another western newspaper, *The Albertan*, ran an editorial on December 30, 1943, that praised the insurance companies as "important" and "well run" and argued that there "is no evidence of exorbitant profits."[16] The editorial concluded that insurance companies are filled with people of "initiative, energy and judgment, as well as a shrewd knowledge of human nature."[17] It then compared those good people to those of the CCF:

These qualities are by no means conspicuous in our present government service. And they would be even less conspicuous among the rabble of soap-box orators, broken down "intellectuals" and Communist fellow-travelers which a CCF government would certainly bring into the public service. Under Socialist management the administration of life insurance would soon become a sorry mess, tangled up with delay and red tape and infested with politics and favoritism.[18]

While most Canadians were enjoying Christmas with their families, the publishers of the *Financial Post* had other matters on their minds. The *Post's* Christmas Day edition ran a front page article entitled, "The CCF Naturally Fights Insurance." It stated that watching the CCF approach a policy on insurance is "like watching a man race along a diving board, take a magnificent leap into the air and plunge down toward a pool—in which there is no water. Mr. Coldwell is acting more and more like a deluded Don Quixote: a sucker for any anti-business yarn anybody tells him."[19] In defense of the insurance industry, the article continued, "Of all business in Canada none perhaps has a better, clearer record of efficient public service than life insurance. None is so strictly controlled, so constantly policed by government, obliged to reveal more about its innermost workings."[20] The article then stated its interpretation of the CCF's motives for its proposed investigation of insurance companies:

Obviously the CCF dislikes a nation of life insurance owners. Because people who buy life insurance believe in sacrifice today for benefits tomorrow: in standing on their own feet. They are people who are not deluded by the something for nothing gospel. They have the energy, courage and personal pride to look after their own responsibilities. Naturally, people with such beliefs are anathema to the CCF. Its hopes lie with the people who don't want to meet their personal responsibilities; people who aren't willing to sacrifice today for benefits tomorrow.[21]

Meanwhile, the insurance companies had joined the fight. The Canadian Life Assurance Company sent a letter to all its Canadian branch managers on December 21, 1943. The three-page letter attacked Shaw's speech, claiming that he was ill-informed and that his facts were unclear or simply wrong. It concluded, "In our opinion there can be no question that all these attacks on Canadian institutions being made at the present time by the CCF party are an attempt to undermine Canadian public confidence and break down Canadian morale."[22]

The Canadian Life Underwriters Association, a national organization that represents, regulates, and educates all insurance company employees, reprinted and mailed the December 22 *Globe and Mail* article to every insurance agent and company employee in Canada.[23] On December 27, 1943, Metropolitan Life sent a letter, over the signature of its Vice-President, E.C. MacDonald, to all its managers and assistant managers. It made suggestions as to how they and their agents should discuss the CCF with policyholders and enclosed the recent editorials from the *Ottawa Citizen, Globe and Mail,* and *Financial Post.* When asked by CCF National Secretary David Lewis about the letter, which encouraged insurance agents to sit with clients in their homes and criticize the CCF and socialist ideas, MacDonald admitted having sent it with the damning editorials attached. He claimed that the action was not political, but merely intended to keep company employees and clients informed as to recent discussions regarding the industry.[24]

The new year saw a continuation of the editorial attacks on the party with the January 11, 1944, editorial from the *Montreal Gazette* criticizing the CCF for stating conclusions about the insurance industry before any research had been done and claiming that the party was wrong in questioning the right of the insurance companies to defend themselves against the nationalization threats. Both accusations were untrue, and a letter from Lloyd Shaw to the *Gazette*'s editor stated that fact.[25] The *Financial Post* dedicated the entire front page of its February 1944 edition to the controversy under the large, bold title, "State Life Insurance Not a Success." In great detail, it examined attempts at state-run municipal insurance programs in the United States and New Zealand in order to make its case that the CCF ideas were dangerous for individuals and for the Canadian economy.[26]

The CCF leadership appears to have been stung by the attacks of the insurance industry and the newspapers. The front page of the April 13, 1944, *CCF News* outlined the CCF's case for the nationalization of insurance and pointed to the scare tactics being used to attack the party and the idea. Coldwell, noting the ideological tone of the insurance debate, assured CCF members and the public that their savings, investments, and policies would be safe with a CCF government. He wrote, "The political servants of capitalism are busy trying to make the electors believe that the CCF is out to destroy your life insurance policies and to confiscate your savings."[27]

Meanwhile, reflecting the growing negative press and the actions of the insurance companies, a number of letters were received by the CCF national executive from party members, suggesting that perhaps it was a mistake to move against the insurance companies. The political problem with which the party leadership had to contend was that insurance companies were an important part of the capitalist system that the Regina Manifesto had promised to eradicate and that current leaders were promising to at least reform. Stuart Jamieson, who had again taken over the post of national research director when Shaw left for the RCAF, explained this fact to many of the worried letter-writers, including Fred Young, the Nova Scotia provincial organizer:

> In other words, it probably wouldn't pay to attack the insurance companies as such because they probably operate more honestly than numerous other types of business and, as they love to point out, are under closer government supervision. Our point of attack is, rather, that they are one of the major keystones of the present financial system which is unable to run the economy adequately.[28]

Meanwhile, despite the misgivings, the party continued its investigations and research. An internal CCF memorandum asserted that, from 1933 to 1942, Canadians had paid $787 million in premiums, but collected only $334 million, or 42% of that amount, in claims. It then listed a number of American cities that had begun saving money through self-insurance. It ended with a note that the last Ontario CCF convention had endorsed the principle of a Province of Ontario Fire Insurance fund that would allow taxpayers to save money by allowing municipalities to self insure.[29]

Finally, in March 1944, Coldwell added gasoline to the anti-CCF fire with a speech in his home riding of Biggar, Saskatchewan. It was the party's first major address regarding plans for insurance since the Shaw speech in Halifax three months before. It made many of the same points that Shaw had made and repeated that the party would be continuing its investigation of the insurance industry.

While the research and debate continued inside the party, the attacks from the insurance companies and newspapers continued unabated. A number of newspapers responded to Coldwell's speech in predictable ways. The April 17, 1944 *Windsor Star* editorial, for instance, attacked Coldwell, the speech, the party, and the idea of publicly owned insurance. While failing to explain where it derived its facts, the editorial stated that the CCF plans would see the government confiscate the assets of all insurance companies and lump all premiums and assets into a large government monopoly. This was not part of the CCF plan. It also stated that insurance companies benefit the country because they invest in a range of areas.[30] As noted in a letter from Stuart Jamieson to W. C. MacDonald of Windsor, "The statements in the *Windsor Star* of April 17 constitute what our opponents *think* [emphasis in original] we are going to do with insurance."[31]

Insurance companies also responded to Coldwell's speech. On April 12, the Canadian Life Insurance Officers Association published a nationally distributed bulletin to its members from association president H. W. Manning. The bulletin, referring to the Regina Manifesto, made the point that the move to nationalize insurance companies should not have come as a surprise. It then put its own spin on the party's motives:

> The point is that the life insurance companies must be discredited if the people are to be persuaded to vote for a party which proposes to take them over and socialize the business; and it is vital to the accomplishment of the program of the CCF to gain control of all the savings of the people in order to gain control of the whole economy…Mr. Coldwell is merely endeavoring to destroy the people's confidence in the great international institution of life insurance so that the CCF can gain control of the vast funds which are held by the companies as security for their policy holders.[32]

The bulletin went on to assure members of the association that Manning was leading the fight to protect the industry from the CCF. It reported that, when Coldwell announced that the insurance industry was under investigation by the party, Manning had issued a press release, which said in part,

> A non-official so-called investigation of the insurance business by one political party cannot be regarded as unprejudiced. Insofar as the announcement may be construed as reflecting on life insurance in Canada, Canadians will undoubtedly bear in mind that the business is under continuous investigation, regulation and supervision by the Federal Government and the Provincial Governments through their several qualified Insurance Superintendents.[33]

It is perhaps interesting to note that the government supervisors to whom Manning referred enforced regulations only with respect to actuarials, to ensure that the companies remained solvent, and nothing more. After perpetuating this misleading argument, the bulletin ironically went on to state that "Most of Mr. Shaw's charges against the life insurance companies were palpably false."[34]

Life insurance companies cooperated to assault the CCF with the creation and publication of an advertisement that appeared in newspapers across Canada in July 1944. Its bold copy posed the question, "What happens to the Life Insurance dollar?" It showed a graph and then stated below, "for every 95 cents received from policy holders, 84 cents was either paid to them or held for their benefit." The phrase "held for their benefit" was not explained. The tag line at the advertisement's bottom stated, "It is good citizenship to own Life Insurance. A Message from the Life Insurance Companies in Canada."[35]

As news of the ongoing CCF investigation regarding the viability of a nationalized insurance industry continued to surface, and rumours of the plans of Saskatchewan's CCF government to create a publicly owned automobile insurance scheme were confirmed, the attacks on the party and the idea intensified. The *Montreal Gazette* published a lengthy article in its February 14, 1945 edition that was ostensibly about the year-end financial report of Sun Life, but was, in reality, a glowing article in support of the company and a denunciation of the CCF's arguments about high premiums and unfair profits. A chart demonstrated that, of all the money that came into the company approximately, 49% went back to policyholders and 37% went to reserve funds to meet future policyholder needs.[36]

Meanwhile, the *Financial Post* continued its support of the insurance industry and capitalism, and its disdain for socialism and the CCF, with a full page article in its April 7, 1945 edition, entitled, "Insurance: Free Enterprise Answer to Problems of Security and Risk." It used a graphic, similar to that used by the *Gazette,* to show how the insurance industry was putting money into victory and government bonds while investing in Canadian industry and in homes for Canadians. The article played on the hopes, fears, and resentments of a country engaged in war, while cleverly portraying the insurance industry as a good corporate citizen for its support of the war effort. It used another graphic to show, in contrast to the claims of the CCF, that the majority of money gathered from premiums is returned to policyholders and another to show the thousands of people that the industry employs. The policyholder is called part of "The life insurance family."[37]

The year 1947 was not a federal election year, but the insurance company's anti-CCF campaign took no rest. On January 22, 1947, Lloyd Hiltz of Chester, Nova Scotia wrote to David Lewis, enclosing a six-page pamphlet that his father had received, unsolicited, in the mail. Hiltz noted that his father was a life insurance salesman and that it was the second of the sort that he had received. The first was from Vancouver, and the latest was from Ontario. Hiltz posed the question, "Do you think the Assurance Company could have sent his name to a mailing list?"[38]

The cover of the pamphlet to which Hiltz referred showed a cartoon carnival barker yelling the title *Let's All Join the CCF!* His podium contained two signs, "Membership Drive" and "Come In and Look Around." Inside were eleven crudely drawn cartoons showing an audience moving past a series of stages. Each cartoon reflected a war-time concern, or an anticipated post-war issue, with government intervention either creating the problem or making it worse. A few of the cartoons tell the tale. The first showed a thin man sitting bare-chested with an empty plate on his lap and the words "Severe Food Rationing" and "British Public" printed beside him, with the barker yelling, "See one of the thinnest men in the world!! He eats barely enough to keep alive!" The second showed a bearded lady with the words "Controls and

Restrictions" written on her beard, and the barker yelling, "The great bearded lady! See her beard actually growing!" Another cartoon showed a man in great pain swallowing a sword, which was much larger than he, with the word "austerity" printed upon it, and the barker yelling, "See the sword swallower attempt the great feat of taking more of this." The pamphlet ended with a man and woman screaming, "Good Heavens!" and "Enough is enough!" rushing out of the tent and pushing the barker out of the way, who is seen saying, "Wouldn't you like to join the socialist CCF circus in Canada?"[39] The cartoons played effectively on real fears and apprehensions about post-war austerity, while dismissing CCF ideas by equating them with a freak show.

David Lewis responded to Hiltz, saying that he was aware of the pamphlet and that they were being distributed throughout the country. He claimed not to know how the mailing lists were assembled but guessed "that they compile them from the records of the large insurance, financial and industrial corporation [sic], Chambers of Commerce, Canadian Manufacturers Association, etc."[40]

The insurance companies increased the volume of the smear campaign in 1948, partly in reaction to the impending Saskatchewan election and partly to the fact that, in May 1945, Tommy Douglas' CCF government in that province had created the country's first publicly owned automobile insurance program. A Saskatchewan government memo explained the move:

> Saskatchewan people were the first in Canada to recognize they were being exploited by the eastern insurance interests and were prepared to do something about the situation. They had seen in a short ten years over $52,000,000.00 of their insurance premiums largely going out of Saskatchewan with only a paltry $19,000,000.00 returned in the form of payments for their losses.[41]

Canadian Underwriter was a periodical of the Canadian Underwriters' Association distributed to insurance agents across Canada. It was at the forefront of the misinformation campaign to discredit the national CCF by bringing Saskatchewan's public automobile insurance system into disrepute. Its August 16, 1948 article entitled "Undemocratic Auto Insurance" made a number of statements that were false or misleading, resulting in a letter of rebuke from G.R. Bothwell of the Saskatchewan Government Insurance Office.[42] Of course, many more people saw, and were possibly influenced by, the lies in the article, than saw the Bothwell correction.

The December 15, 1948 issue of *Canadian Underwriter* contained an article entitled "Let There Be Light." The article received even greater readership when reprinted into booklet form for distribution to insurance company employees, clients, and newspapers across the country. The article and booklet listed a number of figures which seemed to prove that the Saskatchewan public auto insurance office was inefficient and that it could not do what it claimed. Specifically, it argued that the Saskatchewan claim that it was providing the same auto insurance for $6 that other provinces' policyholders had for $45 was false. It asked the rhetorical question, "Who is misleading the country?"[43] It called the CCF figures regarding public auto insurance in Saskatchewan "unadulterated poppycock." Calling up the greater ideological debate at issue, the back cover of the eight-page booklet stated,

> Responsible enterprise has brought Canada and the United States to their present prosperity. This is indeed a proud record. A profit kept reasonable by competition is a thoroughly good thing: it is the essence of sound trading and the stimulus of industry. Profit absorbs far fewer dollars than the inefficiency of monopoly.[44]

A January 1949 Canadian Underwriters' Association press release outlined the article's main points and announced that a copy of the booklet *Let There Be Light* was being sent to every newspaper editor in Canada.[45] The booklet became so widely distributed, and apparently so widely believed, that the CCF national executive decided to confront it with a radio broadcast. In the January 13 broadcast, Coldwell outlined the party's stand on public ownership as stated in the Regina Manifesto, and then assured his listeners, "We intend to socialize only those things where socialization would bring about great benefits to the Canadian people."[46] He went on to outline in some detail the costs of auto insurance in Saskatchewan before and after the government plan was implemented. He spoke of the savings for policyholders, and the benefits for taxpayers as surplus premiums were invested in government bonds. He noted that a similar plan would benefit other provinces since, at that time, many were moving toward making automobile insurance compulsory. Coldwell ended by taking on the insurance companies and the Canadian Underwriters' Association's growing role in the anti-socialism/anti-CCF campaign. He argued that the Saskatchewan success was scaring insurance companies and concluded, "No wonder the insurance companies endeavored to defeat the Saskatchewan government last June."[47] A transcript of Coldwell's address was printed as a small pamphlet and made available to CCF members. Yet it was unlikely that it reached as wide an audience as the association's original booklet.

The radio address may have assured party stalwarts, but it did little to stem the tide of anti-CCF attacks. The negative effects of *Let There Be Light* were still being felt. Two weeks after Coldwell's speech aired, the anti-CCF campaign focusing on public insurance in Saskatchewan was growing with such alacrity that Bothwell felt obliged to write a four-page, single-spaced letter to the new CCF National Research Director, Lorne Ingle, in which he clarified and refuted the entire *Let There Be Light* booklet one paragraph at a time. Bothwell demonstrated how the booklet's statistics were wrong or misleading and that its economic assumptions were false.[48]

The booklet's power is also seen in the fact that two years later, Bothwell's refutation notwithstanding, it was still being reprinted and nationally distributed. Carl E. Seibert, President of the Ontario Insurance Agents Association, wrote a letter to newspaper editors and enclosed a new copy of the booklet, explaining, "during the Ontario provincial elections last year, the CCF devotees repeatedly made inaccurate and misleading statements concerning the Saskatchewan [CCF] Government's automobile insurance scheme vs. responsible enterprise insurance in Ontario. The same statements are still being bandied about in Ontario and elsewhere. For this reason we believe that the truth should be told."[49]

In April 1949, the Montreal-based Dominion Board of Insurance Underwriters responded to Coldwell's January radio address with a leaflet entitled *Coldwell's Misleading Statement*. The leaflet was reprinted by British Columbia's *Financial Times* and distributed across Canada. It claimed that Coldwell was trying to deceive Canadians and disputed his figures and Saskatchewan government reports. It said that the Saskatchewan office paid inadequate claims, that premiums were too high, and that it was avoiding federal rulings that applied to private insurance companies.[50] Again, Bothwell wrote to Lorne Ingle with a detailed response, disclaiming the new leaflet. He created a chart that showed a comparison of provincial automobile insurance rates for collision, public liability, fire and theft, property damage, and accident coverage. In every category, the Saskatchewan rates were cheaper.

It is interesting that Ingle actually welcomed the Dominion Board of Insurance Underwriters' leaflet, for it contained so many blatant inaccuracies that he believed it would prove useful to CCF candidates in upcoming elections as a tool to demonstrate the unfairness of the insurance agencies' anti-CCF campaign. In a letter to Bothwell, Ingle wrote, "This would be exceptionally useful to us in the campaign if we could make it available to our candidates since we have reason to believe that this propaganda sheet of the insurance companies is receiving a rather wide distribution and the false charges it makes should be answered with the facts as they are set forth in your detailed and itemized reply."[51] In November 1949, Ingle had 5000 copies made and distributed to all federal CCF MPs and provincial MLAs and officers.

Speaking in Victoria on June 14, 1949, Coldwell noted that mortgage and insurance companies had paid for the creation and distribution of a pamphlet called *The Saskatchewan Story*. The pamphlet, which he called a "last minute roorback," was full of lies, but was distributed too late to enable CCF candidates to respond to it in full.[52] Through this pamphlet and others, Canadians seeking financial and security advice, whether in insurance offices or at their kitchen tables, had become involved in a ruthless battle for their loyalty to an ideological point of view. Perhaps what made the campaign so effective was the intervention into people's daily lives through their decisions about the mundane, but necessary, matter of insurance. By instilling fear and uncertainty into this decision, the insurance companies were able to score important ideological points.

The Canadian Chamber of Commerce

The Canadian Chamber of Commerce and its local affiliated branches across the country, speaking for the majority of Canadian businesses, were united in their opposition to socialism and the CCF and acted in a number of ways to fight them. At its 1943 annual meeting in Quebec, the Canadian Chamber of Commerce announced that it was forming a new committee, under the chairmanship of Paul Sise, to undertake an "intensive and vigorous" education campaign. The campaign was to use the Canadian Chamber's magazine, *Canadian Business*, as well as membership bulletins and briefs to government agencies, to promote its message. Its message was to emphasize what it considered a proper balance between free enterprise and government regulation.[53]

The Canadian Chamber had long been promoting its views through *Canadian Business*. Its April 1943 edition can serve as an example of its pro-capitalist, anti-socialist, anti-CCF editorial policy. It contained an article by C.W.T. Hollingsworth entitled, "This is the CCF," in which he insulted all those supporting the CCF:

> There's a dictator streak in the best of us—an itch to plan someone else's life. Usually such a streak is harmless and merely serves as a basis for stimulating discussion. Sometimes, however, it becomes belligerent. Then out may pop a strident supporter of Mr. Coldwell's socialist party: the Co-operative Commonwealth Federation.[54]

The article continued with the assertion that CCF planning would lead inevitably to dictatorship and the loss of all the democratic and economic freedoms that Canadians had come to enjoy. It went on to attack party leaders and members as pacifists and isolationists and questioned their patriotism. It praised the party's intellectual leadership, but berated party members, saying they had "lower foreheads." The difference between the leaders and members meant that "The political appeals of the CCF range all the way from wild demagogy to the sly and learned implication of the brain trust."[55]

The work of the Sise committee promised more, and its impressive accomplishments were reported at the next annual meeting. Over the course of a year, literature had been produced and distributed with instructions to local chambers for setting up their own educational programs to promote free enterprise. A 16mm film had been made, telling people that, to save free enterprise, they needed to get out and vote for political parties that supported it. Fifty thousand pieces of literature had been mailed across the country, including publications such as *Canada's Future Belongs to Free Canadians* and reprints of Hayek's *The Road to Serfdom*. Chamber speakers addressing the value of protecting free enterprise had visited local organizations in every province, speaking in schools, service club halls, church basements, and on the radio. Newspapers had been given copies of speeches and articles. "Freedom of Enterprise" clinics had been held in Montreal, Winnipeg, Saskatoon, and Regina. An astounding total of 692,000 mailing pieces had been printed over the course of the year.[56]

The Chamber's annual report of the next year recorded another successful campaign, with 53,100 copies of literature distributed across Canada, including a pamphlet called *Canadian Capitalism and the Menace of a Fifth Column.*[57] In speaking of the more than 100 audiences that had been addressed through the speakers' bureau, the report related that "first, business men were urged and inspired to promote the free enterprise way of life among employees and the public and their advertising audience, and second, generous newspaper and radio reports of these speeches found their way into Canadian homes."[58] To further this end, the report stated that the Canadian Chamber's Department of Economic Development education program had been developing and distributing literature: "It has also placed in the hands of corporate and organizational members, facts and arguments with which the claims of those opposed to the democratic system can be refuted."[59]

Similar efforts were reported in 1946 and 1947; and with 1949 being an election year, the Canadian Chamber increased its propaganda efforts. Its *1949 Reports to its 20th Annual Meeting* spoke glowingly of its National Affairs Committee, which was spearheading 200 national affairs committees operating through boards of trade and chambers of commerce in all provinces. Speeches to local chambers were made in addition to the airing of 900 radio broadcasts and the printing of 11,000 newsletters containing one million reprinted articles. In addition, the "Get Out the Vote Campaign" distributed 750,000 pieces of literatures to homes and local media. It was reported that just one of these pieces of literature was picked up by 63 newspapers, leading to a readership of about 1 million. A short film extolling the virtues of free enterprise was created and shown in about 100 theatres, with an audience estimated to be about 4.5 million.[60]

Meanwhile, many local chambers had followed the leadership of the Canadian Chamber, and they had organized campaigns to promote their political point of view and to criticize both the Communist and CCF parties.

For example, a November 1947 letter from the London Chamber of Commerce to its members drew national notice when it asked its members to complete a form that asked how much of each dollar of sales covered the cost of materials, wages, taxes, and profits.[61] The results of the survey, which were completed by only nine local companies, were published in a quarter-page advertisement in the *London Free Press* on January 31, 1948. It claimed that the figures showed that business profits were fair and reasonable, despite the claims made by CCF and Labour Progressive [Communist] Party candidates. The Canadian Chamber's conclusion was printed in capital letters along the bottom of the advertisement: "DON'T BE FOOLED BY COMMUNISTS OR DEMAGOGUES— LOOK AT THE FIGURES AND THINK FOR YOURSELF."[62]

To make clear exactly to whom they were referring by the term "demagogue," the January 1948 nationally circulated newsletter from the Canadian Chamber of Commerce attacked statements Coldwell had made in a speech the previous month, in which he had questioned the fairness of businesses' pricing practices; the newsletter stated, "The trouble is, statements of this kind—flat, round-figured and demagogic—are difficult to combat."[63] The newsletter went on to argue as fact that the Communists and CCF were merging and had to be stopped.[64]

The Canadian Chamber of Commerce's April 15, 1948, newsletter stated on its first page that it was a lack of self-confidence that was leading too many Canadians to be attracted to socialism. It called socialism "a way of life, something that is foreign and alien to this country.[65] In its next newsletter, the Canadian Chamber took issue with the provincial Crown Corporation, Saskatchewan Industries, as it was in competition with private business.[66] The July newsletter warned that people should not be confused by the political labels of communism and socialism for they were the same. In the context of an emerging Cold War, linking the CCF to Communism could do irreparable harm. The first-page article stated:

> This woolly talk is a symptom of the woolly-headedness which is part and parcel of our time. It is used as a weapon by the opponents of Democratic traditions. It is mistaken as "tolerance" or "broad mindedness" by foggy-thinking disciples of Democratic Socialism."[67]

Another way in which the chambers of commerce were active in the national ideological debate was through the placement of advertisements in newspapers. One such advertisement that can be seen as typical was a quarter-page that appeared in the *Regina Leader Post* on June 18, 1949. The large, bold title screamed "STATE SOCIALISM IS NOT THE ANSWER!" The copy quoted Alfred Edwards, Labour Member of Parliament in Yorkshire, England, who had crossed the floor and retracted his support for socialism. The conclusion drawn from Edwards' conversion was printed in large type along the bottom:

> Socialists everywhere have little understanding of the problems that arise in running a business until they get into business. The more realistic amongst them must admit to disillusionment when they learn the facts. They may remain reformers but, with Mr. Edwards say: "Socialism is not the answer." Freedom of Enterprise is the Only Answer.[68]

The 1949 campaign saw many business owners make direct threats to their employees. CCF stalwart Angus MacInnis spoke of being told of a number of British Columbia employers who threatened to fire employees who worked for the CCF.[69] During that campaign, Saskatchewan CCF leader and Premier Tommy Douglas travelled to Ontario and delivered a number of speeches. Among the issues addressed in his speeches were the anti-CCF activities of the insurance companies and the chambers of commerce. Douglas said, "The CCF party had polled 25,000 votes more in the last Saskatchewan election than they had in 1944 in spite of the concerted campaign against them by both the old line parties, the Chamber of Commerce, Canadian Manufacturers' Association and big insurance companies."[70]

The Canadian Chamber of Commerce continued to organize and finance its anti-CCF activities into the 1950s. Its 1953 report to the annual meeting, held in Edmonton, stated, without going into specifics, that the Canadian Chamber was continuing to protect the freedom of its members:

> Telling blows are being struck on behalf of free enterprise in the face of the persistent threat from socialism and other political economic systems which weaken or

destroy the sense of responsibility and the rights and freedoms of citizens. Many people do not know how our business system operates and have little appreciation of the tremendous benefits it offers as compared to other economic systems. The Chamber, therefore, is using every available channel to set forth the case for liberty and initiative, and to explain the functioning and operation of the free-market economy to employers, employees, teachers, students and others."[71]

In 1959, the last year of the CCF's existence, and with its electoral strength and potential at its nadir, the Canadian Chamber was still sponsoring anti-CCF activities. For example, on May 1, 1959, St. Catharines, Ontario CBC affiliate CKBT broadcast a public service program sponsored by the local chamber of commerce. It was so highly critical of the CCF, and contained such a plethora of factual errors, that party supporters who heard the broadcast believed it would cause serious damage both to the party and to the labour movement. Ontario CCF leader Donald Macdonald received a letter that stated, "It has been the usual, but worse, tirade against labour, public enterprise, creeping socialism, etc. [An unidentified CCF member] thinks other private stations do the same thing and he thinks it's so bad that the [Board of Broadcast Governors] should look into it, he thinks it borders so close to the political that it may contravene the CBC's ban on dramatized political broadcasts."[72]

By 1959, though, the Canadian Chamber of Commerce had changed its education program, from one of propagandizing the Canadian public as to the virtues of the free enterprise system and the vices of communism and socialism, to one more concerned with promoting entrepreneurialism among young people and instructing business people as to ways in which their businesses could become more successful. Pamphlets such as *How To Make Friends for Your Business* and *What About Profits?* became the norm. With the CCF no longer an electoral threat, the Canadian Chamber's anti-socialist/anti-CCF propaganda campaign was wound down.[73]

Newspapers

Through their enthusiastic endorsement of the business community's attacks on socialism and the CCF, as already seen in the support offered to insurance companies in their fight with the party, many Canadian newspapers were influential participants in the anti-socialist/anti-CCF campaign. They were part of the business community, as they were businesses themselves, but they also enjoyed a unique power in that they were the instruments through which most Canadians learned of their community, country, and world. Before the days of television, when many homes still did not even have a radio, newspapers were the most important source of news for most Canadians. Newspapers had to balance their ethical responsibility to truthfully and fairly inform the public against their financial responsibility to protect and enhance their bottom lines. Meanwhile, many were also implicitly, or explicitly, concerned with protecting the country's dominant ideology.

Even beyond their functions as businesses and disseminators and filters of information, newspapers deserve attention because, as Gramsci argued, they can act as "directive forces" appearing to stand outside the political fray while actually being a part of it. They exert an immense and subtle power, as many people believe them to be outside political parties, and thus believe that their content is unbiased and trustworthy. Gramsci argued that the actions of newspapers enable them to assume many of the functions of political parties, and in so doing, they are important players in the constant struggle for consensus in the civil society.[74] As such, their words and ideological allegiances deserve careful study.

Some newspapers played a role in the anti-CCF movement by refusing to print CCF advertising copy during election campaigns and by refusing to print letters to the editor or submitted articles that sought to answer or clarify attacks on the party. They also ran editorials that were equally harsh and biased in their criticism of the party, its leaders and its ideas. One of the newspapers that acted in this fashion was the *Montreal Star*. It printed the advertisements of Gladstone Murray, Burdick Trestrail, and others who ran anti-CCF campaigns that will be addressed later, as well as those we have seen already from the Canadian Chamber of Commerce, insurance companies, and others who also promoted capitalism by ravaging socialism and the CCF. However, when important CCF intellectual leader and noted Canadian Frank Scott wrote a response to a particularly unfair editorial, the *Star* refused to print it. The *Star* then published a new editorial, making the point that all that it had said about the CCF must be true because the party had failed to respond to its charges.[75] While squelching this debate, the *Star* attacked the CCF for its advocacy of socialism, which the paper claimed would do just that—stifle debate. Its January 11, 1944 editorial had attacked the CCF's investigation into the possible nationalization of insurance. The editorial's final point was that the newspaper felt happy to be able pass on its views on the matter, since "under socialism no such editorials would be allowed to appear so there would be none to pass on."[76]

Meanwhile, a similar situation presented a significant obstacle to the party in the Maritimes. In April 1944, Jim Mugridge, the New Brunswick CCF Provincial Executive chairman, was appointed chairman of the election committee for Saint John and County. In his first month on the job he found that T.F. Drummie, the editor of both Saint John newspapers, steadfastly refused to print any CCF copy whether it was political matter or paid advertising. In a letter to Lewis in which he explained his problem, Mugridge wrote that Drummie had told him, "That's not politics; we are doing a public service. You fellows are a public menace."[77] Only after a series of discussions did Drummie agree to take some party advertisements, but advised that he would be the judge as to which he would use and which he would not.

At that point the situation in New Brunswick was already difficult, with the provincial executive having trouble fielding candidates, signing members, raising funds, or generating substantial or sustained interest in the party. With little money and few people to respond to the anti-CCF propaganda that was being locally created or imported from the west, and with many Maritime newspapers playing a role in supporting that propaganda and stifling the party, the anti-CCF campaign had the field to itself. Mugridge made this point in a letter to Lewis, stating, "Our largest public meeting was 300 people. The same faces are seen at nearly all meetings. There are probably over 50,000 people, in this city alone, who have no idea in the world of our message except the unfavorable ideas endgendered [sic] through reading the prostitute press."[78]

Another newspaper that was active in the anti-socialist/anti-CCF campaign was the *Winnipeg Free Press*. Its anti-CCF editorials were scathing, unfair, and numerous. In October 1944, Lloyd Stinson, a CCF Winnipeg alderman and CCF provincial secretary, brought to Lewis' attention that the *Winnipeg Free Press* had printed an editorial in which it stated that the CCF was making an arrangement regarding sharing seats with the Bloc Populaire. No such deal had ever been contemplated. Stinson's frustration with the paper was clear in his letter: "we can't hope to answer all the charges made by their scurrilous, hysterical rag of a newspaper but we feel here that this particular one calls for something from headquarters."[79] Lewis wrote a letter of complaint to the editor of the *Winnipeg Free Press*, but there is no evidence of the letter being printed.

Later that month the paper published two more anti-CCF editorials. The October 12 editorial stated, "No socialist state can be democratic. Socialism and democracy contradict each other; and English socialists are honest enough to admit it frankly."[80] The October 16, 1944 editorial wrote of the CCF plan to "dump into the equivalent of concentration camps everyone whom the Socialists of Canada consider to be chronic idlers, shirkers and obstructers."[81] The editorial writer must have been aware of the emotional power of the term concentration camp, for it would have conjured up in readers' minds both the war's Nazi death camps and the Depression's relief work camps. The writer would have understood not only that what had been written was a lie but also that tying the CCF to these emotionally charged images would hurt the party.

Its attacks continued the next year. Its April 15, 1945 editorial was entitled "The CCF Appeal to Fear" and criticized Coldwell and Douglas for allegedly always beginning their appeals to voters by asking them to remember the hard times of the Depression. It went on to attack CCF ideas to avoid a post-war depression, with special attention to the party's contention that deficit financing might be a tool to fight any future economic downturn. The editorial ignored the fact that deficit financing had been used by Canadian, British, and American governments to fight two wars and the Depression and claimed, "The ultimate end of deficit financing is dictatorship and bankruptcy, which have both occurred wherever nations made deficit financing a continual policy."[82]

An editorial published the next month continued the attack. It asserted, "The multitude of boards which the Russians established, and which the CCF would set up to carry through their master plan, must have authority...The entire coercive power of the state must be marshaled [sic] behind the plan. Opposition must be ruthlessly suppressed, for opposition to the master-plan becomes treason to the state."[83] Using the term "master-plan" was a brilliant propaganda ploy, as it would have played on the lingering fears of the totalitarian Soviet state, of what could happen if Canada were even temporarily allied with the Soviet Union. At the same time, it would have brought Hitler's use of the term to readers' minds.

On the same day that this damning editorial was published, the *Winnipeg Free Press* editorial cartoon showed a ramshackle airplane held together with strings and tape and powered by a bicycle. On the plane was written "CCF Plan For Canada." Its propeller was a cuckoo clock's crazed bird sprung from the front. Coldwell was shown pointing to the plane and saying to a man with Saskatchewan written on his back, "Here's your chance to take the first ride in my new airplane—it's never been off the ground."[84]

The next week the paper raised the bogey of the CCF taking over family farms, playing to direct material concerns in a province where farming was still an important occupation and part of the economy. An editorial entitled "The CCF and the Land" argued that the people of Saskatchewan did not want the government to take over their farms. It noted that Tommy Douglas had insisted that the CCF had no intention to do so, but claimed that he and the party were saying other things in other parts of the country. The editorial reported, without supporting evidence, that the party planned the mass collectivization of farms in a cooperative scheme and that "individual farmers, who cannot compete with the government-subsidized co-operatives, will obviously be forced out of business or into the co-operatives."[85]

The June 11 editorial attacked the party's trade policies by incorrectly asserting that the CCF supported an isolationist policy, which would hurt farmers and the entire Canadian economy. It concluded, "The CCF remains today what it was in the beginning, a party which regards trade as of little importance, a party which lays all its emphasis upon socializing the internal economy of Canada in an effort to isolate this country from the world."[86]

The power of the *Winnipeg Free Press* to sway opinion, and the degree to which the CCF recognized and attempted to address that power, was seen in an exchange between influential Canadian intellectual, labour leader, and tireless CCF supporter Eugene Forsey and *The Economist*, which had a decidedly anti-CCF stance. Forsey was one of the founding members of the League for Social Reconstruction in 1930. Along with fellow Montrealers Frank Underhill and King Jordan, as well as Irene Bliss, Harry Cassidy, Eric Havelock, and others from Toronto, and Hamilton's Kenneth Taylor, the LSR played an enormously important role in establishing the intellectual ideas and credentials of the Canadian left in general, and the CCF in particular. Involved in the early days was a young law student, David Lewis. Forsey was among the most visible and outspoken intellectuals in defence of social democracy and the CCF, and on February 23, 1945, set his sights on the *Economist* criticizing an article published the previous month entitled "Socialism in Saskatchewan." He argued that the article contained a number of errors that demonstrated a lack of careful research. Forsey contended that the article was wrong in its assertion that the CCF's economic policies were based on economic self-sufficiency and that it contained many other inaccuracies regarding the Saskatchewan Trade Union Act, party policy on closed shops, and the Saskatchewan Act regarding a compulsory check-off box for union dues. Forsey concluded that the *Economist's* irresponsible and inaccurate article placed the periodical among those of the press who were a part of the anti-CCF campaign. In his conclusion, Forsey chose to mention only one Canadian newspaper as representative of that effort. He wrote, in reference to the *Economist* author, "His statement is wholly false, a mere echo of the propagandistic twaddle of the *Winnipeg Free Press*."[87]

Another newspaper that played a significant role in the anti-CCF movement was the *Ottawa Journal,* which made no secret of its editorial opposition to the CCF. In a large editorial published on January 12, 1944, it lashed out at the party in particular and socialism in general. Entitled "Please Don't Laugh Everybody—This Thing is Serious," it began by reminding readers that the paper had already criticized Woodsworth and CCF leaders for their stand against the war, but that the *Journal* was also opposed to the assumptions and conclusions of David Lewis and Frank Scott's *Make This Your Canada.* The editorial contended that only unfettered capitalism was good for Canada and that a planned economy offered only "magical" things that would never work. It concluded:

> One can imagine what a mess this CCF program would make of the Canadian industrial and business structure: and yet the CCF wise-acres talk glibly of the vast sums of money they would spend when they get to power... The basic idea of Socialism is to seize all main activities of a civilized country and administer them by government appointed men or boards ("administrative boards," says the CCF booklet) with the idea of leveling society so that the intelligent, energetic and industrious people shall get less, and the lazy, the idle, and the inefficient and the unintelligent shall get more.[88]

In April 1944, Coldwell felt obliged to respond to another editorial attack from the *Ottawa Journal,* in a letter to the editor. The to-and-fro had begun when the paper took exception to a CCF advertisement that contained a cartoon showing a stereotypical capitalist, in a suit and top hat, throwing mud at the CCF. The *Journal's* editorial had made the point that the cartoon was unfair. Coldwell wrote to say that the party advertisement was part of a series of four meant to counteract the anti-CCF campaign. He wrote, "That this campaign against us has been financed by certain big business executives is beyond dispute."[89]

The *Journal* responded in two ways to Coldwell's letter. First, it inserted an editor's note under the letter saying that Coldwell was wrong to assert that the smear campaign against the CCF by business was beyond dispute. The insertion said, "The thing is not at all 'beyond dispute,' rests entirely on the CCF's odd assumption that while it should have complete freedom to attack, nobody should have any right to defence."[90] Second, on the same page as Coldwell's letter, the newspaper ran an editorial under the heading "Mr. Coldwell Missed Our Point." The editorial claimed that the *Journal's* objection to the CCF advertisement was that it suggested that only rich business people were opposed to the CCF, when most people in the country did not support the party. It then returned to a point made in January, contending that the CCF was trying to scare Canadians into supporting its policies. It said, "The economic climate is becoming increasingly adverse to the CCF and the now habitual practice of trying to terrify people with 1933 scarecrows is fairly convincing evidence that the Socialists know it. "[91] In a fascinating conclusion, given all that preceded it, the editorial then called on all of the parties and those people and groups involved in the election to end name-calling.

The *Journal* seemed gleeful about the June 1945 Ontario election, which saw a precipitous reduction in the number of CCF seats and in its popular support. In an interpretation of the federal election, held only days later, the newspaper celebrated the party's failure to win seats in central and eastern Canada and took what it apparently wished to convey to its readers as final shots at the party:

> The danger of Socialism has been checked with a single member elected between the Atlantic and the Great Lakes, the CCF becomes a sectional movement, nationally a spent force...the CCF represented things alien to our Canadian traditions and to the genius of our

people. The CCF with its socialistic jargon, with its foreign accents, represented an intellectual hangover from Europe, was too ideological for our Canadian people, who, whatever their faults, have little use for doctrinaire creeds and isms. A degree of collectivism may prevail in this country, may gain wide favor among many of our people; we have no use for Socialism or for the totalitarian ideas that attach itself to it.[92]

Two days later the *Journal* appeared somewhat less certain about the party's death. Its June 15 editorial criticized the Liberal and Progressive Conservative parties for complacency, and it argued that they were falling back into their normal habits of resting between elections even though the CCF "menace" remained. With humorously mixed metaphors, the editorial stated:

Last week's election did not kill the CCF and the Socialist menace has not passed. While the two old parties are putting off their armor, assuming that their work is done until another general election comes four or five years hence, the CCF is keeping on its armor, preparing to carry on its work and propaganda without stop. While so-called "free enterprise" is going to rest on its oars, satisfied that everything is well, Socialism will go on with its propaganda with redoubled zest.[93]

The editorial extolled both the Liberals and Conservatives to continue to raise funds and to work hard to avoid "being submerged by Socialism."[94]

Some publishers, unwilling to publicly express their personal points of view, acted behind the scenes. Such was the case with Phillip Ross, who published the *Ottawa Citizen* and was one of Gladstone Murray's supporters. His paper published a number of anti-CCF editorials and articles and reported glowingly on many of Murray's speeches.[95]

Meanwhile, other publishers appeared to be quite comfortable in publicly stating their preferences while seeing those preferences reflected in their newspapers. *The Globe and Mail*'s George McCullagh is an example of this type of publisher, his support of and role in the Progressive Conservative

Party being well-known. In fact, during the 1949 campaign, an often-run Liberal advertisement included a cartoon showing the Cabinet in a boat pulling oars together with Prime Minister St. Laurent at the bow with a bullhorn. The CCF ran a similar cartoon, showing McCullagh in a leaky bathtub yelling instructions through a bullhorn at frustrated-looking Ontario Progressive Conservative leader George Drew.[96]

In speeches during that campaign, Coldwell sometimes called attention to certain newspapers and their publishers as being virulently anti-CCF or biased in support of the old-line parties, and McCullagh was a favourite nemesis. In a Windsor, Ontario speech on May 27, for instance, Coldwell made the familiar charge that George Drew and the Progressive Conservatives were controlled by big business and that many worked together in the anti-socialist/anti-CCF campaign. Among the anti-CCF business leaders Coldwell specifically named was a Mr. Wright of certain mining interests, a Mr. Bickle of certain chain stores, and Mr. McCullagh of *The Globe and Mail*.[97]

Under McCullagh's leadership, the *The Globe and Mail* published many anti-CCF articles that went beyond the pale of normal political opinion pieces. Among them was a series by William S. Gibson, who was the president of National Cellulose of Canada Limited and the author of a book entitled *You Knew What You Were Voting For*. The book examined Lewis and Scott's *Make This Your Canada* and took exception to many of the facts upon which they had based their economic arguments. The Gibson series, which consisted of excerpts from his book, included conversations he had undertaken with un-named CCF voters and workers who claimed to understand CCF policy but were, according to Gibson, confused as to the party's dangerous intentions for the country. He argued that CCF economic policies were based on a misunderstanding of basic economic facts. Eugene Forsey, then the director of research for the Canadian Congress of Labour, wrote to Gibson and pointed out, in a rather condescending tone, that it was, in fact, Gibson who was confused:

> Your quarrel is not with the CCF but with the Dominion Bureau of Statistics, and indeed with statisticians and economists generally. You are evidently unaware of what national income figures mean... All this stuff of yours about people lending and borrowing is wholly

beside the point, and has no more relevance to what is discussed in "Make This Your Canada" than a dissertation on hoop skirts.[98]

Meanwhile, *The Globe and Mail* continued to publish his series, as well as a number of anti-CCF advertisements that Gibson had created, until October 1946.

The Globe and Mail also published a great number of editorials attacking the party that were much like those of other anti-CCF newspapers and publications of the anti-socialist/anti-CCF campaign. Beyond its editorial copy, *The Globe and Mail's* editorial cartoons were also scathing. George Boothe's cartoons reflected many of the stereotypes that the anti-socialism/anti-CCF campaign had foisted upon the country. They also took a racist tone when portraying CCF general secretary David Lewis. In his memoirs, Lewis took exception to the cartoons, revealing anger that continued to rankle even decades after the fact. Lewis wrote that Boothe's cartoons "depicted my features in a way which literally rivaled the frankly anti-Semitic cartoons I had seen in *Der Stürmer*, the weekly Nazi publication in the thirties."[99]

Beyond allowing the Boothe cartoons to be printed on the editorial page of his newspaper, McCullagh revealed his support of the anti-CCF campaign by allowing the cartoons to be copied and widely distributed as a 1951 pamphlet entitled *Down the Garden Path*. Even more significant was the fact that Boothe's *Globe and Mail* editorial cartoons graced Trestrail's *Social Suicide*, which was a virulently anti-CCF tract distributed nationally as unsolicited mail.

The Globe and Mail was not alone in having its anti-CCF message transferred to pamphlet form: other newspapers used that tactic to win greater coverage of their negative messages. One of the first was published in 1940 by R.P. MacLean, the editor and publisher of the *Kelowna Courier*. MacLean's 14-page pamphlet was entitled *Reflections of a Wicked Capitalist,* and in it, he pondered how he could run his newspaper if the socialists took power. He predicted that "since the goods which each citizen used every day would be decided for him by experts, and the price of them settled so that they would absorb the proper proportion of his income, there would be no reason for advertising at all."[100] MacLean cited no source for his contention that any of these notions were official CCF policy. In fact, throughout the pamphlet,

MacLean never once referred to any CCF documents, but he made increasingly outrageous accusations as to the fate of the country under increasingly absurd, but supposed, CCF policies. His final sentence questioned the patriotism of CCF leaders and supporters. He wrote of the many brave men and women working to support the war effort, then concluded, "so far as we know there are no socialists among them. Socialist leaders have been too busy with their post-war planning and political propaganda to give their 'expert' services to the war effort except to stir up discontent among war workers."[101] The last point could only inflame opinion at a time when the war was seen as a popular and patriotic necessity.

Another of this type of anti-CCF propaganda, called *Pie in the Sky Socialism*, was published and distributed by the *Regina Leader Post* in 1944. Like *The Globe and Mail*'s Boothe pamphlet, the *Leader Post* reprinted its many anti-CCF editorial cartoons. The pamphlet was dedicated to "all of those who have footed the bills for the Socialist experiment in Saskatchewan—the taxpayers. In short, to U and I."[102] In its opening paragraphs, the pamphlet called the CCF leaders who took power in Saskatchewan "hot-eyed, power hungry left wingers [who] put the squeeze on business [and] restricted personal freedom through the use of compulsion."[103] No evidence or examples of such action are offered. It is unnecessary to describe each of the 44 Charles Bell editorial cartoons that follow. Suffice it to say that each is nasty in its portrayal of Douglas and other CCF leaders and consistent in its ridicule of CCF ideas. Newly written captions were as critical as they were unfair.[104]

Many small-town newspapers also contributed to the anti-CCF movement. While their influence was not on a national scale like *The Globe and Mail* or even regionally significant like the *Winnipeg Free Press,* they nonetheless influenced the ridings in which they were published. One such newspaper that can serve as an example was Ontario's *Peterborough Examiner.* A glance at the coverage of the 1945 campaign illustrates its anti-CCF editorial stand, which was maintained throughout the 1940s.

Its May 18, 1945 editorial hinted at many of the false assumptions and fears raised by the anti-socialist/anti-CCF campaign in its discussion of socialism's anti-Christian beliefs, its anti-Canadianism, and the untrustworthiness of the CCF's leaders. It began by stating that anyone who had followed the newspaper knew that it supported the Liberal government in

Ottawa and went on to praise Mackenzie King's handling of the war and his plans for the post-war economic adjustments. It continued on to claim that

> Mr. Coldwell has had no such experience, and if he were to represent Canada in international conferences we may be sure that he would speak first as a socialist, and second as a Canadian, for socialism is a burning and fanatical faith, and those who profess it dare have no God before it. To let Mr. Coldwell speak for Canada in the council of nations at this crucial period of the world's history would be a most dangerous experiment.[105]

Also on the editorial page that day was an article by local selective service head W.H.L. Mellis, who reported that, based on the predictions made by many business people, the small, industrial city of Peterborough would enjoy full employment when all the servicemen of the area returned home. Mellis concluded that this belief, which was reported as fact, put to rest the CCF "propaganda" that supposed that there could be an unemployment problem in Canada after the war. In a tone that insulted the intelligence of working-class people, while claiming to be concerned with their interests, Mellis wrote,

> The cry of unemployment is a common one with the CCF, and it is a cry which we particularly deplore for it plays upon the fear of people who are especially prone to fear—industrial workers. The CCF which was begotten in the depression of the thirties has talked depression ever since, and has offered to save the workers from further depression by the cure-all of socialism.[106]

In an irony obviously lost on Mellis, he concluded that workers need not worry about the Depression returning or consider socialist ideas because of the "impressive body of social legislation designed to prevent the horrors of the last depression from being repeated."[107]

Opposing the CCF while supporting its policies was an idea to which the newspaper often returned. Mackenzie King would have been proud, for

53

instance, had he read the *Peterborough Examiner* editorial of the next day, for it made the point that, since the prime minister had essentially taken many of the CCF's ideas and enacted them in legislation, that the country did not need the CCF: The May 19 editorial stated:

> The CCF has no concrete advantage to offer to the electors which the Liberal party does not also offer, and the older party has repeatedly forestalled the younger one in matters of social legislation. All that the CCF can offer which Liberalism can not is an extreme form of state control which would, in our opinion, lead to abuses greater than any that capitalism has ever engendered.[108]

The next week the editorial writers returned to their attempts to keep the working class vote from the CCF. Its May 25 editorial claimed that the party was simply wrong in arguing that its voice was the voice of the "working man."[109] Three days later the point was made again in an editorial that quoted American trade union leaders William Green of the AFL and Phillip Murray of the CIO, who had both stated their support for the free enterprise system. It concluded with assertions for which it offered no facts or evidence, while ignoring the British Labour Party and other examples: "Wherever socialism has been given a complete trial it has not only ruined the industrialists, but has also cut the ground from under the unions... Organized labour knows this, and it is working strongly against the CCF."[110] It then listed the occupations of the CCF leaders, apparently to demonstrate that they had no affinity for workers. Coldwell, Knowles, Joliffe, and Lewis were listed as teacher, preacher, lawyer, and lawyer respectively, with the conclusion, "We see no reason to believe that the CCF is more closely representative of the working man (using the expression in their own narrow sense) than the Progressive Conservative or Liberal parties."[111]

Like all newspapers, the *Examiner* often reprinted articles from other newspapers. A number of anti-CCF *Globe and Mail* articles found their way to Peterborough readers. On the same page as the May 28 editorial that attempted to split the CCF from the industrial workers' vote, a reprinted *Globe and Mail* article by W.J. Gartley attempted to do the same for the farm vote. Gartley reported, without evidence, that the CCF planned to nationalize all family farms and end democracy. He wrote of "long haired Socialists running up and down the country with plans for this, plans for that, and a master plan for everybody. The CCF plan would mean that my freedom and individuality would vanish."[112]

The bogey of a CCF dictatorship was repeated in the main editorial the next day. After calling George Drew an excellent premier, the editorial turned to attack Coldwell. It said, "Every time the CCF leader opens his mouth he puts his foot deeper into it. Mr. Coldwell, your arguments don't hold water."[113] It ended by conceding that Ontarians have the final choice of who shall govern them, but ominously warned, "If the people of Ontario want a totalitarian state, it is for them to say so."[114]

Warning its readership of the dictatorial designs of the party was a theme to which the newspaper often returned. On June 1, for example, displaying its editorial writers' determination never to miss a chance to slam the party, the *Examiner* offered a glowing piece praising the number of volunteers that had taken on a wide variety of causes throughout the previous summer to make Peterborough a better place in which to live. It then argued that, under a CCF government, volunteerism would not be allowed, as it would contradict party policies that dictated that all such activities had to go first to unionized workers. Although it would have been impossible to find anything in party policies to support such an idea, the editorial concluded, "Not only could a socialist State not afford to pay for this sort of work; it could not provide the ethical background for it."[115]

On the same editorial page, another article wrote of Coldwell speaking in San Francisco and of his expressing surprise that a CBC reporter was covering his speech so far from home. Echoing arguments made by some of the larger newspapers, the editorial noted that, if the CCF ever came to power, all privately owned news organizations would be put out of business, leaving only the CBC. It stated, "But if Mr. Coldwell had his way, which is the socialist way, nothing but the CBC would be left to them."[116]

The next day, the *Examiner* reprinted a *Globe and Mail* article written by influential journalist Bruce Hutchison, in which he argued that Coldwell was like the Pink Knight in *Alice in Wonderland,* fighting against the capitalist jabberwocky. Hutchison had confused *Alice in Wonderland* for *Through the Looking Glass,* and, further, there was no pink knight, but a red and white one, and neither fought the Jabberwocky. Nonetheless, the article continued with a long poem in which Hutchison stretched the tortured metaphor to the breaking point while misrepresenting a number of CCF policies. The article concluded with an insult to all of those who might consider voting for the party: "Canada, wonderfully rich in energy, strength and resources, is still too small a brain for its immense body. And from intellectual infantilism springs this silly, vengeful talk of voting against something when there is so much to vote for."[117]

Following the 1945 Ontario and federal elections, the *Examiner*'s June 14 editorial called Coldwell and Ontario CCF leader Ted Joliffe "sore losers" and "totalitarian leaders." It then explained why it had taken such a strong anti-CCF stance, repeating the old arguments that its leaders were untrustworthy and that its policies would destroy the economy and lead to dictatorship. It then brought new emotionally charged rhetoric to the debate: "One of our quarrels with the CCF is that it makes a religion of politics as it attempts to make crusades of political campaigns, it vilifies its opponents as heretics and devil worshippers and it puts forward its ideas as mystical beliefs which will right all the wrongs of the world."[118]

The irony of its words seems to have been lost on the editorial writers, as was the irony inherent in the words and actions of business leaders, business representatives, and other highly politicized newspapers; as they spoke of their love for the freedom of democracy and the honest competition of free enterprise, while using all the power they could muster in the ideological battle in the civil society, which sought to limit the freedom of debate and end the competition of ideas.

The actions taken by insurance companies, the Canadian Chamber of Commerce, and some of the country's newspapers, reveal much about the anti-socialist/anti-CCF campaign. The magnitude of the campaign was evidenced by the volume of the material pushed upon the Canadian people. Current issues, such as the war and plans for the post-war economy, were woven into the propaganda. Confusion regarding fascism, communism, and socialism was encouraged, and emotions regarding Stalin, Mussolini, and Hitler were stirred. Some of the links between the people and organizations involved in the many facets of the campaign, and the consistency of its message, words, and images is also revealed. There was no pretence of neutrality or objectivity in the campaign, which was as ingenious as it was brutal.

INTO THE HURRICANE

THE INSIDIOUS CAMPAIGNS
OF MURRAY AND TRESTRAIL

While many Canadian business people undertook direct attacks against the CCF and the ideas for which it stood, many also acted somewhat more clandestinely, using individuals and thinly veiled front organizations to do their bidding. The most important of these mercenaries were the secretive and fascinating Gladstone Murray and Burdick Trestrail. They organized and led two organizations that used money raised primarily from business people to bring pro-capitalist and ruthlessly anti-socialist/anti-CCF ideas to the Canadian public, through speeches to various groups and clubs, media manipulation, advertising, publications, and direct mailings. Their actions were important in that they supported the ideological arguments of Canada's political and business elite, while offering ideas, questions, and vocabulary for those wishing to challenge socialism in general and the CCF in particular. The CCF leadership and rank-and-file recognized the power of the two organizations and made a number of attempts to counter their influence. That the party leadership spent so much time and energy in that effort is evidence of the efficacy of the Murray and Trestrail operations.

Gladstone Murray

Gladstone Murray was an intriguing and mysterious man. He was shameless in his self-promotion, yet his papers indicate that he was also quite adept at controlling access to those parts of his life that he obviously wished to remain in shadow. Murray was born in Maple Ridge, British Columbia, graduated from McGill University, and attended Oxford University as a Rhodes Scholar. He left Oxford, without earning a degree, to serve in the First World War as a member of the Highland Infantry and ended his service as an airman with the rank of Major. Having shown bravery and skill, he earned the Military Cross, Distinguished Flyer Cross, Croix de Guerre, and the Italian Medal for Valour. Murray became a journalist, writing for Beaverbrook's *Daily Express*, then one of the first employees at what evolved into the BBC, eventually being promoted to manager of publicity and industrial relations, and, later, of political relations. He returned to Canada in 1936 to become general manager of the CBC and resigned in March 1943 as the Director General for Programs. Like much of his life, his resignation is something of a mystery. While he was allowed to resign for personal reasons, there were suspicions about his drinking and his possible misuse of CBC funds. Nonetheless, it is significant that, by the time of his resignation, Murray had a resumé that engendered respect in many quarters, and he had a network of friends and acquaintances among Canada's political and economic elite.

Murray's reputation, connections, and qualifications rendered him a natural to lead a national political adventure. That adventure began in late 1941, while he was still with the CBC, and was dubbed "Responsible Enterprise." Its stated purpose was to promote free enterprise, but the means was through an attack on communism and socialism. Since the Communist Party was never an electoral threat, its chief aim was to discredit socialism and the CCF.[1]

Murray's organization was set up so that he was responsible for day-to-day operations, while overall policy matters were approved in advance by those whom he called "participants." He consulted with participants when needed and dispensed advice as to how they could assist in the project through individual initiatives.[2] While no minutes of meetings seem to have been taken, or at least to have survived, there is evidence that, besides meetings with individuals and small groups of business people, Murray also hosted annual meetings of his supporting participants.

The "founder participants" set the project's budget and terms of reference. In a 1943 letter soliciting support from a business leader, Murray explained the necessity of the participants maintaining control of the organization's expenses and mandate, stating, "This was a consideration of the founder participants when they limited the project to a three-year period and an expenditure of $100,000 with the expectation that this amount would be forthcoming from a relatively few leaders in industry and finance representing a cross-section of business throughout Canada."[3] Beyond this initial contribution, participants were sometimes called upon to make special contributions-in-kind to defray costs of the campaign. CPR President N.R. Crump, for example, agreed to provide Murray with free rail transportation to British Columbia.[4]

While Murray's actual expenses are not known, they must have been enormous, for, as will be seen, he would have needed funds to cover his salary, along with expenses for his offices, secretarial assistance, postage, printing, travel, accommodation, research, and more. That the campaign was well-financed is demonstrated by the fact that all of these, and related, expenses were covered, and, at the same time, even though Murray undertook an ambitious schedule of speaking engagements, he was always able to waive his speaker's fees. Correspondence between Murray and many of the groups to whom he spoke indicated that this practice increased the scope of the campaign, as many of those groups allocated his speaking fee to other groups that were trumpeting the same anti-socialist/anti-CCF message.[5]

By August 1943, Responsible Enterprise was thriving. A 1943 letter to Ontario Progressive Conservative leader George Drew, inviting him to join in the anti-CCF campaign, revealed the depth of business support Murray had assembled. He explained, "The project has been undertaken at the initiative of a group of representative leaders in industry and finance."[6] Murray enclosed a partial list of participants, which included business leaders from public utilities, finance, mining, insurance, and industry. There was a suggestion that there were more supporters still but that they wished to remain anonymous (see appendix 2).

Murray pursued his goals, and those of his benefactors, in many ways, but the activity that served as the base for the whole campaign was his speaking tours. Murray addressed a number of audiences from 1943 to 1962, with his busiest schedule in the crucial years from 1943 to 1950. He spoke to service clubs, church groups, professional organizations, legions, chambers of commerce, and more (see appendix 3). For nearly every speech, he prepared copies as pamphlets that he distributed to his audience, with extras for those who could not attend. He sought membership lists with which he could mail additional copies of his speeches and from which a mailing list for other publications could be created. His experience in radio allowed him to skillfully use newspapers to advertise and publicize his speeches, and, in many cases, to have them broadcast. He also published a monthly newsletter and published and distributed pamphlets by others with similar messages.

Murray's well-prepared and articulate speeches were all ostensibly about the role that capitalism and liberal democracy played in the development of Canada's culture and economy and in the promotion and protection of all that was and had ever been right and good in the Western world. The speeches then always moved on to discuss the forces that threatened those systems, values, and Canada's way of life. Considering that his speeches began during the Second World War and continued into the Cold War, it is interesting that, while he portrayed fascism and communism as dangerous, he insisted that his greatest fear for the country was from socialism and, specifically, the CCF. He insisted, in fact, that there was little difference between the beliefs and goals of those ideologies. Murray's portrayal of socialism and of the party were seldom accurate and always sensationalist.

One of Murray's favourite bogies, and the one most often used to attack the CCF, was collectivism. In a speech that he delivered in slightly different forms throughout Ontario during the fall of 1943, he defined collectivists as those "who believe that the profit motive, free enterprise, and capitalism are the real obstacles to progress... The collectivists say in effect, 'we shall continue and extend the war controls and the war management by government agencies. Hand over your banks, insurance companies, communications, important industries and agriculture.'"[7] Standing against the collectivists, he argued, were individualists who wanted free enterprise and a maximum degree of freedom in society. The struggle that Canada would undertake at the war's conclusion, he contended, would be between individualists, who had faith in the Canadian political and economic systems and in Canadian values, and the collectivists, who did not.

Demonstrating his ability to bend his themes to his audience, Murray ingratiated himself with members of the Canadian Shorthorn Association at the outset of his February 1945 speech at Toronto's Royal York Hotel, by relating stories of his childhood days on a farm in the Fraser Valley and of the day he accepted the responsibility of leading a shorthorn bull calf 20 miles to the provincial exhibition in New Westminster. Those experiences, he claimed, taught him the importance of individualism and self-reliance, which were values, he argued, that were shared by all in the room and all those involved in agriculture throughout history and throughout the world. Why then, he pondered, would anyone want to surrender those values to those who attack them? He warned:

> After the war we shall be invited to discard the creed of the free individual by those who tell us that salvation rests in collectivism. They say that freedom has been tried and found wanting; that the all-powerful state is the solution; that the profit motive is wrong; that private ownership is wrong. Make no mistake about the effect of such a policy on the farming community. Realizing that farmers are sturdy individualists, the advocates of fundamental change pretend that farmers may remain an isolated island of freedom in a sea of state socialism.[8]

At the Royal Connaught Hotel in Hamilton, Murray addressed about 400 members of the Purchasing Agents of Canada at their annual conference in November 1944. The title of his talk was "Problems of the Canadian Economy." He mentioned several problems regarding the re-establishment of commerce and trade in a post-war world, such as adjusting to the influx of immigrants, which he saw as a positive factor, and the long-running tension between French and English in Canada. Toward the end of his speech, he came to the most dangerous threat to the Canadian economy, which he characterized as "state worshippers," or those who believe that the state can look after the affairs of citizens better than citizens themselves:

> The state-worshippers are split into numerous factions that seem to hate each other more than they hate freedom itself. The two main divisions are the Socialists

and the Communists. The Socialists are generous enough to say that they will not abolish freedom until they get a mandate from the voters... Make no mistake about it, these enemies of freedom are a menace to the future of our economy... To "sell out" to the state-worshippers would guarantee the doom of the future economy of Canada.[9]

A speech to the Canadian Corps Association of Toronto, in November 1943, introduced another of his themes and an idea that was to be a significant part of all anti-CCF propaganda. Murray argued that the danger posed by the CCF, insofar as it supported collectivist ideas, was that, if it came to power, it would enact policies that would lead inevitably to revolution, chaos, and possibly communist, fascist, or totalitarian rule in Canada. To a receptive audience of military personnel, Murray referred to a speech by communist Leslie Morris at the founding of the communist Labour Progressive Party the previous August in Toronto. In that speech, Murray claimed, Morris said that the election of a CCF government would be the first stage in establishing a communist Canada. Murray explained:

> He minced no words about the CCF. They were a necessary transitional stage; their part was like that of the Mensheviks in Russia under Kerensky. But even if the CCF could avoid control or direction by the extremists, its programme could not be framed and applied without the employment of totalitarian methods and the enforced suppression of all opposition.[10]

Murray developed this theme in a February 1944 speech to the Kiwanis Club of London, Ontario, noting that many people of the province seemed to be considering voting for a change in government. He bluntly warned his audience about the dangers of considering the CCF, saying, "There has emerged a new political party which advocates policies that cannot be carried out within the framework of existing free democracy."[11] He then examined CCF policies in detail but twisted them beyond recognition, in accord with his sincere belief, or cynical contention, that all were derived from communism. He then upped the ante by contending that a Canadian dalliance with the CCF would not only lead to communism but inevitably to fascism. His alarming conclusion for the audience was, "It is something more than coincidence, however, that when Hitler was appealing for the votes of the Germans on behalf of his National Socialist Workers' Union, his propaganda had much in common with that of the advocates of socialism in Canada."[12]

Days later, Murray addressed the Toronto Kiwanis Club at the Grace Church of the Hill. He assailed the CCF directly and from the very first words of his speech. Again bringing the Hitler comparison to the fore, he said, "and, by the way, although the party is both national and socialist, the CCF leaders are strangely tender about being called National Socialists."[13] To another Kiwanis Club he repeated his warning that a CCF government would be a transitional, or Kerensky, government, and he accused all Canadian socialists of being "chameleon communists" and "appeasers."[14] He ended with a direct plea to his audience to defeat the CCF at the polls, concluding, "Its defeat requires the thought and action of every Canadian who has genuine concern about the future of the country and of the British Commonwealth and Empire."[15]

Three years later, Murray was standing firm in his contention that socialism, through support of the CCF, would lead to the harder stuff of communism and fascism. In March 1947, Murray spoke to the Conservative Progress Association at Toronto's Albany Club. The association comprised important members of and contributors to the Progressive Conservative Party. Its honorary presidents were former Prime Ministers R.B. Bennett and Arthur Meighen and future federal PC leaders John Bracken and George Drew. In his speech, entitled "How to Save Freedom," he said that he preferred communists to socialists, as they were more honest in their goals and tactics. He argued:

> But the Socialist has built up an elaborate façade of sweet reasonableness. He says he will seek power by democratic means and apply his measures only by the mandate of the people When the Socialist argues thus, he conveniently ignores the fundamental truth that Socialism and Democracy are intrinsically incompatible... The CCF in Canada are doing a good job of softening up resistance to Collectivism; but if they

do gain power, they will be brushed aside as were the
Kerenskyite Social Democrats in Russia.[16]

Murray's solution to the threat posed by the CCF was for Canadians to express their love of freedom by defending their institutions from those who would destroy them. He also urged the two old-line political parties to fight socialism. Further, he argued that industries should provide fair wages and good working conditions to keep workers happy and, thereby, fight the development of class consciousness.[17]

Another theme of his speeches rested on the argument that the CCF's adherence to fascist policies led to its disdain for the profit motive and to its goal of taking over all areas of economic activity, from bank ownership to land ownership. At Toronto's Bathurst Auditorium in October 1944, for example, Murray's short introduction took his audience back to the days of the cavemen, who discovered that those wishing to survive had to accumulate excess fuel and food for the coming winter. This metaphor led him directly to current economic systems, in which, he claimed, monopolistic practices and cartels were properly controlled, but the profit motive, quite rightly, in his opinion, was allowed to continue as a motivator for pursuing the "Common Good." It was at this point that he began his attack on the CCF, as part of an ideology that wished to destroy thousands of years of economic and social progress by removing the profit motive from society. He equated that CCF desire with the policies and goals of both Nazi Germany and Communist administrations, saying, "that democratic socialism, the great 'Utopia' of the last few generations is not only unachievable, but that to strive for it produces something so utterly different that few of those who now wish it would be prepared to accept the consequences, many will not believe till the connection has been laid bare in all its aspects. Germany is the prototype of this development."[18]

Murray took great care to ensure that his speeches reached far beyond his assembled audiences. Often, the organizations to which he had spoken acted as his anti-CCF agents and co-conspirators, as they undertook to distribute hundreds of pamphlets of his speeches to members, friends, and supporters. A few examples illustrate the point: R.J. Johnston of the Bank of Nova Scotia Accountants Club wrote to Murray, saying, "It may interest you to know that your talk has stirred up a great deal of interesting discussion and many members have expressed the opinion that they now have a much clearer view of the Socialist aims of the CCF and the attending dangers. The Club would like to take advantage of your kind offer to furnish us with a few printed copes of your recent address before the Queen's Alumni Association."[19] Two hundred fifty copies of a speech were sent to members of Montreal's Kiwanis Club who had missed it, pamphlets were sent to all of the members of the St. Catharines Rotary Club, 200 copies of his May 1947 speech were sent to members of Oshawa's Kiwanis Club, copies of his speech to the Ontario Medical Association were distributed to every doctor in the province, and 125 copies of his December 1947 speech to the Junior Investment Dealers Association in Toronto were distributed to all its members.[20]

It was not only the large numbers of pamphlets distributed, but also who they reached, that was significant. As an illustration of this point, on May 30, 1958, Murray spoke to the Canadian Roofing Contractors Association in Toronto, which in itself ensured national exposure to his ideas. Prior to the engagement, 25 copies of his speech were mailed to each member who was not planning to attend. More significantly, following the speech, Murray mailed copies to the presidents of 21 companies, including British Petroleum Canada, Canada Permanent Mortgage Corporation, Cities Service Oil Company, Crown Life Insurance Company, Dominion Rubber Company, Donnacona Paper Company, Goodyear Tire and Rubber Company, Great Lake Paper Company, Harris and Partners Limited, Hollinger Mines, Moore Corporation, National Life Assurance Company, Procter and Gamble, Alphonse Raymond Limited, Silverwoods Dairies, Sun Oil Company, Toronto General Trusts Corporation, Union Carbide Canada, Union Gas Company of Canada, and the William Weld Company.[21] The list reveals the extent of Murray's business contacts, supporters, and audience. Even if it had only a small effect on the beliefs and actions of the leaders of these businesses, the pamphlet was significant.

There was often a seamlessness between the anti-socialist/anti-CCF campaign and many business leaders' professional lives. This fact can be demonstrated by the results of Murray's March 1946 address to Toronto's St. George's Men's Club. One of the prominent members of the club was Mr. M. Fraser, who was also an executive at Canadian General Electric. After the speech, Fraser wrote Murray asking for copies of his speech: "If you will be good enough to send me fifty copies of your talk, as given to the St. George's Men's Club, very good use can, I think, be made of them."[22] It is interesting that Fraser's letter was not on his club's stationery, but, rather, on Canadian General

Electric Head Office letterhead. Presumably, Fraser, like other audience members, took the message directly to his daily business life, spreading Murray's ideas at General Electric.

Murray exploited this seamlessness as he also organized a sophisticated convergence of communications that advertised, disseminated, and afforded credibility to his ideas, far beyond his speeches and pamphlets. Part of the operation involved having his speeches excerpted or reprinted in corporate newsletters. The Association of Ice Cream Manufacturers, for example, reprinted Murray's December 9, 1952 address, entitled "Business and Welfare," in their nationally distributed *Canadian Dairy and Ice Cream Journal*.[23] The Canadian Banker Association reprinted and distributed his February 1953 speech to Toronto's St. George's United Men's Club as an article in *The Canadian Banker* newsletter, then reprinted and nationally distributed the speech again as a separate pamphlet.[24]

Another part of this clever web of communications organization involved radio. There are records of the broadcast of at least seven of Murray's speeches. The first was his June 19, 1944, address to the Life Underwriters Association of Canada in St. Catharines. The 30-minute segment broadcast live on CKTB; after the speech, and at Murray's request, the association's chairman William Gray sent Murray a copy of the names of those at the head table and a clipping from the *St. Catharines Standard*, which had covered the speech.[25] Two days later, Gray wrote again, thanking him for his speech and asking for additional copies. He also told Murray that the association's president, Mr. Tucker, had arranged to have a copy printed in the association's national magazine called *Life Underwriters' News*.[26]

The activity surrounding one speech can serve as an illustration of the complexity of Murray's communications strategy. On January 27, 1944, he spoke to the Toronto Board of Trade. Even before he made the speech, his anti-CCF message was afforded credibility through a front page article in the organization's newsletter: it announced the upcoming speech, provided a picture of Murray, praised his war record and distinguished career with the BBC and CBC, recounted a glowing assessment of his Responsible Enterprise activities, and concluded that members should attend and bring friends to the speech, as "Mr. Gladstone Murray is one of Canada's most illustrious citizens."[27] The speech was carried live on CFRB, which at the time was Toronto's most-listened to radio station, and it was also covered in Toronto's newspapers.

Three weeks after his address, Murray received a letter from E. Prittie, secretary of the Property Owners Association of Toronto and member of the Board of Trade, with a request for over 10,000 more copies of the pamphlet that Murray had handed out to members of the audience that night. Mr. Prittie promised a wide distribution.[28]

The complex communications strategy seen in the Board of Trade speech was used throughout the campaign and was made even more effective by the network of Murray's business and media connections. For example, in February 1948, Murray addressed the Harcourt Lodge at Toronto's Masonic Hall. Here, there was pre-speech advertising, pamphlet distribution to the audience, and, finally, post-speech newspaper coverage. The Masonic Lodge member who invited Murray to speak was George Clark, who also happened to be president of the Canada Life Assurance Company and one of the leaders of the insurance industry's attacks on the CCF. After the speech, Clark wrote to Murray requesting 150 additional copies of the speech and explaining that he had managed to ensure that the speech was widely covered in newspapers and broadcast on the radio.[29]

While in cases such as this, others did much of his communications work, Murray often personally wrote or telephoned local and national newspapers in advance of his speeches, then mailed follow up letters in which he often enclosed pamphlet transcripts of his remarks. His personal attention to these details increased in the 1950s, as the business community's support for his activities began to wane. His personal work to ensure press coverage is revealed in a July 16, 1953, letter from F.C. Murray of Belleville's Rotary Club, in which Murray is thanked for his letter and phone calls regarding upcoming press coverage of his speech. He was assured that both local newspapers, as well as the nearby Trenton newspapers, would cover the speech.[30]

Instructive in this regard are the actions taken surrounding his speech to The Sons of England in Orillia on April 23, 1953. In the days leading up to the event, Murray prepared copies of his speech and had them delivered to 53 newspapers in Ontario, including *The Globe and Mail* and *Toronto Telegram*. He also sent copies to the *Montreal Gazette* with special attention to John Bassett and to the *Montreal Star* with special attention to J.G. McConnell.[31]

Murray's concern with his press coverage was evident throughout his campaign and is revealed in his sharp reaction to bad reviews. For example, on November 24, 1943 he spoke at the Canadian Club in Morrisburg, Ontario, and it later came to his attention that he had been unfavourably reviewed in the local newspaper. On December 1, he wrote to D.K. Stewart of the Bank of Montreal, his contact at the Morrisburg speech, noting the bad review, asking for a clipping, and inquiring as to the reporter's name so that he could send him a copy of the speech.[32] Stewart had obviously responded quickly, for, only a couple of days later, on December 4, a letter to the editor from Murray appeared in the local newspaper. Murray equated his critic with Communists of the Labour Progressive Party, a form of red-baiting that was designed to discredit any opposition to him or his message:

> I note that you say your impression of my address at the Morrisburg District Canadian Club was one of deep "disgust." This is precisely the way in which my statement is met in the *Canadian Tribune*: the organ of the Labour-Progressive Party, formally the Communist Party of Canada. No doubt the method is a convenient substitute for argument against an incontrovertible case.[33]

While it is important to see that his speeches were covered by the media, it is important to understand, too, that the media was often biased in support of the points Murray was making. This bias made Murray an even more potent factor in the anti-socialist/anti-CCF campaign. For example, on November 15, 1946, Murray spoke in Toronto at a meeting of the Workers Educational Association, in debate with George Grube (CCF) and Michael Freeman (LPP). The next day, the *Montreal Gazette* reported on the debate, but its two-column article quoted only Murray. The reporter perhaps had used the pamphlet that Murray had provided to the audience, as the quotes in the article were taken verbatim from it. While faithfully and accurately relating Murray's words and views, however, the article did not even mention points made by Grube or Freeman, or print a word of their remarks.

The collusion with Murray was seen again in the preparations for his November 1946 appearance in Montreal, where he was to debate Eugene Forsey, political science and economics professor and intellectual gadfly, who lent support to the Canadian labour movement and the CCF. On November 19, the editor of the *Montreal Gazette* wrote to Bill Fraser of *The People's Forum*. He noted that "a group" had been "turning left" lately and that the trend needed to be rectified by stacking the audience with planted questions. In a conspiratorial tone, hinting that the suggestion had come from unnamed others, he suggested:

> Some of the questions could be directed at Mr. Forsey to embarrass him or point out the errors he has made; others might be with the intention of elaborating some point of your own, or bringing up some subject that you omitted for any reason. You will see the object without forcing my point. Would you be willing to do this, please? It might be both stimulating and helpful. It is, course, a ramp; but it is precisely the sort of thing the socialists do all the time. Sauce for the goose.[34]

CCF members, workers, and candidates could not help but see Murray's anti-CCF storm raging around them. The party's leadership recognized it and addressed it in many ways. The CCF's *New Commonwealth* wrote often of Murray's speeches and pamphlets, including an article in the December 9, 1943 edition, noting that there had been people and groups who had unfairly and libelously attacked the CCF before and that the party had come to expect such attacks. However, it observed that, beginning in 1943, the ideologically driven anti-CCF campaign was different from what had been henceforth seen:

> This time the uproar against the CCF is organized. Gladstone Murray…is in the role of Dr. Goebbels and has been provided with a great deal of money to direct the campaign. Much of the absurd anti-CCF material now being spouted by Tory orators, or reproduced in the press, is inspired by Murray—at a fat fee. Since it is recognized that the old party leaders have lost touch with the thinking of the people, Murray is supposed to advise the Tories (and some of the Liberals too) on how to frighten and bamboozle the masses. It is a well known Fascist technique.[35]

If one jumps ahead to the 1949 campaign, the CCF can be seen still fighting against Murray's propaganda and doing so, partly, through a number of advertisements. One such advertisement that ran in British Columbia was entitled "Government Can Work For You." It stated that the province's greatest asset was its working people and that a government should represent those people. It then responded directly to the anti-socialist/anti-CCF campaign, stating, "British Columbia labour is not going to be fooled by the high pressure 'Free Enterprise' propaganda campaign designed to protect exorbitant profits and to retain the advantages for a few."[36]

After the 1949 election, Murray continued to publish a scandalously brutal anti-CCF tabloid called *Outlook,* which repeated many of the ideas he had developed in his speeches. He maintained ties with, and influence in, the Progressive Conservative Party.[37] By 1955, however, his business benefactors had left him. More speeches were made and more was written, but with the CCF ceasing to be the electoral threat it had been, the need for Murray's campaign waned. Yet the damage had been done.

It is important to see that this damage to the party and its ideas was effective because of the scope and context of Murray's attack. As Gramsci argued, civil society was one of the most important areas for political discourse. Murray used service, professional, social, and church club meetings held in auditoriums, church basements, and meeting halls. He also used newspapers and radio, and provided short, easy-to-read publications distributed by friends, neighbours, employers, and co-workers. His energy, message, words, and images inspired and encouraged others who were acting against the CCF in the same areas of the civil society. There was no better place and no better way to stage and influence an ideological fight, and Murray was not the only one in the ring swinging.

Burdick Trestrail

In terms of their financing, organization, breadth, and effectiveness, Burdick Trestrail's mercenary efforts in the ideological battles of the 1940s stand second only to Murray's Responsible Enterprise campaign. Trestrail was born in Kansas City, but moved to Canada during the First World War and became a Canadian citizen. He claimed to have made a fortune in the twenties, but to have lost it in the Depression. He found his feet again as a Toronto advertising man, and he became relatively well known for assisting in the organization of a successful Victory Bonds drive near the outset of the Second World War. In the early 1940s he worked for the John Inglis Company, which was later one of Gladstone Murray's supporters, and also did work as a free-lance industrial relations counsultant, helping companies with long-range economic planning. These activities would have allowed Trestrail to cultivate a wide and important range of contacts in the Ontario business community. Beyond that he is an enigma. He left no papers.

In late 1943, the Toronto Board of Trade asked Trestrail to lead a campaign meant, initially, to ensure that CCF municipal candidates were unsuccessful in the upcoming municipal election.[38] To fulfill his mandate, Trestrail created the Society for Individual Freedom Against State Socialism, but its early success led to a broader mission. In early 1944, the organization was reborn as the Public Information Association, and it developed national connections and support. The operating agencies that handled the financing of the Public Information Association's many activities were called General Relations Service Limited and the Industrial and Merchandising Council. The purpose of the Public Information Association was to attack socialism and smear the CCF.

In preparation for his national campaign, the Public Information Association undertook a number of interviews in the greater Toronto area in the spring and summer of 1944. About 3,000 people representing six distinct groups were polled, allowing Trestrail to conclude that from 25% to 40% of Canadians could be dissuaded from voting for the CCF in the next election.[39] He also wrote a short book entitled *Stand Up and Be Counted,* which attacked the CCF with out-of-context and false quotes from party documents, false assumptions about and extrapolations from party policies, and libelous slurs directed at party leaders, members, and anyone who was considering casting their vote for the party.

Stand Up and Be Counted tried to stir interest in the upcoming election with the prediction, "The next Federal Election will decide the destiny of Canada and its people—politically, economically and socially—for at least five or ten years and perhaps for generations."[40] It went on to use language similar to Murray's and many others of the anti-socialist/anti-CCF campaign, arguing that the party wished to create a totalitarian state where all political and economic freedom would be lost. Trestrail also used the old canard that the party employed Nazi tactics to dupe its followers and to attract more:

This foxy flexibility is designed, of course, to provide a method of attracting and intriguing all types of citizens who are either discontented; or who are sort of semi-socialistic; who are sincere social reformers and are disappointed with the performance of our present political parties or who are just "agin the government"— and so to substantially increase their following. This is the same sort of slippery technique used by Hitler in building up his Nazi Party in Germany.[41]

Trestrail heaped abuse upon CCF leaders and ridiculed party members in his attempts to portray them as susceptible to tricky intellectuals thinking only of themselves. He saved a special insult for women who considered supporting the party. Perhaps he imagined his construction of their essential maternal nature would appeal to women, even as he criticized them. His categorization of women revealed traditional conservative views about their instinct and maternalism:

Women seem to be singularly susceptible to the siren song of State Socialism. This is partly because of their instinctive sympathy for the underdog, those whom they feel that fate, or social order, has dealt with unkindly or unfairly. Add to this their natural motherly instinct, which seeks protection and security for themselves and fairly, far more than for opportunity or ambition, and you have a combination of traits which, while very worthy and noble, make women particularly vulnerable to the pleasing platitudes and plausible promises of the Socialists.[42]

He also provided quotes from pro-capitalist articles, such as Ayn Rand's "The Only Path to Tomorrow," from the January 1944 *Reader's Digest*, in which she discussed the threat of totalitarianism from the left. Quotes from Edgar Queeny's book, *The Spirit of Enterprise*, praising competition in the automobile industry as reflecting the glory of capitalism, were also used.

In 1945, during the weeks before the writs were issued for the June 4 Ontario election and the June 11 federal election, then with increased fervour

73

during the campaigns, Trestrail oversaw a coordinated campaign of newspaper and radio advertisements, pamphlet and booklet publication, and, most devastatingly of all, the production and national distribution of a 25 page pamphlet called *Social Suicide.*

Social Suicide was merely a shortened version of *Stand Up and Be Counted.* The pamphlet's cover used the menacingly bold red, white, and black of the Nazi flag and carried the subtitle "A Message that has opened the eyes of 50,000 Canadians." Even larger than the title was a glaring red subtitle along the bottom which said "$500 Cash Award." The subtitle referred to a contest outlined on the back cover in which readers were asked to invent the best title for a cartoon. The cartoon showed a worried man with "CCF" written on his chest who is standing rather unsteadily on a ball on which is written "First Term Plan." He is standing on one leg while David Lewis holds his other and commands him to "Hold it." Meanwhile, the man is balancing a stick on his chin, upon which he balances yet another stick with four balls perched on top; on the balls are written "Provincial Program," "International Affairs," "Civil Socialist Program," and "National Administration." Further, the man is juggling four more balls on which are written "Credit and Banking," "Production," "Full Employment," and "Distribution."[43] Like other cartoons of the campaign, it portrayed the party and its ideas as foolish and its leaders as cynical manipulators asking Canadians to take unfair and silly risks.

The booklet's foreword attacked CCF leaders not only for their ideas, but also for having the temerity to have proposed them during war time. It then pointed out that several of the CCF leaders were foreign born and leaned toward a racist slur in introducing all party leaders but mentioning only David Lewis' ethnicity as a Russian Jew.[44] It purported to outline the history of the CCF and the ideology upon which the party was based, while warning the Canadian people about the dangers posed by both. The foreword set the stage for what followed in terms of tone, style, and sophistication. Its fourth paragraph began:

> The issue is briefly this: Shall we Canadians throw up our hands and say that our democratic system is a failure; that it can't be made to work, and that we are therefore going to substitute for it a system of "State Socialism" (as proposed by the CCF), under which we hand over to a Central Bureaucracy the complete ownership, operation

INTO THE HURRICANE

and control of our industry, commerce, agriculture, finance and natural resources, not to mention the regimentation of our lives and the careers of ourselves, our children and their children?[45]

It is interesting that the crux of Trestrail's argument was the danger of state socialism, but that his definition of the concept was weak and divorced from the party's actual policies. Trestrail defined state socialism as:

Ultimate government ownership, operation or control of ALL industry, commerce, finance, utilities, transportation, agriculture, mines, fisheries, forests and services. All production, distribution, and employment would be regimented under a "National Plan." Under this "plan" all competition and all profits would be totally eliminated.[46]

The booklet went on to discuss, in equally inflammatory words and phrases, the threat that state socialism posed to Canadian society. It concluded that every individual, group, and corporation must rise up and fight state socialism by fighting the CCF. Its concluding paragraph was as inaccurate, poorly written, and scurrilous as all that proceeded:

BUT—above all—the red-blooded Canadian wants his Freedom! And, gild it as you will, State Socialism Spells Slavery—social and economic slavery, because, if the "National Plan" of State Socialism is ever put into force, every third citizen will be a government employee appointed to administer the "plan" and every fourth citizen will be a COP!—to enforce it.[47]

In many of the points it made, and with its veiled racism, scandalously inaccurate portrayal of party policies and goals, and emotional incitement to avoid supporting the party, *Social Suicide* was not unlike many of the other publications that had been presented to Canadians. But *Social Suicide* was different in that, in mid-May 1945, in the middle of the federal election campaign, Trestrail had it mailed to every English-speaking address in Canada.

Many business people who were either partners in or sympathetic to the anti-socialist/anti-CCF campaign were quick to use *Social Suicide* and assure it an even broader audience. Moreover, their status as influential business leaders perhaps afforded it credibility. Hugh Millar, for instance, was president of Montreal's Lyman Tube and Supply Company. On June 5, just days before the federal election, Millar arranged for a letter, over his signature, to be placed with his employees' pay-packets. The letter said that, for their business, a planned economy would mean more bureaucracy, overwork, more forms, and more taxes. The letter continued:

> We all have a clear duty to VOTE, and it is not my privilege to tell anyone what party to vote for, but I do want everyone to know that I regard the CCF programme as a deadly danger to our future, not only in the matter of jobs, but the world we live in outside our jobs. So whichever way you want to vote is your business, but it is my firm belief that if the CCF should prevail, none of us will ever have a chance to cast a ballot again.[48]

To further assist his employees with their electoral decision, Millar helpfully included a copy of *Social Suicide* with each letter. His letter ended bluntly: "Be sure to vote—but don't vote CCF."[49]

The effect of *Social Suicide's* unsolicited mass mailing was significant. A number of CCF candidates and riding association officials wrote to the CCF's national executive explaining how support suddenly dried up and negative attitudes toward their candidacies increased the day it arrived in mailboxes. Halifax CCF candidate Lloyd Shaw, for example, wrote to David Lewis explaining that, after the publication swept every household in his riding, the tension could be "cut with a knife."[50]

The national executive and constituencies across Canada also received a flood of letters from voters and CCF members seeking clarification of party policy in light of *Social Suicide's* claims. The booklet's power to affect political discourse was seen in the fact that many of the questioners employed Trestrail's language in posing their queries. One typical letter is a quaint, hand-written note from a Simcoe, Ontario Canadian National Railway employee named Ray Thorne, dated May 20. Thorne explained that, the day they had received

Social Suicide in the mail, he and his co-workers had talked at work about the CCF, and they had some questions. Among his questions were, "Is every CCF candidate committed to a complete programme of State Socialism regardless of his personal views or statements?... Under State Socialism could the small business man be sure he would not be taken over by the government?... Under the system of State Socialism, now in force in Russia, can the people displace the government by ballot if they so desire?"[51]

That the party leaders clearly understood the enormous negative effect of *Social Suicide* on the election in the short term and the party's future in the long term is seen by the actions they took, first to try to stop it, then later to try to address the damage it caused. Days before *Social Suicide* was mailed, news of its creation and proposed distribution, and even copies of the pamphlet itself, had reached the national executive. On May 7, Lewis had received a letter warning him that Trestrail had sent a letter to business executives across Canada, informing them of the planned mass distribution of *Social Suicide* and providing them with advance copies.[52]

Two days later, Lewis sought to have its mass distribution stopped by having the action declared illegal. He wrote to Canada's postmaster general, asserting that the distribution of the pamphlet violated the Dominion Elections Act and the Defense of Canada Act because it did not contain the name and address of the publisher.[53] The assistant postmaster general replied the next day that it was his interpretation that *Social Suicide* was not in contravention of the postal law or regulations but that it indeed appeared to contravene the Defense of Canada Act and the Dominion Elections Act. He promised to refer the matter to the deputy minister of justice.[54] It appears that Lewis' request was lost in a bureaucratic shuffle, however, for it went from the assistant postmaster general to the deputy minister of justice, then to the chief censor of publications, then to the minister of justice, where the trail goes cold. No action was ever taken.[55]

Unable to stop *Social Suicide*, Lewis tried to deal with its effects. He asked Dudley Bristow, a party organizer who would later do grassroots party work in northern Ontario, to create a formal response, but it was not ready until three months after the election. Bristow warned in a cover letter, however, that a response was difficult, as the party had to refute lies and present the CCF's real policies while at the same time avoiding digressing into criticizing the

Communists or big business and becoming guilty of slander. It is interestingly ironic that while Bristow was attempting to attack lies with the truth, he suggested using a pseudonym as the author. He suggested, "pseudonym of author to conjure a kindly impression of average reader. For this; I favour Scotch names."[56] The idea of using the Scotch alias perhaps reflects a belief among some in the party that the anti-CCF campaign's branding the party as foreign was having an effect.

Bristow's pamphlet, *Who Paid For the Lies They Told?*, stated in its introduction, "Our purpose here is to show how many false statements Mr. Trestrail crammed into *Social Suicide* and to connect the Trestrail campaign of distortions with the determination of Big Business to continue to rule the Canadian people by keeping one or other of the old parties in power all the time... Once we realize who is paying for this expensive campaign against one political party it will be easier for us not to be fooled next time and for us to help other people not to be fooled."[57] He then outlined all of the errors, exaggerations, and lies contained in *Social Suicide*. Bristow's approach to counterpunching Trestrail while promoting CCF ideas can be best seen in his response to the accusation that the CCF was akin to Germany's National Socialists:

> It is common knowledge and it is a fact that the big industrialists and financial moguls of Germany paved the way to power for Hitler by making huge donations to the Nazi party. The so-called National Socialist party was the tool of Big Business to beat the genuine socialist party...Nazi Germany was a capitalist dictatorship the exact opposite of the socialist democracy toward which the CCF aims. The danger of fascism comes from the Right not the Left.[58]

Bristow also caught *Social Suicide*'s veiled racism, noting that Trestrail mentioned David Lewis' Jewish ancestry a number of times but failed to refer to the ethnicity of any other CCF leader. Further, while mentioning Frank Scott, a university professor who was influential in the founding of the CCF and, for a time, acted as its national chairman, as often as Lewis, he notes Scott's Scottish heritage, but ignores his father's career as a poet and chaplain in the

First World War. Bristow concluded, "In all cases Trestrail picks, he chooses and twists his facts to produce the sort of picture he wants to present. Such Hitlerian techniques are an offense to the Canadian people."[59]

A second response to *Social Suicide* was prepared by Eugene Forsey. It answered all of Trestrail's arguments and stated that, while claiming to present facts, the booklet was actually crammed with exaggerations and falsehoods. Forsey addressed the definition of state socialism and explained how the CCF platform did not fit Trestrail's definition. He noted many of the same factual errors that Bristow had mentioned in his response, dismissed Trestrail's equation of the CCF with Hitler, and challenged his twisting of facts regarding the comparison of Canada to New Zealand, which the party had been using as an example of democratic socialism in action.

Bristow's response and an abridged version of Forsey's response were mailed to all CCF candidates and released for publication in newspapers. Some newspapers printed at least portions of the responses, but many that were known to be either sympathetic to or in support of the anti-socialist/anti-CCF campaign, most notably among them, *The Globe and Mail* and the *Winnipeg Free Press*, did not.

Among the many editorials and articles that were written in the wake of the mass mailing and the party's later response, there was one of special interest because Trestrail saw fit to respond. The *Vancouver Sun*'s Elmore Philpot wrote a piece after the federal election and after the initial fervour caused by *Social Suicide* had waned. His June 14 article criticized Trestrail for his smear campaign and for the false logic and inaccuracies of *Social Suicide*. He condemned Trestrail for his anti-Semitism and teased him for merely being the voice of big business. Trestrail took up the challenge, and, in a July 3 letter to the editor, claimed that he had taken the reasoned approach in debating the CCF in the recent campaign, and it was the CCF and its apologists who had reduced themselves to mudslinging. Trestrail went on to brag of his past accomplishments, then addressed the issue of the funding of his campaign, asserting that big business had little interest in his activities and contributed only 10% of his operation's costs. Rather, he claimed, it was nearly 1,000 individuals whom he had met on a tour of 26 cities who contributed the necessary funds. He did not mention who had funded the tour.[60]

The publication and mass mailing of *Social Suicide* would have been sufficient to render Trestrail an important player in the campaign, but there was more. He also organized a massive effort that saw viciously anti-CCF advertisements placed in newspapers across the country in the weeks leading up to the 1945 summer elections. Many of the advertisements contained copy and cartoons either taken directly or adapted from *Social Suicide*. Trestrail, as a former advertising man, understood that the ideas of *Social Suicide* would become more powerful for two reasons. First, people who chose not to read the booklet when it arrived free in their mail would be nonetheless exposed to its ideas through their newspaper. Second, the anti-CCF ideas and vocabulary would become more deeply engrained in Canada's political culture through sheer repetition.

There were many advertisements, of varying characteristics and size, but each contained a footing banner listing its source as "The Public Information Association, PO Box 178, Toronto, Ontario, B. A. Trestrail, National Director." A look at a few is sufficient to understand the campaign. One effective advertisement was entitled "Our Next Big Threat" and showed a crude drawing of a black, evil-eyed octopus wearing a mortarboard with a sign on its stomach that read: "State Socialism." Its tentacles were grasping the words "Finance," "Farms," "Education," "Production," "Distribution," "Resources," "Industry," and "Occupations." The copy stated, "The most important issue confronting Canadians in the coming election is 'State Socialism'—as proposed by the CCF party."[61] It stated as fact that the party planned to take over the eight parts of the economy cited in the cartoon and that Canada would end in a dictatorship.

The ad then announced a contest open to all Canadians. It asked people to send for a copy of *Social Suicide* and to send names and addresses of "boys and girls in the armed services" so that a copy could be mailed to them as well. The contest listed ten questions that could only be answered if one read all of *Social Suicide*. Correct answers could lead to prizes ranging from $5 to $1000, which were substantial sums in 1945. All copies of *Social Suicide*, the ad promised, were free and would be mailed free of charge.

The octopus advertisement was clever, and its effectiveness was revealed by the fact that David Lewis personally commissioned a response ad. In a witty parody of Trestrail's ad, the CCF national executive approved an advertisement with the same dark octopus, but with "Monopoly Control" written across its stomach and its tentacles gripping the words "Resources,"

"Science," "Labor," "Health," "Agriculture," "Education," "Recreation," and "Distribution." The copy used words similar to Trestrail's, speaking not of free enterprise, but of free exploitation, where monopolies take over Canadian lives. It claimed that the CCF was dedicated to ending monopoly control and, again aping Trestrail's ad, quoted from letters thanking the CCF for promising to free the country. It ended with the statement that the CCF did not have the money of the monopolists, so a contest was not possible, but anyone wishing to support the CCF program could send donations to its Montreal office.[62] In a twist that reveals much about the obstacles before the party, a number of newspapers refused to print the CCF response ad.[63]

Another Trestrail advertisement that used a crude cartoon bore a drawing of an index finger hosting three strings with the title beneath, "3 Things For Voters To Remember." These three things were essential to be kept in mind by those planning to vote for the CCF, even, it added, if only as a protest vote:

1. You are voting not merely to change the Government but to change our entire system of government—substituting a foreign-born scheme of "state Socialism" for our democratic way of life.
2. You are voting to turn over to the CCF politicians complete control of our lives.
3. The CCF program of "State Socialism" can only be carried out under absolute dictatorship.[64]

On May 18, Canadians across the country who were reading one of a number of newspapers saw another advertisement that bore the title, "A Solemn Warning...To All Voters." Those not wishing to read the full copy could glean the advertisement's point simply by scanning the large bolded subtitles that said, "Remember Italy," "Good-bye Freedom!" and "So Vote Against the CCF!" The main point made was that the CCF was led by theorists with no practical experience, which was the same type of people that had led Italy down the road to dictatorship under Mussolini. The ad stated, "Mussolini, Laval, Quisling and other dictators all started as Socialists—posing as the friend and saviour of the so-called 'common people.' Their promises all ran parallel with the present CCF program."[65] The copy concluded with a, perhaps not surprising, warning: "Hence if you want to preserve your liberty of action—your individual freedom—where to work—where to live—where and how to spend your money, you simply cannot vote for ANY CCF candidate—even though he be your personal friend—because every CCF candidate is definitely committed to that program."[66]

Another of Trestrail's nationally run advertisements was directed at women and was headed "A Challenge to the Women of Canada." The June 1 ad began by praising the many contributions that women had made to the war effort, both at home and overseas. It then argued that a new contribution to Canada was being asked of women: to stand against the hordes that were promoting state socialism. The advertisement focused on issues that Trestrail obviously believed would attract women's attention, saying that under state socialism the CCF would control all that could be manufactured, "from pills to petticoats, from jam to jewellery the Government would control everything."[67] The advertisement ended by repeating news of the quiz contest and the promise of free copies of *Social Suicide*. Ignoring the fact that many CCF candidates were women, it then stated, "Urge all of your friends to vote against the CCF candidate—no matter who he is—because he is positively committed to State Socialism."[68]

While all of Trestrail's advertisements used ideas, cartoons, and phrases from *Social Suicide*, some simply reprinted a page or a section from the booklet. Such was the case with an advertisement that appeared in newspapers in the first week of June under the heading, "To Voters, Wise Words of WARNING!" It was a reprint of the inside cover of *Social Suicide*. The advertisement showed images of Abraham Lincoln and Winston Churchill, and the copy warned about being hypnotized by the "lavish promises" of the CCF. It quoted a Lincoln speech in which he argued that the wealth of others should not be used to inspire violence or resentment; it should inspire those of more modest means to work harder. Churchill is quoted as extolling individualism. The irony of criticizing the CCF as standing for foreign-born ideas, then bringing foreign leaders to support his views, was apparently lost on Mr. Trestrail. The text drew the following conclusion from Lincoln's and Churchill's words:

> There, from the lips and hearts of two patriots, comes
> the whole gospel of democracy—a gospel which needs
> now to be spread again before Canadians of every class
> and creed—for the simple reason that it is founded on

plain, common sense. On election day Canadians will be asked to decide whether or not they want Canada to embrace "State Socialism"—hence they should appreciate its meaning and OBJECTIVE.[69]

On the day of the federal election, Trestrail ran a nation-wide advertisement headed "Election Day is another 'D-Day' for Canada." It equated the "Christian" world being saved by the soldiers at D-Day to Canadian democracy being saved on voting day. The copy warned that a CCF victory would spell totalitarian control and listed ways that the CCF apparently wanted to install economic and social controls on Canada's economy and society, concluding:

> All of these and other controls and regulations will become a permanent part of our existence, as decided by the CCF politicians and administered by a vast army of Government Agents. Under any such system we would become like animals in a zoo. We would lose our individual freedom just as completely as though we have lost the war.[70]

It is clear that the Trestrail campaign influenced the 1945 federal election. Following the campaign, CCF leader M.J. Coldwell stated in a CBC radio broadcast that the CCF's showing in the election was negatively affected by the, "tissue of lies and distortions of Trestrail and his employers."[71] The Trestrail attacks also influenced the Ontario election. The Ontario CCF issued a statement after the campaign in which it listed three reasons for its failure to meet its electoral goals. Its second and third reasons were the actions of the communists and the weakness of its own organization. The reason listed as first and most important was the effectiveness of the anti-CCF campaign.[72] In his memoirs, David Lewis noted the devastating effect of *Social Suicide*, arguing, "The effect of *Social Suicide* was immediately noticeable. From the plants and the streets we had reports of people turning away as they were no longer ready to keep their promise of support. I could sense it in Hamilton West, as could our candidates everywhere."[73]

Dr. Lorna Thomas was the CCF provincial candidate in Peterborough, Ontario. She was an impressive candidate and a well-educated woman, having earned a master's degree at the University of Toronto and a PhD in economics from Columbia. During the campaign, the local newspaper, the *Examiner,* had run a number of Trestrail's advertisements; after the election was over and the Liberal candidate won, Thomas wrote to the newspaper, criticizing its decision to run ads that had so obviously been inaccurate and biased against her campaign.[74] The *Examiner* responded the next day with an editorial defending its actions and stating that, in the interest of fairness, it had in fact refused to print one of Trestrail's advertisements, as the editorial board had found it "a scurrilous attack on the CCF."[75] This exchange of letters is interesting in that it serves to show that candidates appreciated the negative affects of Trestrail's actions and that even a newspaper that was as determinedly anti-CCF as the *Examiner* found some of his advertisements to be over the ethical line.

Following the 1945 election, Trestrail moved his Toronto offices from 51 King Street to a larger space at 229 Yonge Street under the name General Relations Service Limited. His organization remained in the anti-CCF business and prepared for the next election. Its preparation was complicated, expensive, and professional. It involved undertaking new interviews and sample group meetings. In the Toronto area, in the spring of 1948, more than 3,000 people were asked a series of questions and presented with information about Trestrail's version of CCF policies and beliefs.

At the conclusion of his field research and other preparations, Trestrail issued a document that outlined his conclusions and plan for the new struggle, entitled *General Outline of the 7 Point Educational Program.* Trestrail repeated a prediction, similar to that made in 1943, that, according to his sample groups, between 25% and 40% of women, farmers, and workers could be swayed from voting CCF through providing them with what he called "proper information in the proper manner."[76] The document continued:

> All the evidence indicates that *Social Suicide* was the most effective piece of educational propaganda ever produced in Canada. Based as it was on a carefully pre-tested pattern, its effectiveness was forecast almost on the nose. For example, our tests indicated that 30% to 35% of potential Socialist votes could be converted. And that is exactly what happened.[77]

The document also noted that there were 27,000 entries to the contest and that 3,000 of those offered to pay an annual membership fee.[78]

A May 1949 letter from Trestrail to all subscribers and supporters announced the beginning of the new anti-CCF battle and the launching of a new weapon. Based on the success of *Social Suicide*, he promised that a new 16-page booklet, entitled *Is Democracy Doomed?*, would be mailed to one million English speaking postal addresses. The letter claimed there was no time to do independent fund raising for the new project, but that half the funds needed were already in hand. He asked for new donations.[79]

When finally published, the new booklet was actually 32 pages long and entitled *Is Democracy in Canada Doomed?* The cover showed a price of ten cents, but there is no evidence that anyone ever paid for it, as it appeared as unsolicited mail across Canada in early June 1949. Evidence that the CCF national executive had acted to stop it's publication and distribution was seen on its cover, which stated in large letters, "This is the 'smear' which the CCF warned you about!"[80] There are indications that Trestrail's organization was even better funded than in 1945, for the front cover carried an announcement of a new contest offering $2500 in prize money. As with *Social Suicide*, the contest took up the entire back cover and involved a quiz that could be answered correctly only if one read the entire booklet.

Is Democracy in Canada Doomed? began by recounting that the Public Information Association had begun four years before to stop "State Socialism" and referred to its use of *Social Suicide* as a means to do so. It noted that the 1945 election saw the Canadian people reject the socialism of the CCF. The problem, it claimed, was that the country was still falling prey to "creeping socialism." If this trend was not checked, it warned, democracy was doomed. It cried, "Democracy as we know it will die! Not by the ballot or the bullet but because of the apathy, inertia and disinterest of the people—or the narrow selfishness of pressure groups trying to get an 'edge' by putting across a pet program of government aid or subsidy or restriction."[81]

On the booklet's first page, Trestrail attacked CCF leaders. He criticized David Lewis for publicly warning people about the anti-CCF campaign and, surprisingly, for having obtained copies of his organization's materials. He wrote, "This is not the first time that the CCF boys have purloined communications of ours."[82] Trestrail also noted what Coldwell had said at an Ottawa press conference on April 8: that his main worry in the upcoming campaign was the anti-CCF actions by the Public Information Association. Trestrail crowed that Coldwell's fears were well-founded.[83] Trestrail's only quibble with Coldwell was with regard to his estimates of the smear campaign's costs and its donors.

The main text of *Is Democracy in Canada Doomed?* began with a historical look at the 6,000-year evolution of freedom and democracy up to the point where North America became home to the freest and richest people in the world. The five devils that threatened that freedom and wealth were listed as communism, state socialism, bureaucracy, pressure groups, and public apathy. Each of the devils was then addressed. The devil of state socialism led Trestrail to attack the CCF, its guiding ideas, and its leaders:

> This threat to democracy is officially crystallized in Canada in the form of the political party known as the CCF. The voters of Canada have so frequently and so emphatically rejected the advances of the CCF that you'd think they'd get discouraged, but the movement is quite a luscious breadbasket for a lot of men and women who might find it difficult to live very comfortably if thrown on their own resources so they keep "holding out the carrots" to their followers, who are bears for punishment.[84]

The assault then moved to organized labour, and in so doing, continued the attempt to sever union members from both the party and their union leaders. Trestrail noted that the CCL-CIO had designated the CCF as its political arm and thus had forced their membership to help fund the party. He then claimed that union support was prompted only by the egos and personal ambitions of union leadership, not because the membership supported the move. Trestrail concluded, "In any event it's not the welfare of the workers that the CCF and CCL candidates have at heart. It's their own personal desire for power, glory and perquisites."[85] The booklet ended by returning to its frontal assault on CCF policies, such as public ownership, and concluded, "To vote for any candidate who is committed to State Socialism (as is the CCF) is like stabbing yourself."[86]

The CCF national executive was appalled at the renewed campaign in general, and *Is Democracy in Canada Doomed?* in particular. In July, Lewis travelled to Toronto and met with the party's solicitor F.A. Brewin; the two discussed the possibility of taking legal action against Trestrail.[87] Due perhaps to a lack of funds, or to lessons learned from the 1945 attempt to have Trestrail's mass mailing stopped, no action was taken.

Trestrail's 1949 campaign re-ran many of the same messages in newspaper and radio advertisements that he had employed in 1945. Rather than again examine those advertisements and radio broadcasts, it will be more instructive to turn to the question of the sources of Trestrail's funding and support. It is clear that Trestrail operated with the support of, and funding from, a national network of business people. Just days after the mass mailing of *Social Suicide* in 1945, CCF research director Stuart Jamieson had found himself answering many letters from members, supporters, and others about the pamphlet's accusations, and he was careful to note his belief that big business was behind the Trestrail campaign. Jamieson estimated that *Social Suicide* cost ten cents per copy to print and one and one-half cents per copy to mail; with five million mailed across Canada, then supported with radio and newspaper advertisements, the campaign needed a budget of about $500,000.[88]

In his official party response to *Social Suicide* that was released to riding associations, CCF clubs, and newspapers, Eugene Forsey also estimated the cost of Trestrail's operation to be approximately $500,000.[89] He claimed to have secured evidence which indicated that the money had come from "S. M. Wedd, president of the Canadian Bankers Association, D. C. Betts, president of Canadian Breweries; F.H. Marsh, president of the Bank of Toronto and Excelsior Life; E.G. McMillan, director of Algoma Steel; R.A. Bryce of the National Trust Company; E.G. Burton, director of Simpson's; and more."[90] Others that were listed in an early draft of his response included Clifford Sifton of the Sifton newspaper chain, H.M. Turner of General Electric, Burnam Mitchell of the Royal Bank, A.L. Ainsworth of John Inglis Co., H.D. Burns of the Bank of Nova Scotia, E.A. Gaby of British-American Oil Company, H.T. Jaffray of the Imperial Bank of Canada, and former president of the Canadian Bankers Association, J.G. Parker of Imperial Life, and Robert Ray of the Dominion Bank.[91] It is interesting to note that many of the gentlemen named were also among those whom Gladstone Murray had claimed in a 1943 memo to have been the founders and supporters of his organization.

Lewis and Coldwell issued similar press releases in which they estimated that the Public Information Association spent $1 million dollars on the 1945 campaign—about $500,000 to $700,000 of which was spent on the printing and distribution of *Social Suicide*. Lewis and Coldwell also claimed that *Social Suicide*, and the original *Stand Up and Be Counted*, were printed in government-owned war plants, meaning that taxpayers had also subsidized the Trestrail campaign.[92]

Even before *Social Suicide* was mailed, Lewis had been told, and had in turn made CCF leaders aware, of the role that business was playing in Trestrail's operation. Lewis had been informed that between two and three million copies of *Social Suicide* were lying in warehouses belonging to Simpson's and de Havilland Aircraft of Canada awaiting mailing. This allowed Lewis to conclude that at least these two corporations were directly involved, but also that many others had to be tied to the operational side of the Trestrail organization.[93]

Trestrail's reaction to the CCF's accusations regarding his well-heeled supporters demonstrated that the CCF's attempts portray him as a puppet of big business obviously struck a nerve. In a rather weak defense, a Trestrail advertisement published three days before the 1945 federal election claimed that *Social Suicide*'s printing and distribution costs were merely one-tenth of the entire campaign and one-eighth of what Coldwell had stated. The advertisement claimed that, to raise the money, Trestrail had visited 26 cities and delivered speeches on the evils of the CCF, and from these appearances, individuals, as well as small and large businesses, contributed to his cause.[94]

Trestrail's "Octopus" advertisement revealed the extent to which the CCF's responses to the Trestrail campaign were leading to bothersome questions about big business' involvement in his campaign. A paragraph in the advertisement stated,

> You will be told that these advertisements are the voice of "vested interest"—that the Public Information Association is sponsored and controlled solely by "big Business." Such statements are designed solely to keep you from reading and heeding our message. The

campaign is the result of hundreds of letters from boys overseas, from farmers, women and workers, urging that the people be told the truth about State Socialism before it is too late… The campaign is made possible by the voluntary support of individuals and companies both small and large from coast to coast who are sufficiently concerned over the threat of dictatorship to do something about it.[95]

A later advertisement in the 1945 campaign responded again to the CCF attempts to weaken Trestrail's campaign by linking him to big business and having people understand the suspected sources of his funding and support. Under the glaring heading "A Shocking Exhibition of ABUSE!" the copy protested, perhaps a little too vehemently:

In a desperate attempt to stop our effort to tell Canadian voters the true objective and ultimate consequences of "State Socialism," CCF leaders, speakers and supporters are resorting to tactics and talk that literally "reek of the gutter." This Association, its Director and supporters have been publicly branded as "liars, gangsters, rogues and racketeers." The cost of our Educational Campaign has been multiplied into fantastic figures; gross, false charges have been made as to the source of our support and our messages have been branded as pure "capitalist propaganda." Vicious, however, as has been this public slander, it pales into nothing compared to the foul, obscene, disgusting language used by the supporters of the CCF Socialists in the anonymous communications to us by mail and by telephone.[96]

In a somewhat amusing spin away from the CCF accusations the advertisement continued,

Which of us is the biggest liar, rogue, rascal or racketeer is of little consequence and will be forgotten by all within a few weeks after the election, —but, neither you or your children will ever forget it—if you should vote for "State Socialism" (CCF) because, regardless of who is a liar or who is paying for either our campaign or theirs, or how much it costs, these three incontestable facts remain.[97]

Trestrail protested the CCF's accusations until the end. His final advertisement of the 1945 federal election, which appeared on voting day, had as its last line, "This Association is not sponsored or controlled by any group, nor is it connected directly or indirectly with any political party."[98]

However, there is more evidence than conjecture regarding business support for Trestrail's anti-CCF campaign. Notice that the 1949 campaign was about to commence, for instance, came with letters that Trestrail sent directly to a number of business people across Canada, under the General Relations Service Ltd. letterhead and over his signature, including one that announced:

Starting in May a mass educational campaign will be launched from coast to coast by the Public Information Association to acquaint every Canadian with the truth about State Socialism… This campaign, an outline of which is enclosed, will be based on the findings of surveys covering more than 3,000 Canadians in all walks of life. The material to be used has already proven its effectiveness. Now it is merely a question of how comprehensive the campaign will be.[99]

The letter went on to explain that Trestrail's organization had spent the time between the two elections meeting with business supporters in 22 cities across the country, and it had received financial support from "hundreds of individuals and business leaders."[100]

The organization was sufficiently well funded to have representatives in 22 cities to solicit funds and coordinate the dissemination of information. In the spring of 1949, Trestrail's regional officers were active in publicizing the new attack and soliciting funds. An example of this activity can be seen in the actions of Winnipeg's D. A. B. Murray, who in March 1949 issued a letter on his company letterhead:

> You probably will recall the outstanding job the Public
> Information Association did to combat the threat of
> Socialism in the Federal election of 1945 with its tabloid
> "*Social Suicide*," and ita [sic] radio broadcasting and
> newspaper advertising. They are going into action again
> shortly with an education campaign as outlined in the
> enclosed bulletin. The campaign will be conducted by
> the Public Information Association but will be financed
> by the General Relations Service Limited, Public and
> Industrial Relations Counsel. At a recent meeting of a
> group of Winnipeg businessmen it was decided to get
> behind this campaign and this letter is to solicit your
> support by engaging General Relations Service Limited
> as Public Relation Counsel for a subscription of $200.[101]

The reader was instructed to complete an enclosure and mail it to George Keates of Manitoba Cartage and Storage Limited. It concluded with the prediction of upcoming provincial and federal elections with the ominous warning, "an adverse result in either of these elections could mean a staggering blow to free enterprise."[102]

Those signing the enclosure enlisted the services of General Relations Service Limited as Industrial and Commercial Counsel and promised to remit a monthly fee. In return, the subscriber received a monthly bulletin summarizing labour and industrial relations, a monthly report on new developments and post-war activities, use of the Industrial Research Library, telephone discussions when required, consultation when needed, and public relations activities, including "educational campaigns, to combat confiscatory economic programs."[103] Trestrail also met personally with business people in 16 cities in Ontario, as well as 6 cities in the Maritimes, and he reported to have received endorsements of the plan at each stop. He also solicited funds and gathered volunteers, hoping to have 100,000 volunteers working on the campaign.[104]

Again and again the CCF were made aware of, and in turn made public, the web of business and political connections financing and supporting Trestrail's campaign. In a Hamilton speech during the 1949 federal campaign, Coldwell spoke bluntly about the ties between the old-line parties, big business, and the smear campaigns of Trestrail and Murray. He said that a number of businesspeople who were members of the CCF had received appeals to fund the campaigns. According to Coldwell, the appeal had been to "wage a campaign of vilification against us as in 1945 and again stuff the mailboxes with propaganda."[105] Coldwell specifically named Trestrail and Murray as leading the 1945 anti-CCF campaign and claimed the two played "big business for suckers, because they work for the old parties for a month before an election and receive enough money to live in comfort for the rest of the year."[106]

Trestrail echoed the themes, language, and tone of the insurance companies, Canadian Chamber of Commerce, and the anti-CCF newspapers. Gerald Caplan called the Trestrail campaign the "most intensive, and, it is arguable, the most effective attack on any party ever undertaken in Canada."[107] The CCF leadership and rank-and-file understood the power of the Trestrail campaign and their inability to successfully respond. In his memoirs, Lewis suggested that, if the Trestrail campaign had been all that the party was fighting at the time, perhaps the challenge could have been met. However, he conceded that, because Trestrail was not alone, but one more voice in the anti-socialist/anti-CCF campaign, his actions were devastating. With special reference to the mass mailing of *Social Suicide*, Lewis argued, "partly because its appearance was the culmination of fully two years of an intensive and extensive campaign, it acted as the final roll of the anti-CCF drum."[108]

The Murray and Trestrail campaigns were similar in their vitriolic anti-socialist/anti-CCF messages and in their celebration of liberal democracy and capitalism. They used similar language and metaphors. Both men stirred and exploited the fears and insecurities of Canadians by linking the CCF to fascism, communism, and the totalitarianism of Hitler, Stalin, and Mussolini. They both brilliantly used the tools of mass communication. Finally, they were similar in that both were spokespeople for business leaders who financed their operations, while also providing contacts and other support. Murray and Trestrail both damaged the CCF through the individual actions they took and as parts of the larger campaign that filled the avenues of communication in Canada's civil society.

4

PARTY AND PULPIT: THE PROGRESSIVE CONSERVATIVE PARTY AND RELIGIOUS LEADERS JOIN THE ATTACK

Two important arenas of public discussion that were identified by Marxist intellectual Antonio Gramsci, and are also important in understanding the ideological debate that raged in Canada's civil society in the 1940s, are parties and pulpits. Pulpits suggests the role religion played in the anti-socialist/anti-CCF campaign. There is a great deal of scholarship addressing the degree to which religion was a motivating factor in the political decision-making of Canadians in the 1940s. Historian Ivan Avakumovic, for instance, has argued that religion was a major factor in distracting working people from socialism, as both the Protestant and Catholic churches provided a similar code of behaviour that, while expressed and enforced in very different ways, held a quiet, obedient respect for authority at its core.[1] In this way religion plays a role in ideological debates. As Terry Eagleton has written, from a Gramscian perspective, "Religion…is probably the more purely ideological of the various institutions of the civil society."[2] In examining the role of religion in the anti socialist/anti CCF campaign, it is relevant to focus on the degree to which it became one more theme that was presented to Canadians as part of the overall campaign, while bringing more organic intellectuals, that is, societal leaders one might encounter in everyday life, to the debate. In this way, the role of religion in the campaign can be explored through an examination of the actions taken by the Catholic Church, by Protestant clergymen whose titles and affiliations perhaps afforded weight to their messages, and by those of the campaign who articulated religious ideas.

At the same time that the anti-socialist/anti-CCF campaign used religion to persuade Canadians to consider the spiritual health of society when making political decisions, it also involved political parties which sought to persuade voters to consider the country's political wellbeing. Political parties are significant actors in democratic societies and deserve careful study. They fulfill organizational functions, working to win and retain power; and sociological functions, allowing competing groups to create consensus in the civil society to promote their short- and long-term interests.[3] In the 1940s, Canadian political parties went beyond the pale of normal political debate, discourse, and maneuvering. The Liberal and Communist parties gained by the anti-CCF campaigns, and they were not above using clever tactics and dirty tricks. However, the Progressive Conservative Party went even further, committing illegal acts and becoming a participant in the activities of Gladstone Murray and his big business masters.

Those using pulpits and parties to attack socialism and the CCF used rhetoric similar to that of others involved in the exercise. They exploited people's fears of communism and fascism, and of a world in which the values inherent in liberal democracy and Christianity were under threat. They used similar tactics in taking messages to the civil society: through church services and communications; and through political speeches, official party pamphlets, and third-party publications. Those using pulpits and parties to participate in the anti-socialist/anti-CCF campaign added strength to that campaign, as they were more voices, repeating similar warnings.

Parties

In the ideological debate raging in Canada in the 1940s, there was no more potent weapon to use against socialism and the CCF than the accusation that both were tied to, similar to, or fronts for communism. As has been seen, this confusion was sometimes initiated, and ruthlessly exploited, by the words and actions of big business and their spokespeople, Murray and Trestrail. The Communist Party of Canada (CPC), which later became the Labour-Progressive Party (LPP), also intentionally contributed to this confusion in order to further its own goals. As will be later explained, in its many guises, the LPP was an enemy of Canada's many small labour and socialist parties, including, and especially, the CCF, as it was the largest and most successful of those parties.

It fought the CCF from the left as part of its struggle to win the allegiance of the Canadian working class and secure influence in the labour movement. Canadian political scientist, and son of communist Jake Penner who became a "Red" alderman in Winnipeg after the 1919 General Strike, Norman Penner has written, "The founding of the CCF brought about a torrent of abuse by the Communist Party, the most virulent it had ever directed at social democracy."[4] While antagonism changed to calls for cooperation during the Popular Front period of the 1930s, and again in the late 1940s, social democrats and communists were deeply hostile to each other, each promoting very different views of socialism.

The Progressive Conservative Party played an important and assertive role in the anti-socialist/anti-CCF campaign, attacking socialism and the CCF from the political right. It not only supported the anti-CCF campaigns, but worked with them and exploited the cracks in the CCF and Canadians' interest in socialism when they appeared. It actively adopted the campaigns' techniques, such as the use of surrogates and inflammatory pamphlets, as well as their messages and language. The Ontario Progressive Conservative Party even participated in illegal activities.

One propaganda piece the Progressive Conservative party was involved with was *What the CCF Plans to do With Canada*, a collection of articles written by George W. James and originally published in the *Canadian Statesman* of Bowmanville, Ontario, in 1943. It was later re-published as *Canada Faces Dangerous Political Program: Socialism as planned by the CCF Menaces Freedom of Labourer, Farmer and Businessman* and then, in 1944, under the more succinct title *The Menace to Canada*.

In its many forms, the pamphlet was rife with misrepresentations, exaggerations, and lies. The most fundamental problem with the original articles in the pamphlets was that they consistently quoted two sources when addressing CCF policies: *Social Planning for Canada* and *Democracy Needs Socialism*, although neither book was an official publication written or endorsed by the party, and neither book totally or accurately reflected the party's beliefs or policies. The articles claimed that the party wished to abolish newspaper advertising and to ration paper to newspapers in order to control content. They said that the CCF wanted to take control of all business and expropriate all land, that it had no use for unions, and that it wished to take away the rights of workers to own their own homes. Further, they said that the party would dictate wages, limit how much businesses could spend on capital investment, and even forcibly relocate and re-educate workers, making them surrender much of their wages to the state for social security. It was piffle, and obviously so to anyone with even a cursory knowledge of the CCF.

However, the James pamphlets received the endorsement of the Progressive Conservative Party. PC leader John Bracken wrote a glowing introduction which appeared as each edition's first page. Bracken wrote in the form of a personal letter to the author:

> May I take this opportunity to say I think you have rendered a signal service to your readers and the people of Canada… I would hope that every Canadian could read your enlightened exposition of the CCF… The value of your service, it seems to me, is in pointing out not only the virtues but the fundamental fallacies of the CCF preaching. It is only when the defects as well as the merits of an issue are presented to the public that it can, with wisdom, determine its future course.[5]

Eugene Forsey wrote a response to *The Menace to Canada* that he forwarded to the CCF national executive and to newspapers. In that response, he argued that the Progressive Conservative Party had financed and organized the re-issue and distribution of the pamphlet. Forsey's response, in true form, then tore into the errors and lies in the work. It also commented on Bracken's introduction and inferred that, if Bracken sincerely believed what he wrote—that James had completed a careful and accurate analysis of the CCF platform—then Bracken could not possibly have read the Regina Manifesto. Forsey concluded:

> Stuff like *The Menace for Canada* is a disgrace to any party, and a threat to the very foundations of democracy. Unless the opposing parties can discuss each other's programmes in terms of what those programmes actually contain, and of the relevant facts, the basis of rational argument disappears, and with it all hope of orderly social development in this country.[6]

Another propaganda initiative of this type began in British Columbia in late 1945, with a series of pamphlets by a man about whom little is known, named Joe Paynter. Paynter's 24 page *Masters of Misjudgment—The CCF's Record in War and Peace* began, "The booklet gives chapter and verse to show how out of place their brand of political thinking is in big, free democratic Canada."[7] He went on to accuse the party of a number of crimes, including being "shifty" in that it supported the war effort in some cases but not in others, being "unreliable" in that it purported to support democracy but did not, and being "dangerous" in its plan to confiscate all businesses, farms, and private property.

Another of Paynter's pamphlets, called *We Can Learn a Lot from Russia*, walked much the same path, but in this work, he tied the CCF to communism and Russia. Paynter wrote in his introduction of the importance of his pamphlet and his cause: "Its importance lies in a number of related facts—that the dream and the hope of the USSR lies in a socialist world state; that the Socialist-CCF Party is working unceasingly for the establishment of a full socialist state in Canada; and that unless the most complete information available is put before Canadians, both democracy and individual liberty may be lost in Canada."[8]

Paynter's pamphlets did not indicate who had financed or published them, offering only an address: 216615 West Pender Street, Vancouver. The pamphlets said nothing about the author. Despite the fact that the pamphlets had a five-cent price printed on the cover, they were distributed free of charge.

By December, the Paynter pamphlets had blanketed British Columbia and were showing up in mailboxes across the country. The CCF's British Columbia secretary, F.J. McKenzie, reported to the national executive that they were being released from sources in Toronto, Montreal, and Winnipeg, and everyone on the Progressive Conservative Party's mailing list had received copies from Bracken House, PC Party headquarters in Ottawa.[9] The accusation of PC involvement had already been confirmed in a letter from CCF member John Robbins, who had written to CCF national research director Donald Macdonald stating that he had completed a form to receive literature from the Progressive Conservative Party and, shortly afterwards, had begun to receive a number of anti-CCF pamphlets from Toronto, Winnipeg, and Vancouver, some of which were the Paynter pamphlets.[10] Other letters to the national executive office confirmed that Paynter's pamphlets were also distributed as free unsolicited mail from the Progressive Conservative party in the Maritimes, Ontario, and Quebec.[11]

While flummoxed regarding the origins and funding of the Paynter campaign, CCF leaders seemed in agreement about its efficacy. In a letter to national executive member Lorne Ingle, British Columbia's CCF leader, Harold Winch, wrote, "It is my opinion that these things are even worse than the Trestrail affairs and much more effective."[12]

The Paynter story ended unresolved. Winch's detective work determined that Paynter and partner Austin Campbell ran an organization called Facts Publishing. The company began in July 1945 and was owned by Paynter, Campbell, and a lawyer named R. Farrow. Winch was convinced that they were being financed by outside sources, but could not discover them. Winch expected no more pamphlets, however, as Paynter died of a heart attack on November 15, 1945.[13]

Both the James and Paynter publications demonstrate the role of the PC party in the anti-socialist/anti-CCF campaign. More important in understanding that role were the Progressive Conservative Party's dealings with Gladstone Murray, as seen through the actions of two prominent Progressive Conservative leaders, federal PC leader and Prime Minister John Diefenbaker and Ontario premier, and later federal leader, George Drew.

John Diefenbaker attended at least one of Murray's speeches, at the Rideau Club on April 29, 1947. He also met with him at least once, in Toronto in 1946, and was a frequent and warm correspondent. Diefenbaker purchased and distributed Murray's pamphlets and encouraged him to continue his anti-CCF efforts. Diefenbaker's first contact with Murray appears to have been through a January 29, 1945, letter, in which he asked for 1,000 copies of *Things To Know About the CCF,* written by Rev. John W. Hamilton.[14] Diefenbaker must have made use of the pamphlets, for the next month he wrote again from Prince Albert, but this time on his House of Commons letterhead, exclaiming, "I think these pamphlets are remarkably effective and would appreciate it if you would forward me 200 copies. Cheque for $10.00 is sent you herewith."[15] Later, in the heart of the 1945 campaign, Diefenbaker wrote again, through Murray's secretary Marjorie Lamb, "I wish to thank you for forwarding me 600 copies of 'Tricks and Traps,' which I am making use of in my campaign. You might express my appreciation to Major Murray."[16]

A letter from Diefenbaker on March 23, 1946, thanked Murray for the material he had forwarded to his Parliament Hill office and encouraged him to continue his anti-CCF work. Diefenbaker wrote, "I wish to thank you for the material which you have sent me from time to time in connection with the campaign waged by you against Socialism in this country. I have made wide use of your material, and have found it most effective... I hope that you will continue to give wide circulation to the literature that you are putting out."[17]

In August 1948, Murray wrote to Diefenbaker, stating he had heard that Moscow Radio had mentioned the CCF in Canada, which, in Murray's mind, linked the party to communism sympathizers.[18] Diefenbaker was impressed with Murray's observations in this matter and with the copy of *Outlook* that he had enclosed. Diefenbaker wrote, "Have you any objections to my using parts of it providing I give credit to whom it belongs? ...I intend to be in Toronto on the 10th of September and will be seeing you at that time if I may."[19]

Diefenbaker also made effective use of Murray's material in the 1949 campaign. He was experiencing some electoral difficulty, partly due to the redrawing of his constituency's borders, which had brought a number of CCF supporters into his riding. Diefenbaker wrote to Murray expressing his concern: "However, I am having a real fight in this constituency where, of course, the CCF is very strong."[20] In an attempt to help, Murray forwarded samples of what he called propaganda, promising that great quantities of whatever Diefenbaker chose would be forwarded to him free of charge. Murray also offered an interesting warning: "I have a feeling, however, that you should be careful at election time to avoid being in any way identified with the 'Spokesman of Big Business'; perhaps therefore the material should be adapted to your own use. Either way, I am at your disposal."[21] Earlier, Diefenbaker's brother, Elmer, had written to Murray asking for a supply of an anti-CCF cartoon booklet which Murray had published.[22] After his victorious campaign, Diefenbaker wrote to thank Murray, explaining, "I based my whole campaign on the preservation of free enterprise and Parliamentary Government and found that the people understood the issues... The literature put out by your organization was most helpful. The cartoons were the best and most effective that I have ever used."[23]

Diefenbaker's reliance on Murray for thoughts on the CCF did not end with his ascendance to the prime minister's office. On September 24, 1957, under the letterhead of the Office of the Prime Minister, Diefenbaker wrote to

Murray to thank him for an advance copy of *Outlook:* "I have read with interest the extracts you have marked and will keep them in mind for future reference."[24] How much Murray's ideas shaped Diefenbaker's government is an interesting question for another study.

Another important Progressive Conservative leader, with even closer ties to Murray, was George Drew. Drew had been a correspondent of Murray's from the late 1930s, when Murray was with the CBC and Drew was Ontario's PC Party leader and leader of the opposition. Most of the early letters essentially praised each other for work well done. They met several times, sometimes in each other's offices and sometimes for lunch or dinner.[25] Murray even arranged to pay Drew's expenses to attend conferences and to deliver speeches when Drew was the Ontario opposition leader.[26] Murray began to introduce Drew to the idea of his anti-CCF campaign in February 1943. Initially, Drew expressed reservations and only tepid support, conceding in a letter to Murray, "You are moving into uncharted waters but waters through which we must sail and which certainly do need some careful sounding."[27] Murray urged Drew to join the campaign, encouraging him with a long list of corporate sponsors that were supporting Responsible Enterprise. The list could not have left Drew unimpressed.

Drew's speeches soon began to be peppered with anti-CCF arguments that seem to have been taken verbatim from Murray. During the 1943 Ontario campaign, for example, Drew lashed out at the CCF as a threat to Ontario's freedom and prosperity, and he equated the Communist Manifesto to the Regina Manifesto. At the same time, he confused fascism with communism, using indications of the former as a scare tactic: "The decision rests between freedom and fascism right here at home...it is time to stop talking about fascism having been destroyed. This is fascism."[28]

By November 1943, Drew had moved from a reluctant supporter to an enthusiastic exploiter of, and participant in, Murray's project. Drew and Murray exchanged many letters in which information was shared and sought. They often met in person and spoke on the telephone.[29] Drew had even begun to use Murray as an ex-officio researcher, as can be seen in the many letters the two exchanged, including one in which Drew asked Murray to seek information on organized labour and the CCF. As Drew noted, "I am hoping that before too long we may get something a little more definite about the activities of the CCF in relation to the CIO and the Communist Party."[30] Their relationship became increasingly cordial, to the point where many letters were hand-written with first-name salutations.

JOHN BOYKO

Three weeks before the 1945 Ontario provincial election, CCF candidate Agnes Macphail was told by one of her supporters, who was also an Ontario Provincial Police officer, that Premier Drew had created a special branch of the provincial police force to spy on the CCF and forward reports to himself and the attorney general, as well as to Murray and another big business anti-CCF propagandist named M.A. Sanderson, who led an anti-CCF organization in Toronto. Such a unit was obviously illegal, as it operated beyond the mandate of the OPP and was funded without the approval of the legislature. Macphail told Ontario CCF leader Ted Jolliffe who, on a May 24 radio broadcast, told the country. Jolliffe was quite specific: he was able to state the Toronto address of the secret operation's office and that its leader was William J. Osborne-Dempster, who wrote memorandums to the premier using the code name D.208. Jolliffe further claimed that the purpose of the secret and illegal operation was to report on CCF activities and to harm the party by linking it to communists in the LPP and organized labour. Jolliffe claimed that the secret operation smacked of the Nazi Gestapo, and in so doing, gave the scandal a name—the Gestapo Affair. Jolliffe's radio address ignited a storm of denials by Drew and accusations from others that the CCF was inventing the story out of desperation. Drew created a commission to investigate the charges, but ensured that its work would not be done until after the election.

The CCF's leadership had known of George Drew's character and political habits long before the scandal broke. Years prior to the Gestapo Affair, Eugene Forsey had written a memo to the national executive in which he outlined policy points that he believed should be pursued in the impending 1940 election. Forsey also made a rather damning assessment of Drew, writing, "a dangerous man, who should be attacked and debunked at every opportunity. I rather hope we can make gains in Ontario, provincially at any rate, by pointing out to decent people that unless they vote CCF they have no choice but to elect a thug as premier of the province."[31]

The scandal was national news, and it affected the federal CCF in the simultaneous national campaign. In the June 2, 1945 edition of the *Manitoba Commonwealth*, there was a picture of John A. Rowe, former special assistant to Osborne-Dempster, who had filed an affidavit that supported Jolliffe's contentions.[32] On the last page was an article that linked the Progressive Conservative Party to the anti-socialist/anti-CCF campaigns of Murray and

Sanderson and referred to R.G. Hall, who had also submitted an affidavit in support of Jolliffe's charges.[33] The article explained how Hall's affidavit confirmed suspicions that Sanderson and Osborne-Dempster had planned the anti-CCF advertisements that had appeared in Toronto newspapers on the eve of the 1944 municipal elections. It explained the successful suit brought against Sanderson by CCF candidates regarding those advertisements. Jolliffe's speech and related articles stated publicly what many in the CCF had known for some time: that in the anti-socialist/anti-CCF campaign, there were undeniable links between big business; those who fronted the campaign, such as Murray and Trestrail; and the Progressive Conservative Party.

The CCF attempted to exploit the Gestapo Affair, and to counter the new nation-wide storm of anti-CCF attacks it had inspired, by running advertisements which explained these links. One such CCF advertisement stated:

> A great national movement is being attacked by the most unscrupulous campaign in Canadian history. Every possible lie, distortion and slander is being used by Big Business and its political parties against the thousands of Canadians who form the CCF. The CCF has not the money to buy enough space to answer all of the misstatements. Here are the answers to a few of the more glaring falsehoods.[34]

A box at the bottom of the advertisement was entitled "D.208—THE DREW GESTAPO." It stated that Drew had been using taxpayers' money to illegally spy on the CCF and other citizens. The copy read:

> This exposure discloses that the paid agents of Big Business have been working hand in glove with Drew's secret police. It shows how far Big Business is going in its campaign to stop the CCF at any price. The lies about the CCF shown above in their advertisement are part of the same campaign. The coast-to-coast advertisements, broadcasts, and literature distribution "front" organizations are also part of the same slander and falsehood financed by Big Business at a cost of millions of dollars.[35]

Meanwhile, newspapers that were already in the anti-CCF camp remained there and used Jolliffe's accusations as new ammunition to hurl at the party. The reaction of one such newspaper is a sufficient illustration. The May 26 edition of the *Peterborough Examiner* ran the story on its first page, with a quote from Drew in which he stated, "I will show in terms that leave no doubt that Mr. Jolliffe is an unvarnished liar."[36] That day's editorial offered no evidence as to why it believed Drew's defense and not Jolliffe's accusation, but nonetheless concluded, "The charges made against Mr. George Drew by Mr. E. B. Jolliffe are as serious as any which can be brought against a public official and we most emphatically do not believe them."[37]

Two days later, a new editorial took up the case again, stating categorically that Drew simply could not be guilty.[38] Despite the fact that Jolliffe had released affidavits from police officers who had been involved in the special unit, another editorial the next week maintained, "The Jolliffe charges have all the earmarks of a gigantic Roorback—one of those prolonged hoaxes which are designed to distract attention from the real issues in an election.[39] The affidavits were dismissed as simply not to be taken seriously. Other editorials made similar points. With intentional blindness to the anti-CCF barrage against which the party had been fighting, and in which the *Examiner* played a role, the paper published an editorial after the federal and Ontario elections that actually blamed Joliffe and the CCF for the harshness of the campaigns: "The fact that the CCF did not win a single seat in Ontario is further indication that Mr. E. B. Jolliffe's conduct in the provincial contests was not to the taste of the provincial electors."[40] As seen in the *Examiner*'s coverage of the Gestapo Affair, the truth did not seem to matter in the ten days between Jolliffe's announcement and the election; however, Jolliffe did have the truth on his side.

The public papers of both Drew and Murray validate all of Jolliffe's accusations. For example, a year before the scandal broke, a May 13, 1944 letter from D.208 to Drew outlined in detail the proceedings of the Second National Congress Canadian League Against War and Fascism and brought Drew up to date on Tommy Douglas' role in the CCF in the next election.[41] That Murray was involved is seen in a number of letters, including a November 1943 letter from Murray to Drew forwarding information about a meeting involving CCF members. Murray wrote, "I think it is important for you to get hold of a copy of a [sic] the draft as soon as possible. It is available from D.208."[42] This and other letters make it clear that, from the secret operation's inception,

Murray was receiving the D.208 reports, he was advising Premier Drew on their significance, and suggesting courses of action based on the intelligence.

After the Ontario election, Drew's commission began its work. Chairperson Mr. Justice A.H. LeBel called a number of witnesses, including Drew and Murray. Premier Drew swore under oath that he had no connection with the "special branch," as it had come to be known; had learned only of such things from Jolliffe's radio broadcast; and had never received reports from D.208.[43] Gladstone Murray was also called to testify and he too claimed to have no connection with the operation and to have never received reports from Osborne-Dempster.[44] George Drew lied. Murray lied too. The Royal Commission exonerated Drew and let Murray and others slip off the hook.

Drew later became leader of the federal Progressive Conservative Party and, as such, continued to echo the arguments, and even the phrases, of Gladstone Murray. During the 1949 federal election campaign, for instance, Drew used the old saw that the CCF's brand of socialism would lead to communism, ignoring the intense antipathy between social democrats and communists at that time. For instance, in a May 30 speech delivered in Kelowna, B.C., Drew said:

> I am opposing socialism because socialism has been a failure wherever it has been tried. I am opposing socialism because in nation after nation it has opened the door to communism and I will do everything I can to prevent that happening here.[45]

Meanwhile, the Progressive Conservative Party continued its connection with Murray, even as the threat it perceived from the CCF declined and Murray's anti-CCF campaign was winding down. This connection can be seen through its support of Murray's monthly tabloid, *Outlook*. It began publication at his Richmond Street offices in April 1948 and ran until 1962. The six- to eight-page tabloid was densely worded and contained no pictures. Its articles often quoted directly from his speeches, making the same points regarding his support of free enterprise and disdain for socialism and the CCF. Compared to his speeches, *Outlook* was less polite, less historically based, and more direct in its blunt, scurrilous slams against the CCF. It used misleading quotes from CCF documents and members' and leaders' speeches, and it often resorted to patent untruths.

The inaugural April 1948 edition, for instance, intentionally perpetuated the confusion regarding the CCF and communism. The cover article concluded, "Moscow has decreed that in Canada its spear-head of attack is to be the CCF."[46] An August 1948 cover article warned, "If the CCF were to come to power and apply the policies now being ventilated, Canada would be moving straight in the direction of the totalitarian police-state, in which, incidentally, organized labour is stripped of its rights."[47]

Outlook was distributed across Canada and used by those who wished to crush the CCF. Newspapers received free copies of *Outlook*. Membership lists acquired from groups to whom he had spoken became the core of Murray's mailing list.[48] As late as August 1955, it was clear through cordial correspondence between Ontario Progressive Conservative Communications Secretary Harry Robbins and Murray that the party was still using Murray's material and was grateful for it.[49]

The PC-Murray ties continued even after the creation of the NDP. On June 1, 1961, Robbins wrote to thank Murray for having provided 250 copies of a newsletter, which copied *Outlook* in style and content, called *Responsible Enterprise*. Robbins explained that the stridently anti-socialist/anti-NDP newsletters would be distributed at the annual meeting of the Young Progressive Conservatives meeting in Atherley, from June 9 to 11, and he was profuse in his thanks: "I am deeply indebted to you for your kindness in supplying us with the material mentioned which will be most helpful in the battle against Socialism."[50] Shortly after the PC Youth meeting, Robbins followed up, thanking him again for the material, noting that it was well received, and that he still often used quotes from *Outlook* in his work for the Progressive Conservative Party.[51]

In taking the actions that it did, the Progressive Conservative Party moved beyond fair political play. It moved beyond the normal, clever, Machiavellian maneuvering of parties intent upon attaining, enhancing, or preserving power. The party's participation in the anti-CCF campaign was another sign that the ideological struggle in which Canada was involved went much deeper than normal tactical maneuvers or political debates and that there were few limits on the means that would be used in that struggle.

Pulpits

The importance of religion in debates regarding socialism and the CCF was revealed in a comment by a CCF candidate who reflected on his win in the 1943 Saskatchewan provincial election: "You can say anything you want about capitalism, the banks and so forth. Be as radical as you want. But you can't speak here of socialism... Socialism to them means Russia and anti-religion."[52] Religion certainly played a role in the development of the CCF. The party's first leader, J.S. Woodsworth, was a former Methodist minister who was respected as a man of faith. The CCF espoused many of the beliefs of the Social Gospel movement, most importantly the intellectual move away from seeking individual salvation, toward a belief that all of society must first be reformed. When religious issues surfaced in political debate, CCF leaders insisted that it was their sincere belief in Christian values that led them to see the unfairness of the capitalist system and to their desire to bring about a better society that could be consistent with those values.[53] As Tommy Douglas had predicted, "The religion of tomorrow will be less concerned with the dogmas of theology and more concerned with the social welfare of humanity."[54]

Regardless of the party's origins, beliefs, and secular nature, some of those who attacked the party used religion, and particularly Christianity, as a weapon against it. Socialism, and through it the CCF, was sincerely believed by some, and cynically portrayed by others, to be anti-Christian and anti-religious and, consequently, to be rejected by those who loved Christianity and the society that was founded on Christian values.

One individual that played a role in bringing religion to the ideological debate and anti-socialist/anti-CCF campaign was Reverend J. E. Branch. Branch was a Presbyterian minister who ran an organization called Radio and Press Publicity, located in Gravelbourg, Saskatchewan. He hosted a radio show every Thursday evening, published a weekly magazine called *Our Way of Life*, submitted a regular column to twelve Saskatchewan newspapers, and published pamphlets. His purpose was clearly stated in a form letter soliciting financial donations: "We are the only organization in Western Canada actively and daily counter-attacking socialist propaganda, by radio and press since 1942, and before that date, on a smaller scale."[55]

By 1949, Branch had begun to publish books as part of his operation, and, even more significantly, he had moved beyond Saskatchewan. His national presence was seen in a circular sent to homes in Ottawa from an office on Rideau Street. The mailing sought funds for his campaign and promoted his cause, imploring readers to keep socialism out of Ottawa and Canada: "socialism will strangle Canada and prepare this country for Communism... If you are interested in keeping socialism out of OTTAWA then help us to extend our campaign in favour of our Canadian WAY OF LIFE."[56] This move from a western rural base to an eastern Canadian city suggested that religion acted as one of the links that brought the urban/rural and regional cleavages together in the anti-socialist/anti-CCF campaign.

Reverend Branch's magazine, *Our Way of Life*, began in 1944 and advertised itself as "a digest of anti-Socialist and anti-Communist articles and literature."[57] Each edition contained a number of articles by several authors, photographs on its inside covers, and a number of advertisements from businesses in cities and towns across Saskatchewan. All editions contained a preponderance of articles extolling the free enterprise system and harshly critical of socialism and the CCF. The November 1948 edition is typical. It contained one article criticizing Karl Marx, and others more specifically aimed at discrediting the CCF, entitled, "An Experiment in Socialism," "Uncurbed Labor Can Be Danger Too," "The Socialist Way, Red Journalism," "Experiment in Education," and "Socialist Premier Seeks Aid of Capitalists." An article entitled "Thanks for Everything," which like the others argued that CCF electoral success would spell the end for Canada's freedom and way of life, was a transcript of one of Branch's radio addresses. It began by noting the great popularity of his recently published booklet, *Is This Tomorrow?*, which was about socialism leading to the "inevitable" communist takeover of Canada. The article claimed that it had become necessary to reprint the booklet because of its overwhelming popularity. Also in that edition was a publisher's note that made a commitment for the upcoming new year: "'Our Way of Life' will continue its crusade for our free and democratic way of life, fighting communism and socialism, in so far as socialism leads to communism."[58]

Meanwhile, Reverend Branch's popular syndicated radio show continued to air every Thursday night. The broadcasts were a mix of old-time religion and ruthless anti-socialist, anti-communist, and anti-CCF diatribes. For example, speaking one evening in January 1944 on CHAB in Moose Jaw, and also broadcast on CJGX in Yorkton, Saskatchewan, as well as a number of other stations, Branch appealed to the families of soldiers and to all of those who supported the Canadians fighting in Europe. It is significant that his words, cited below, were also reprinted and distributed across Canada in Trestrail's *Social Suicide*:

> Our fighters are not looking for charitable hand outs; but what they claim, they will get. We owe it to them. A dozen of them have more sense than all the Socialist clique put together. Our men are reasonable—they went out to fight for Canada, all Canada, and they do not want to come back to any Socialist mess.[59]

Also involved in the anti-socialist/anti-CCF campaign was M.A. Sanderson, president of Reliable Exterminators in Toronto. It was this position that earned him his nickname—the Bug Man. It is clear from letters exchanged between Ontario Premier George Drew and Gladstone Murray that Sanderson was involved with one or both of them, and he received information from D.208 as part of the Gestapo Affair.

Sanderson used religion to attack the CCF. He published a number of newspaper advertisements that slammed the CCF for its alleged beliefs, focusing on its supposed anti-Christian religious policy. Typical is a quarter-page advertisement that appeared in *The Globe and Mail* during the 1943 Ontario election. Entitled "Sugar Coating the Arsenic," the advertisement made note of the fact that one of the CCF's Toronto candidates was a veteran of the First World War and leader of a Bible class at his church. Even in his campaign literature, it stated, the candidate claimed to believe in the Christian way of life. Sanderson's response was:

> Tut! Tut! Tut! In fact, a flock of tuts! Does he really believe that the CCF with such a hook up can possibly embrace the Christian way of life?... Does he not know that the CCF is just another organization "fronting" for the Communists and that men of his type are wanted and needed to adorn that "front"?... Doesn't he know that a vote for the CCF is a vote against the "Way of Life" for which he stands?[60]

Sanderson used the religious argument in another highly effective anti-CCF action. As previously noted Sanderson placed advertisements in *The Globe and Mail* and the *Telegram* during Toronto's 1944 municipal elections. The advertisements contained vicious lies that besmirched and questioned the Christian character of every CCF candidate for municipal office. On the day of the election, he ran an advertisement under the title "This Is The Slate To 'Rub Out'—New Year's Day." The advertisement then listed every CCF candidate and accused them of being Communist dupes.[61] After the election, the candidates launched a lawsuit against Sanderson that they eventually won. However, Sanderson's campaign had already done its job: every CCF candidate had failed to win a place on Toronto City Council.

Gladstone Murray also brought religion into many of his speeches, using the Christian faith as a link between many of his themes. For instance, in an address to Toronto's St. George's Men's Club, he argued, "Next to spiritual health, and akin to it, I place freedom of the individual. The sovereignty of the individual soul is fundamental to the Christian faith and to the Jewish faith."[62] He went on to list factors that presented obstacles to spiritual health, pointing especially to the lack of "conscience" on the part of socialists: "And now we come to the obstacle of perverted politics… If most citizens want to have Communism or Socialism they will vote that way, and they will get what they want. Those leaders of organized Labour who induce workers to go on strike in order to force Socialism or Communism on the community are as dangerous a menace to the well-being of workers as are the predatory employers without social conscience."[63] Murray returned to this point in speeches made throughout the year. In his November 1946 speech to Toronto's Keo Club, for instance, Murray utilized references to Christian "light" and the preservation of the soul to link his warnings about Socialism with Christian values: "Individual freedom in the future will depend more upon religion and education than upon policy or organization… Where the flame of Christian thought is kept burning, where the spirit of classical antiquity is preserved, the sanctity and the sovereignty of the soul of the free citizen are impregnable."[64]

Murray's attempt to connect pro-Christian thought to an anti-CCF orientation was made clear again in a February 1947 speech to the Welland Rotary Club, entitled "The Message of Responsible Enterprise," in which he wrapped up his remarks by exclaiming,

I come, in conclusion, to the most important part of the message of Responsible Enterprise—to restore and strengthen the spiritual foundation of our society. Observe how the Socialists and Communists concentrate on material solutions, either ignoring or contemptuously rejecting the spiritual side. This is a strange inversion of values. The concept and charter of liberty derive from the Bible wherein are proclaimed the sovereignty and sanctity of the individual soul. The sacredness of the individual is common to all three great faiths— Catholicism, Protestantism and Judaism: it is denied by all collectivists—Socialists and Communists—in practice, if not in theory.[65]

Murray also published and distributed a series of small pamphlets written by Reverend John W. Hamilton of Ancaster, Ontario. The first in the series, entitled *Things To Know About the CCF,* appeared in 1943. Its introduction noted that the CCF's goal was to create a socialist, un-Christian state in Canada. It then outlined the purpose of the publication: "It is only because evil and not good would befall the people of Canada if such a Socialist State were set up that these facts and arguments are advanced."[66] The pamphlet went on—in short sentences and with a liberal use of upper case letters, bold print, and exclamation marks—to equate the CCF with Hitler, Stalin, and Mussolini. It argued that the CCF was based on foreign, non-Christian ideas and meant to overthrow the Canadian constitution, to enslave the Canadian people, to destroy self-respect and the integrity of the individual, and to eradicate the middle class, while ensuring that no one in Canada owned a business or land.[67]

Typical of the Hamilton series was a five-page pamphlet, published four years later, entitled *I Want Socialism?* Hamilton took a satirical approach and explained that he had come to embrace the socialist ideology. He explained that he wanted business owners to have their companies confiscated and wanted citizens to lose their freedom. He saw the advantage of Canada becoming like the totalitarian states it had defeated in two wars. He supported closing churches and denying people the freedom to worship as they wished.[68] In his conclusion, he warned that all of these things would come to pass if the CCF ever formed the government in Ottawa.

Beyond the actions of these well-connected individuals, and those whose words surely carried weight in the religious debate because they had the title "Reverend" before their name, the Catholic Church played a considerable role in the campaign. Its stance was an important factor in keeping the party from enjoying electoral success in Catholic Quebec and in the many urban areas populated by immigrants from predominantly Catholic countries who settled in those ridings in the post-Second World War years.

The Catholic Church in Canada was obliged to enforce Vatican directives regarding socialism, and thus the CCF that espoused it. A papal encyclical issued by Pope Leo XIII in 1891 supported the concept of private property and ordered Catholics to oppose communism and socialism as threats to that concept. It was followed by an encyclical from Pope Pius XII in 1903 and repeated in 1912, reiterating the Vatican's directive that Catholics were to reject communism and socialism.

In the United States, the influential Cardinal O'Connor was blunt in his support of the Vatican's directives and had a letter read in churches throughout the Boston archdiocese in December 1912 that stated, "There cannot be a Catholic socialist."[69] Similar actions were taken in Canada. In Quebec, the École sociale populaire studied the Regina Manifesto; Chairman Père Georges-Henri Lévesque's March 1933 report stated that the CCF's program was in opposition to the teachings of the Catholic Church. Accordingly, in February 1934, Cardinal Monsignor Georges Gauthier issued a pastoral letter that was read from every Catholic pulpit in Quebec, stating that Roman Catholics were forbidden to join or support the CCF. The Church indicated that a person could not be a good Catholic and a socialist at the same time.[70]

The Church's ruling affected many areas of everyday life. For instance, students at Collège Notre-Dame in Montréal, like many students then and now, were politically active and many had joined the CCF. They were told by the priests who made up the school administration that they were to quit the CCF or face immediate expulsion.[71]

In 1944 Jim Mugridge was the New Brunswick CCF Provincial Executive chairman, and in April was appointed chairman of the election committee for Saint John and County. He wrote to Coldwell expressing regret over an article in the British Columbia edition of the *CCF News* in which Coldwell is reported to have made uncomplimentary comments regarding the Catholic Church. The comments, Mugridge argued, were causing trouble in

New Brunswick. Coldwell responded that he and others regretted the publication of the comments, and he reiterated that the Regina Manifesto stated that the CCF supported religious liberty for all. Two days later David Lewis wrote to Mugridge asking him not to publish Coldwell's letter, as it would only serve to further publicize the problems the party was having with the Catholic Church hierarchy. Lewis suggested that Mugridge show the Coldwell letter to the Archbishop.[72] The problem, and the letters exchanged to address it, indicate the degree to which the CCF leadership thought the Catholic Church's beliefs and actions to be important to the party's electoral prospects.

The Progressive Conservative Party was quite willing to use the Catholic Church's disdain for socialism and the CCF to its ends. As part of this tactic, it published a two- by three-foot campaign poster for the 1945 Ontario election, with French on one side and English on the other. It began by reviewing the Vatican stances against socialism, then introduced the Canadian context, proclaiming in large print:

> In the forthcoming Ontario election, socialism rears its ugly head through the doctrinaire preaching of the CCF Party... The following warning against Socialism is taken from the Joint Pastoral letter of His Eminence the Cardinal Archbishop of Quebec and Their Excellencies the Archbishops and Bishops of Quebec and Bishops of Ontario, whose jurisdiction extends into the Province of Quebec, on the occasion of the anniversary of the Encyclicals "Rerum Novarum" and "Quadragesimo Anno." The letter was dated March 11, 1941. Like Pope Leo XIII, Pope Pius XII vigorously rejects Socialism and Communism. He analyses both to show their profound errors. He pays attention particularly to the socialism which presents a more tempting aspect. He condemns it even in its mitigated form where it waters down its old dogmas of class war and the suppression of private property. [Pope Pius XII said] "Religious Socialism and Christian Socialism are expressions implying a contradiction in terms. No one can be at the same time a sincere Catholic and a true Socialist."[73]

The religious issue arose again in a minor exchange involving the British Columbia executive two years later. In April, there was a heated meeting of the executive council with members of the Parliamentary Caucus in Ottawa. Quebec CCF member P. Laroach had pointed out that the British Columbia edition of the January 30 *CCF News* had contained an editorial regarding the death of Quebec's Cardinal Villeneuve, in which the writer had been critical of Cardinal's stand against the CCF. Laroach feared that the article could be interpreted as being too critical of the Catholic Church. When *l'Action catholique* reprinted the article, Laroach reported, it had caused trouble in many Quebec ridings and considerable dissension among CCF members. The national executive expressed regret that the editorial had appeared and hoped that all sections of the party would be careful not to jeopardize the position of other sections by the expression of personal viewpoints through the medium of their publications.[74] The incident speaks to the sensitivity of the CCF leadership to the religious issue, and its caution regarding anything that could harm its chances of electoral success.

In the summer of 1948, the Catholic Church hierarchy made a direct foray into the ideological battleground and spoke to the anti-socialist/anti-CCF campaign that was using the Church and religion for its ends. The *Canadian Register* was the official weekly newsletter of the Ontario Catholic Archdiocese. Its June 19, 1948, issue contained an article entitled "Political Confusion and Religious Scandal." In it, the archdiocese sought to clarify the Church's position with respect to the CCF, stating that the Catholic Church stood in opposition to communism, as it was an atheistic philosophy. Communism, the article continued, worked against the goals of the Church. However, it explained that too many Catholics had been misled into believing that the CCF was a communist party. It specifically referenced the anti-CCF campaign and listed three widely publicized falsehoods regarding the party. It referred to CCF responses to each lie and concluded:

> We hold no brief for or against the CCF. But we must affirm with all emphasis that it is false, unjust and dangerous to say that the CCF is Communist or to confound the CCF with Communism. Smearing the CCF only tends to whitewash Communism.[75]

This statement was noteworthy, given the Catholic hierarchy's long-standing and public condemnations of the CCF at the national and parish levels. However, its anti-CCF past could not be quickly erased. This fact was discussed at length at the CCF national executive meeting on June 27, 1948, and it was decided to issue a statement to support and publicize the Church's stand. The statement revealed the damage that the party recognized had been done by the Church and by those who exploited its years of opposition to communism and socialism:

> In view of the fact that the alleged support of the CCF by the Communists had harmed the CCF vote in some quarters, particularly in Catholic communities, it was resolved that the national office prepare a factual memorandum of the CCF record with regard to Communism and the Communist Party, for distribution, particularly in Catholic communities.[76]

In 1949, the national executive felt that enough Canadians still believed that the Catholic Church opposed the CCF that another advertisement to address the issue was needed. In June, it ran an advertisement in a number of church publications and newspapers that stated that the party supported the Christian notion of living in brotherhood rather than in competition and that the party sought to bring a higher standard of living to Canadians so that they could live in security, health, and fellowship. The advertisement quoted a Coldwell speech delivered in July 1948 at the Rideau Summer Conference in which he acknowledged that Christian values do, and should, inform political discussions, and he argued that the CCF's policies were consistent with those values.[77]

Only a week later, the party ran another advertisement addressing the religious issue. This announcement repeated the party's assertion that it was not an anti-Christian communist party, but rather, had been fighting communists and their beliefs throughout its history. The advertisement quoted Coldwell:

> While no truly democratic party can claim a monopoly of Christian motives, I am confident that the CCF has as

good a claim as any to be considered a party based on those fundamental principles which we associate with Christianity. We (the CCF) believe that voluntary co-operation rather than individual competition is a fundamental implication of Christian doctrine—that we are all brothers of another.[78]

Despite the statements of the Catholic Church and the party's actions to support those statements, the religion issue remained a sore point for the CCF. The toxicity of the issue was seen in many party communications, including the January 1955 *Farm Report*, which listed a number of problems that the party was having winning the farm vote. The report's author, F. Von Pilis, suggested that many farmers still feared state socialism, the power of organized labour, and the notion that the CCF was anti-religious.[79]

The long-standing instructions of the Catholic Church, and the fears and uncertainties about the CCF and socialism raised by Protestant clergymen such as Branch, and others, such as Sanderson and Murray, would have resonated with those holding sincere Christian beliefs. The religious argument would also have been significant for Canadians without such beliefs, as it was presented as yet one more reason to fear and reject socialism and the CCF. The presentation of the issue by those with status, and the message's repetition through numerous avenues of communication, augmented its persuasiveness.

It is clear that, in the 1940s, political parties actively sought to confuse voters regarding communism, fascism, and socialism in order to hurt the CCF and augment their own electoral success. More significantly, the Ontario Progressive Conservative Party involved itself in illegal activities meant to harm the CCF and joined the federal party in its direct involvement in Gladstone Murray's anti-CCF campaign. These actions resulted in Canadians being exposed to rhetoric that asked them to question the CCF's plans regarding Canada's political values. Meanwhile, the Catholic Church, some members of the Protestant clergy, and others presented Canadians with similar rhetoric, but added concerns about the CCF's designs on Canada's religious values. The messages from the parties and the pulpits resonated because they came from people and organizations that enjoyed status in civil society. They were also powerful because they repeated and supported many of the words and arguments that Canadians were also hearing from many business leaders and their employers, reading in many newspapers, and discussing at social and professional meetings. These voices, using many of the same words and metaphors, and repeating the same message over and over again, were as relentless and unforgiving as the raging winds of a hurricane.

5

ATTACK FROM THE LEFT:
COMMUNISTS AND ACCOMPLICES

So far this study has been examining the attacks on socialism and the CCF from the right of the political spectrum. But we must not ignore the fact that the Canadian left joined in the fight. In terms of its goals and players, the political left of the day was as diverse as the right; the primary difference is that those on the Canadian political left, including the CCF, were fighting to win the support of the same people, those who were seen as a natural constituency, whose unique interests would be best protected and served by rallying to one flag or another for the march forward down the left side of the road.

While acknowledging the left's diversity, the attacks from the left upon the CCF can be best understood by examining the actions of the Communist Party of Canada and the ways in which it worked with the Liberal Party of Canada, organized labour, and, to a lesser extent, the Progressive Conservative Party. To see the attack from the left through this prism is useful for, as we have already seen, one of the most persuasive arrows that pierced the heart of the CCF was the confusion among voters regarding the communist and democratic socialist ideologies, and the Communist and CCF parties. Some of that confusion is easy to understand, as both pledged to rid Canada of capitalism, thus turning the Canadian political culture on its head; however, as will be demonstrated, the Communist Party played an important role in creating and exploiting this confusion that was as important as that of the anti-socialist/anti-CCF actors from the right.

Barely mentioned in this analysis is the role of organized labour. In all countries that struggled through the challenges and opportunities of 20th century industrial development, organized labour was an important factor in the political culture, and particularly in the chorus of voices heard from the political left. All countries saw unions either form a political party, as happened in Britain; concentrate on industrial matters and leave politics to the socialist or communist parties, as happened in most of Europe; or gradually integrate themselves into the political sphere by becoming increasingly tied to or a part of existing political parties, as happened in Italy, France, and, eventually, Canada. The period under investigation witnessed Canadian organized labour moving from the second to the third model and, accordingly, become increasingly important in political discourse. However, the points that need to be made in this analysis are adequately made, not by delving deeply into that development, but, rather, in exploring how the Communist and Liberal Parties used their influence with organized labour to take actions against socialism and the CCF while the CCF was, itself, attempting to increase its influence in unions across the land.

The purpose of a political party is to win and retain power. One can not criticize a political party for taking actions to fulfill its purpose. However, it is valid to note actions taken by political parties that are beyond the pale of accepted political debate and discourse. The Communist Party of Canada, along with its co-conspirators, the Progressive Conservative and Liberal Parties, took many such excursions in their reactions to and attacks upon the CCF, to the point where their language and tactics mirrored those of all the other anti-CCF activists. In this way, the actions of the party added legitimacy and clout to the anti-socialist/anti-CCF campaign.

The Russian Revolution and civil war ground to a bloody end in 1922. Even while fighting the war, Vladimir Lenin had afforded energy to the struggle of promoting communism around the world. That struggle began a process through which the Soviet Comintern gave encouragement, leadership, and money to individuals, groups, and parties in many countries. One of those parties was the rather small Workers Party of Canada which, in a barn outside Guelph, Ontario, in May 1921, became the Communist Party of Canada (CPC). From the outset, the CPC was the child of the Soviet Comintern, which communicated either directly with Canadian party leaders or through the Anglo-American secretariat. The party's initial goals, as dictated by the Comintern, were to become the voice of the Canadian working class and to work in concert with other socialist groups as a united front.[1]

Those goals changed, however, when Josef Stalin took power in the Soviet Union and established an iron control of the Comintern, resulting in the CPC becoming not only a tool of communist ideological desires but also of his real politic maneuverings for the good of his regime and of the Soviet Union's changing international goals. In 1928, the Comintern, as directed by the Sixth Congress of the Communist International, decreed that socialists were the enemy of communists and the working class. Socialists were deemed to be the last vestiges of the old capitalist order which needed to be swept away for the good of the communist cause. Communist parties in all countries were directed to unmask and destroy socialists and other left-wing groups and parties.[2] In 1929, and again in February 1931, Stalin ordered increased direct attacks on socialist parties, calling them the most destructive force harming the working classes.[3] The Communist Party of Canada thus saw the birth of the CCF as a new negative force in its struggle to free the Canadian working class and as an enemy to be crushed.

In 1971, Soviet leaders admitted that the attacks on social-democratic parties had been a mistake. The Central Committee of the CPSU wrote:

> Equating Social-Democracy, however, with fascism and advancing the slogan of dealing the main blow against its left elements, who could become the allies of Communists in the fight against reaction and fascism, was a mistake which hindered fulfillment of the task set by the Plenum, namely that of winning the majority of the working class.[4]

But the fact remains that throughout the CCF's history, the Communist Party of Canada, in its many guises, was an enemy of Canada's many small labour and socialist parties, including, and especially, the CCF, as the largest and most successful of those parties. Norman Penner wrote, "The founding of the CCF brought about a torrent of abuse by the Communist Party, the most virulent it had ever directed at social democracy."[5]

The CPC often aimed its attacks on the CCF at the party's leadership, in an effort to divide it from the membership. Even before the creation of the CCF, the CPC had set its sights on the CCF's first leader, J.S. Woodsworth. Woodsworth had solid credentials as a friend of the working class through his involvement in the Winnipeg General Strike and his election to parliament as one of only three representatives of the Labour Party. Woodsworth had written extensively about his goals for the working class and had even written in the Communist Party organ called *The Worker.* Certainly the CCF's Regina Manifesto, speaking of the eradication of the capitalist system, should have put him in good stead with the Communist Party, which shared that goal. However, the Communist leadership was ruthless in their attacks on Woodsworth. Former independent Labour candidate and the CPC's first secretary, John Macdonald, wrote that Woodsworth used "The hocus pocus of the bourgeois pacifist who plays the most damning role in the ranks of the workers today."[6] Powerful, ambitious, and charismatic communist leader, Tim Buck, wrote in *The Worker* that Woodsworth was "the most dangerous enemy we have at the present time. The eyes of our party membership must be focused upon the menace of social reformists."[7]

The CPC worked to defeat Woodsworth in his Winnipeg riding in the 1930 federal election, while conspicuously not running Communist candidates in the ridings of the Liberal leader, Mackenzie King or the Conservative leader, Bennett. The money spent and the volunteers pressed into action against Woodsworth were unprecedented. Communist Party members told reporters that working people found Woodsworth to be a "faker," "labour misleader," and a "social fascist."[8]

Meanwhile, the CPC's strength and influence in national affairs increased. It was seen most explicitly in its leadership of the "On To Ottawa Trek" and its drive to recruit volunteers for the Mackenzie-Papineau battalion to fight fascism in the Spanish Civil War. These high-profile actions, as well as its grassroots organizational efforts and growing inroads into the Canadian labour movement, allowed it to grow increasingly popular among many of the Canadians that the CCF was attempting to attract. While never broadly popular, the CPC earned significant support in small pockets throughout Canada. It was strongest in parts of Quebec, Manitoba, Saskatchewan, and British Columbia, with its largest area of support in Ontario. The party's strength was found mostly in industrial and recent immigrant-settled areas, especially in Winnipeg, Montreal, Toronto, Thunder Bay, Hamilton, and Windsor.[9]

However, like the CCF, the CPC's views and actions earned it a range of powerful enemies among the Canadian establishment. Actions taken against the CPC demonstrated the fear of new, left-wing ideas and the determination of the establishment to deal with those promoting them. From the party's creation in 1921, the RCMP had harassed its leaders, confiscated its literature, and disrupted its meetings. In August 1931, Prime Minister R.B. Bennett had CPC leaders Tim Buck, Tom McEwen, Malcolm Bruce, Sam Carr, John Boychuk, Matthew Popovich, A.T. Hill, and Tom Cacic arrested for belonging to an unlawful association and being part of a seditious conspiracy as interpreted under Section 98 of the Criminal Code. Section 98 had been created after the Winnipeg General Strike to give the government the power it needed to round up communist and foreign agitators, but until then, it had not been used.

After only two and one-half years, in November 1934, the eight were released. Tim Buck staged a triumphant return at a successful rally at Maple Leaf Gardens, where 17,000 people packed the arena and 8,000 more were turned away at the door. It is interesting, given the events that followed, that Ontario Liberal leader Mitchell Hepburn appeared on stage with Buck at the rally.

Bennett's arrest of Buck and the others can be seen to have actually helped the CPC, as it afforded a great deal of publicity for the leader and the party and is generally credited with assisting its electoral attractiveness in the next federal election.[10] This publicity was also credited with leading to a number of CPC members being elected to municipal offices in 1935. In that year, 25 CPC members were elected to municipal councils and school boards. In Blairmount, Alberta, a full Communist slate was elected, and its first action was to rename Blairmount's main street "Tim Buck Boulevard."

For years following Buck's release from jail, and the further consolidation of his leadership, the Communist Party held to its goal of destroying the CCF. It took a two-track approach to attain that goal. On the one hand, the Communists cynically pledged cooperation with the CCF in their common fight against capitalism. On the other hand, it confronted the CCF through infiltrating the party, alienating it from organized labour and the voters, splitting its leadership from its members and supporters, and, finally, allying itself with the old line parties. The two-track cooperation and confrontation strategy was quite effective in inflicting great harm on the CCF.

The cooperation track was initiated by the 7th Congress of the Comintern. It weighed the policy of attacking socialist groups against the growth of the pro-union New Deal in the United States, the ravages of the Depression, and the growing willingness of unions to accept communists as union leaders.

While the establishment of communist parties as the only true voice of the working class remained the goal, its tactics to pursue that goal changed. In May 1934, the Comintern ordered the creation of the World Congress Against War and Fascism as a reaction to events in Spain and to Hitler's becoming chancellor and re-militarizing Germany. It was to unite working classes and those who spoke for them, including socialists, against the growing threat of war and the anti-communist fascist parties that were gaining popularity in Europe, especially in Germany and Italy. This new tactic of attempting to create a united front with socialist parties as a way to infiltrate and overwhelm them was a foreshadowing of things to come.

At its 7th Convention, in July 1934, the CPC responded to the Comintern's shift in tactics and direction by creating the Canadian League Against War and Fascism. Its founding convention took place on October 6 and 7 and was chaired by communist leader A.A. MacLeod. The CCF was invited to join and participate, in an attempt to have CCF leaders and members see that the common enemy of all Canadians was war and fascism and that to defeat both necessitated a united front. Woodsworth responded to the invitation to join the League in a letter to communist spokesperson and organizer A.E. Smith:

> It has seemed impossible to work closely with those who persistently denounce us as enemies of the working class… It was the Communist Party that disassociated itself from me and denounced me.[11]

Later, using language sure to infuriate communists at home and abroad, Woodworth was quoted in a *Daily Clarion* article as saying, "If the Communists are so keen for a united front, why not begin by having a united front of the Stalinists and Trotskyites."[12]

While the new cooperation track was established, the old confrontation track continued. This fact was evident throughout the period of the incarceration of Buck and the other CPC leaders. On January 13, 1934, communist leader Stewart Smith, using the pseudonym B. Pierce, had written an article in *The Worker,* entitled "The Struggle For Marxist Leninism." He argued that the CCF was simply a capitalist front that needed to be crushed. He expanded on his ideas in an anti-CCF book published later that year, entitled *Socialism and the CCF.*

The two-track approach to the CCF was evident in that the same 7th CPC Convention that had created the Canadian League Against War and Fascism, and had asked the CCF to join, had also seen the passage of a motion in which all true friends of the working class were asked to leave the AFL, ACCL, and the CCF and join with the CPC in a united front. This invitation was repeated in an article in the September 15, 1934, edition of the *Worker*.[13] The CPC Manifesto mentioned the CCF directly, but in claiming to wish to speak for the working class with one voice, it was actually asking for it to abandon its core values and policies and for its members to abandon their leaders. The motion said:

> The Communist Party declares there is no way out except the way of revolutionary mass struggle against capitalism and the final overthrow of capitalism. All the deception of the social reformists of a promise of socialism through parliament is only a device for maintaining capitalism and rendering the masses helpless before increasing capitalist misery… We say to the Workers and farmers in the CCF: Form together with us the united front struggle against poverty, fascism, and war in spite of and against the will of your leaders, who oppose the united front.[14]

Tim Buck maintained the harsh confrontational line in an article he wrote for the January 9, 1935 edition of the *Worker*, entitled "Statement to the Working People of Canada." He argued that the CCF leaders were "social reform charlatans" who participate in "fascist methods of deception." The article continued, "We call upon the CCF, the A. F. of L., and the ACCL and all working class organizations to form united fronts on all battle lines of working people against the new attacks of capital and for the immediate interests of the toiling people."[15.]

Many actions taken against the CCF were less public and more effective. One of the most disruptive actions involved infiltrations, and the CPC was open about its goals and tactics in this regard. Its organizational secretary wrote in the *Worker*, "We need strong party factions composed of active workers inside the trade unions, the CCF clubs, Social Credit groups and incipient fascist organizations in order to check the necessary instruments for winning the masses of Canadian people."[16] In 1929, before the CCF was created, the CPC had set a goal to establish communist labour cells in factories across the country, and its success in doing so was seen in its claim that by 1933 the Communist Party would be entitled to legitimately brag about having played a role in 75% of the strikes in Canada.[17]

The years between 1938 and 1943 witnessed the largest growth in labour membership in Canadian history; from 383,000 to 664,000 members.[18] Again, it was the communists who played a large role in contributing to that trend.[19] The fiercest battle between the CCF and the CPC for labour support came in 1940 with the merger of the ACCL and the CIO that formed the new and powerful Canadian Congress of Labour. Despite mammoth efforts on behalf of many CCF leaders and workers, by 1945 the Communists controlled more than one third of all CCL memberships and many positions of leadership, through which it was able to forward union funds to communist candidates, causes, publicity, and the publication of the *Canadian Tribune*, while at the same time taking actions against the CCF.[20]

Concurrently, communist influence in the working class beyond the CCL fight was increasing and further robbing the CCF of the support of one of the most important organizations in the trade union movement: the Trades and Labour Congress, a small but powerful craft union organization with influence mostly in Ontario. In 1921, the TLC had formed the Canadian Labour Party, but when that party failed and splintered into small and largely ineffectual political groups, the TLC retreated and became ostensibly apolitical. CCF attempts to win the support of the TLC, while struggling against communist influence in, and control of, many other sectors of the labour movement, were a constant, expensive, and distracting factor throughout most of the CCF's existence.[21]

While immensely successful in the union movement, the communist infiltration tactic was also successfully used directly against the CCF. It often involved simple patience. For example, a small group of Communist Party members would make a plan, then show up at a CCF constituency or club meeting, arriving and sitting as individuals. They would each then propose motions or engage in long debates and discussions that would prolong matters, until finally, in boredom or weariness, people would begin to drift from the meeting. At the appropriate time, one of the infiltrators would propose a motion, such as advocating closer ties with the Communist Party or voting one of the group into a position of leadership, and, with infiltrators in the majority, see the motion carried. This simple but brilliant strategy was used many times in ridings throughout the country, but was especially effective in Ontario. In London, for example, communist infiltrators used the tactic in a way that led that riding's CCF club voting to stand with the Communist Party of Canada in supporting prominent communist A.E. Smith, who was then facing jail time for sedition.

By 1936, the Ontario CCF found itself either unable or unwilling to deal with the problem of Communist Party infiltration, which had reached the point where the provincial party appeared to be poised on the brink of being taken over. The harm caused to the Ontario party by the communist infiltration tactic was one of the main reasons for Woodsworth having to take an action that was somewhat out of character for him: dissolving the Ontario CCF. Its reorganization was overseen by the National Executive; one of its first moves in rebuilding was to combat communist infiltration by tightening membership rules so that, throughout Canada, CCF members could not simultaneously be members of another political party. The communist infiltration campaign none the less continued to inflict serious and irreparable damage to the CCF in Ontario and elsewhere.[22]

The Communist Party also adopted clever tactics at election times to hurt the CCF. In the 1935 federal election, it undermined the CCF leadership's attempts to distance itself from the communists by releasing a list of CCF candidates who had answered a CPC questionnaire that had shown by their answers that they accepted communist ideas and thus were endorsed by the CPC. Those candidates included E.B. Jolliffe, King Gordon, Grant MacNeil, Graham Spry, E.J. Garland, and H.E. Spencer. Gordon and Spry both made a difficult situation worse for the party by speaking publicly in favour of creating a united front with the communists. The CPC then withdrew its own candidates from those six ridings while running strong candidates against Woodsworth, Heaps and McInnis, who had all spoken against the united front and had continued their anti-communist statements. Meanwhile, the communists expressed outrage that A.A. Heaps would not withdraw from his North Winnipeg race when the CPC nominated Buck to run in the riding. From the CCF's point of view, Heaps was an important CCF leader running for one of the few seats in Canada where the party had a chance, and that chance was being compromised by the CPC parachuting its Toronto-based leader into the contest.

All the work that the CCF had done to differentiate itself from the communists was not helped by important Communist Party spokesperson Stewart Smith stating during the election:

> The CCF and the Communists are both in favour of genuine unemployment insurance, of a large scale building program, of the abolition of slave camps, of increased wages and increased relief, of a moratorium on farmer's debts, higher prices and security for the small businessman. We are both in favour of steeply graduated income tax to force the rich to pay the costs of the crisis. Second, both the CCF and the Communist Party are for the repeal of Section 98, the reform of the electoral system to provide proportional representation... Thirdly, the CCF and the Communist Party meet on common ground in the fight for peace.[23]

The election saw Heaps win with 12, 093 votes, and Buck come third with 7,276. Of the six CCF candidates who moved toward cooperation, only MacNeil was elected.

Woodsworth and Lewis saw the CCF members who supported the united front as guilty of insubordination and tried to stop them. Woodsworth contended that the CCF already represented a common front of farmers, workers, and intellectuals. Further, he said the CCF could never unite with the communists, as they continued to support violence. Woodsworth stuck by the words he had spoken at the party's founding conference, "The CCF advocates peaceful and orderly methods. In this we distinguish ourselves sharply from the Communist Party which envisages the new social order as being ushered in by violent upheaval and the establishment of a dictatorship."[24]

David Lewis also spoke out against the united front. In the September 1936 *Canadian Forum*, he wrote:

> A fusion of the CCF, Communists, Social Credit, Reconstructionists, and left liberals—which is what the Communists advocate—would under present Canadian

conditions, create confusion, compromise the socialist objective of the CCF as a party, and might even, by way of reaction, call forth a strengthening of the right forces.[25]

At the CCF's 1936 National Convention, the motion advocating a rejection of the CCF-CPC united front won 88 votes to 7. However, the long and often heated debates at the convention showed again that the CCF had been hurt by the united front movement and the fight between the leadership and members that it created. Many CCF members were later expelled for ignoring the convention resolution when they continued to support the united front movement. Other CCF clubs and riding associations followed the resolution's instructions, but began speaking publicly about the CCF having too much centralized power. Meanwhile, the CCF was also hurt by the fact that those who were already opposed to, or actively fighting, the party used the internal debates as evidence that it was even closer to the communists than they had already suspected.[26]

Recognizing the harm that the communist cooperation-track efforts were inflicting on his party, Lewis threw a bone to the advocates of the united front by proposing a motion by which groups and individuals could cooperate with others in their communities in activities that promoted CCF ideas. This was interpreted by some as meaning that CCF members could participate in events such as the seemingly innocuous, but actually politically charged, May Day parades without risking the wrath of the CCF leadership.

The actions of the Communists, Liberals and anti-CCF propagandists meanwhile continued to frustrate the CCF's ability to make inroads with organized labour and working-class voters. The frustration was evident in many letters and publications. For example, *New Commonwealth Jr.* was a pamphlet published every two weeks by the CCF's *New Commonwealth*. A spring 1937 edition stated that there were many ridings in Ontario that could elect a CCF candidate, but that potential was being jeopardized by the Liberal-Communist strategy of nominating two or three supposed pro-labour candidates in the same riding. The article argued, "There are seventy ridings in which no Labor man could possibly achieve victory. The Canada-wide situation is much worse… We suggest to Ontario Labor that it not be misled by agents of the bosses who would encourage duplication because they realize that duplication means defeat."[27] It went on to explain the forces against which labour and the CCF had to fight:

> Every once in a while, certain members of the organized labor movement seem to derive satisfaction from poisoning fellow members' minds with the obviously untrue story that the CCF is opposed to organized labor. Those who spread such lies fall into three divisions. Firstly: political scabs, whose employers shudder at the thought of the growing tide of Labor-CCF action. Secondly: members of organizations foreign to our traditions who, seeking to make their trade union movement here a mere adjunct of a political machine, frightened of the progress of the world's social-democratic governments (in New Zealand, Sweden etc.) as compared with the terror now existing in Europe, are fighting desperately to delude labor men into the belief that their nations are "friends of democracy." Thirdly: honest men who have been misled by the former persons and who have not stopped to consider the obvious foolishness of the arguments advanced against the CCF.[28]

At this time, CPC leaders had come to the conclusion that, despite their small but growing popularity, the communist name did not help its electoral or organizational efforts. Its goals, it was decided, could be better pursued if the party changed its name and even acted under different names. In Ontario in 1937, for example, the CPC organized under names such as Labour Party, Labour Farmers, and the Labour Progressives. This tactic hurt the CCF, as it suggested that there were a number of worker and farmer organizations that the CCF did not support and which, in turn, did not support the CCF. It further hurt the CCF when members of such groups appeared at CCF nomination meetings and in campaigns opposing CCF candidates and arguing that the party did not speak for workers or farmers. Many working-class voters turned away from the party and, in many ridings, the vote was split, thereby reducing the chances of CCF electoral and fundraising success and organizational progress.[29]

With respect to organizing, an example can be made of the frustrations experienced by national organizer Grant MacNeil, who believed that his troubles in organizing in the small industrial town of Galt, Ontario, were due almost exclusively to the widespread, but erroneous, belief that the local organization was full of communists. The CCF had been kicked out of its quarters due primarily to suspected communist ties. MacNeil tried to remain confident, but acknowledged the problem in an April 1942 letter to Lewis. He wrote, "difficult to secure new active workers due to intimidation practiced by employing interests, and general prejudice against CCF as 'red' though confident they can retain popular support already gained at polls."[30]

With respect to fundraising, it was common for many of the party's provincial executives to fail to meet their annual quotas, and many local and regional CCF leaders blamed the communists for exacerbating their money problems. Communist influence in these matters was revealed in the spring of 1942, when Alistair Stewart was attempting to organize and raise funds for the party in Winnipeg and came to the conclusion that the communists were nearly defeated in that city. He argued in a letter to Lewis that, with the communists gone, perhaps those who had donated money to them could be persuaded to give to the CCF. He wrote, "There's no reason on earth why we shouldn't get the money which has been going to the C.P.... I'm convinced that there's at least a thousand bucks in it if we have enough warning to do the requisite organizing."[31]

A particularly effective tactic used to attack the CCF was for the Communist, Liberal, and Progressive Conservatives to actively coordinate or in some cases allow coordinated efforts. This tactic was seen in the 1937 Ontario election, in which the communists used newspaper advertisements to urge voters to support Liberal candidate Arthur Roebuck in the Toronto riding of Toronto-Bellwoods. Stewart Smith explained the communist intention to unite with the Liberals against the CCF in an article in the October 10, 1937 *Daily Clarion.* He wrote, "Liberals and Labour are duty bound to vote together and elect proven champions of the people's rights."[32] Two years later, in April 1939, Norman Freed, the executive secretary of the B.C. Communist Party, spoke in Nanaimo and announced that the Communist and Liberal parties would cooperate in the upcoming BC election. The pattern was repeated in many ridings and in many elections throughout the country. The June 3, 1944 *Canadian Tribune* contained an article in which Tim Buck praised Liberal party policies, claiming that they were quite close to those of the communists.[33] The Liberal party made no official responses to these words or actions. Any Liberal response would, in fact, have been irrelevant.

Cooperation between political parties is not unethical and can often bring benefit to not only the parties involved but to the governed. The CCF itself was involved in negotiated and successful a coalition. In October 1940, Manitoba's Progressive Conservative premier, John Bracken, ended a long process of negotiations with the CCF, Liberals, and Social Credit to create a coalition government for his province; this allowed Manitoba to end partisan politics temporarily and concentrate on the war effort, while allowing Bracken to avoid a provincial election that was due the next year. The move was quite popular in the province. The October 28, 1940 *Winnipeg Free Press* editorial praised the move, saying, "Politicians will be interested in the effect that the coalition will have upon the future of their own parties. They would be well advised to forget these considerations for the time being."[34]

Many CCF leaders initially opposed the idea. The highly regarded Angus MacInnis, for example, was among those who argued throughout most of August, while the negotiations were transpiring, that a deal would ultimately hurt the party.[35] On the other hand, many supported the idea, such as the equally respected Frank Scott, who argued that a coalition should never be dismissed out of hand because, with the CCF in the cabinet, Bracken could possibly be moved to the left. The National Executive was eventually convinced by Scott's arguments and Lewis urged the Manitoba executive to negotiate with Bracken in good faith.[36]

The difference between the Manitoba coalition and the cooperative efforts of the Liberals, Progressive Conservatives, and Communists is that the former was done in a public and transparent fashion and motivated by a desire to do positive good for people. The latter were nearly always secret, anti-democratic, conspiratorial, and motivated by a desire to inflict damage on another party by tricking voters.

Given the strategic links between the Liberal and Communist parties, it is richly ironic that on June 6, 1940, the Communist Party of Canada was declared illegal by Ottawa's Liberal government. The arrests of CPC leaders began on June 11 under Section 21 of the Defense of Canada regulations, which had been passed in September 1939 and included the language that hung the CPC. The CPC leaders were found guilty of acting in ways that threatened the safety of the public and the state. The party, however, merely continued to operate under new names and from within front organizations, with the main party later officially adopting the name Labour-Progressive

Party. The declaration of the CPC as an illegal organization and the ensuing arrests, however, did not seem to bother leaders of the Liberal Party, who did not stop cooperating with the communists in the struggle to control and exploit organized labour while attempting to outflank the CCF.

By the 1940s, nearly all leaders of the Trades and Labour Congress were either Communists or Liberals so that the Liberal–LPP alliance was strong enough that all TLC decisions between 1943 and 1945 were influenced by that alliance. When the Liberal Party and the LPP stated publicly that they supported labour unions that were not allied with any political party, the TLC, perhaps not surprisingly, announced agreement with that policy and a refusal to negotiate ties to the CCF. However, the LPP encouraged the creation of labour representative associations, and many were set up. The biggest and most influential was the Toronto and District Trade and Labour Council. It supported the LPP's trade union director, J.B. Salsberg, as its candidate in the Toronto riding of St. Andrew's. The decision hurt the CCF because to run a candidate against Salsberg would make it appear that the party was opposing the wishes of labour. David Lewis suggested not running a candidate in the riding, but Coldwell was furious and overrode Lewis' idea. Coldwell argued, "Whatever steps the Communists made to improve their relations with the CCF, let alone bring about some kind of united front during this period, were in effect abandoned because of the hostility between the CCF and CPC, in the trade union movement."[37]

Sowing even greater confusion among workers and in the labour movement were a number of increasingly rabid anti-CCF articles and advertisements that began to appear in Liberal- and Communist-dominated union publications and newspapers. The *Canadian Labor Press* attack was especially ruthless during the 1943 Ontario election: it placed a quarter-page advertisement in a number of newspapers in July with the large title "Why is the CCF Wrong?—CCF Against Workers' Interests—Sound Reasoning Condemns Whole Idea." The copy warned of the CCF menace, called CCF ideas bunkum, claimed that the party was trying to create race hatred, and predicted that CCF success would lead to dictatorship. It concluded, "The average Canadian worker and farmer knows that Canada has been and is blessed with good sound government as represented by the Progressive Conservative and Liberal Party, beneficial to all classes and representative of all classes."[38]

Just two days later, another advertisement paid for by *Industrial Worker* appeared, entitled "Don't Be Fooled By the CCF—It Cannot Help Canadian Workers." The copy stated that electing the CCF would be a retrograde step, in that it would hurt the Canadian economy and Canadian Workers. It made an ominous accusation: "We are speaking plainly and will admit that there are certain foreign elements in our midst that are using the CCF for all that it is worth to try to gain dominion over our Canada."[39] As in the previous advertisement, the conclusion was that voters should choose either of the old-line parties over the CCF:

> The truth is that the Progressive Conservatives do not make any promises that are not in the best interests of Canadians as a whole and that cannot be carried out and the same applies to the Liberals... Promises made by CCF opportunists are based on mirages, fantasies, fairyland stuff and what they think the people like to hear. The sugar-coated hodge podge of drivel handed out by the CCF is hard to stomach in these critical war days. To make sure that Canada does not land in a morass of dictatorship, confusion and poverty, Ontario will show the way on voting day, August 4th, by shunning like the plague, the candidate who has CCF after his name.[40]

The CCF leadership began to see even small matters through the prism of the unions and parties acting against them. For example, in 1943, it was suggested that CCF members and affiliated unions participate in a fundraising campaign in which workers contributed dimes to the party. Ontario CCF Labour Committee organizational director Oliver Hedges supported the idea, but warned that no solicitation of funds should be done during working hours. He warned that those seeking contribution, must take great care, for "There is naturally the possibility that a supporter of either the old parties or the L.P.P. will use this means to discredit the CCF."[41]

The August 4, 1943 Ontario election saw many communists run as labour candidates in strong CCF ridings; in fact, A.A. MacLeod won Toronto-Bellwoods and J.B. Salsberg won St. Andrews. Meanwhile, prominent Liberals, among them Paul Martin, Mitch Hepburn, and Percy Bengough, cooperated with communists to weaken the CCF in their ridings. The LPP met the promise of its platform which had stated, "The Labour-Progressive Party will advance its criticism of the CCF policies to combat the CCF's opportunist policies and tendencies."[42]

Despite these efforts, the CCF won 34 seats. The electoral victory was an important factor in the CCL adopting the CCF as the political arm of labour at its 4th Annual Convention and calling on its locals to affiliate with the CCF. Meanwhile, there were members of the TLC who maneuvered to pass a similar motion at its annual convention, although LPP members and the many Liberal Party members who were prominent in the TLC joined forces to keep the motion from coming to the floor. Instead, motions in 1943, 1944, and 1945 called for the creation of political action committees to work for the election of candidates that best promoted the needs of workers as suggested by the TLC leadership. None of those candidates would be from the CCF.[43]

The Labour-Progressive Party held its founding convention in August 1943 in Toronto. Five hundred delegates attended and proclaimed Tim Buck as their first leader. Four months later, international events affected the relationship between the CCF and the communists. In 1939, the Comintern had directed that the slogan for the next federal campaign would be "Withdraw Canada from the Imperial War"; however, in June 1942, Hitler had invaded the USSR, and in December 1943, Stalin had met with Churchill and Roosevelt at Tehran to discuss a united war strategy and sign the Tehran Agreement. Part of the agreement saw Stalin issue a decree to communist parties throughout the world, stating that their new goal would be to unite behind the current government in their host country in an effort to defeat the fascists and win the war. The incitement of class conflict and attacks on the capitalist system, he decreed, should end. The LPP had little choice but to adopt and implement the new directive. In the April 1944 edition of *National Affairs Monthly*, Tim Buck and Sam Carr wrote:

> We must develop working class support for national policies
> which make Canada a driving force for progress… We must
> not delude the workers with assurances that we shall have
> Socialism in Canada after the next election.[44]

Stalin's directive altered the united front campaign, increased LPP cooperation with the Progressive Conservative and Liberal parties, and witnessed a new spate of attacks on the CCF. This time, however, it would be different. The communists had argued before that the CCF was dangerous because it was not socialist enough, as it had not advocated revolution to immediately overthrow capitalism in Canada. It began to argue that the CCF was dangerous because it was too socialist in advocating changes to the capitalist system that threatened the war effort.

This shift in communist tactics presented a fresh challenge to the CCF. The LPP offer of a left-wing alliance to win the war hurt the party in the eyes of many Canadians whose first concern was, indeed, winning the Second World War. Further, the CCF found itself caught in a delicate dance of maligning the LPP for its ties to the Soviet Union while having to avoid criticizing Canada's new ally. This balance was made even more difficult by Woodsworth's principled but unpopular refusal to support the war back in September 1939. The LPP exploited the CCF's new vulnerability. In the July 1944 *National Affairs Monthly,* the LPP's Fred Rose wrote, "The CCF policies are a mixture of morbid defeatism and featherbrained utopianism."[45] In the House of Commons, Communist MP Fred Rose used the war to attack a CCF proposal to reduce the powers of the chartered banks. He completely ignored the fact that the idea was part of his own party's policy, saying, "The key issue at the present stage of the war is not to play into the hands of those who want to make an issue of socialism."[46]

The CCF's difficulties in this area, and the continuing Liberal-Communist tacit alliance, combined in Ontario's Grey North by the time of the election of February 1944. In his attempt to wiggle out of his promise to avoid conscription, Prime Minister Mackenzie King had fired his National Defense Minister and replaced him with General Andrew McNaughton. In the hastily arranged by-election to win McNaughton a seat, the general faced Conservative and CCF opposition. The CCF matched the Liberal war hero with their own, nominating Air Vice Marshal Earl Godfrey. The LPP did not run a candidate, but sent volunteers to the riding to defeat Godfrey and campaign for McNaughton. In the January 13, 20, and 27 editions of the *Canadian Tribune*, the LPP wrote specifically to those in the riding and urged "all Workers and all members of trade unions to reject and defeat the most harmful and reckless policy of the CCF."[47] The Liberal-Communist cooperation was seen again in an advertisement that was run in the Owen Sound *Daily Sun-Times* and signed by a number of prominent communist labour leaders, urging voters to support McNaughton.

The advertisement was paid for by the Liberal Party and the signatories were Pat Sullivan of the Trades and Labor Congress and C. S. Sullivan and George Harris of the United Electrical Workers.[48] In this case the coordinated effort backfired, as the split in the working-class vote was credited with the victory of Progressive Conservative candidate Garfield Case.[49]

Shortly afterwards, communist leaders Buck, Sims, and MacLeod sent a letter to the CCF National Executive asking it to suspend its calls for the creation of a socialist Canada and asking that the party join with the LPP to act with the Liberals for the good of the country and to seek victory in the war. Many CCF members were moved by the offer. The British Columbia Provincial Council established a committee to explore the idea, and a number of CCF members appeared before the committee expressing support. Vancouver East CCF MP Angus MacInnis was the last to speak. His words reflected the opinion of Coldwell and Lewis: "I would not appear with members of the Communist Party under any circumstances whatsoever. I do not trust them… Any man who would do what Tim Buck did—appearing on a public platform with Mitchell Hepburn—is the scum of the earth—I cannot associate myself with him."[50] The BC Council voted to reject Buck's offer. Similar discussions were held in other provinces and all voted to reject cooperation with the communists.

However, these votes should not be construed as meaning there was unanimity in the ranks. Many CCF councils, clubs, and riding associations were split by the offer. Many CCF MPs and MLAs put their careers and futures with the party on the line and spoke publicly in support of Buck's invitation. Many of those who stuck to that view were expelled from the party, including Ontario MLAs Leslie Hancock and Nelson Alles and Manitoba MLA D.L. Johnston.

Dorise Nielson makes an interesting study. The North Battleford provincial CCF riding association decided to run Nielson as a unity candidate representing the CCF and Communist Party. The CCF's National Executive and Provincial Executive refused to support the idea, but she nonetheless ran and was elected as a member of what she called the Unity Party. Buck claimed she was a communist Member of Parliament. She said she was an independent, but also maintained her CCF membership and remained a part of British Columbia's CCF Provincial Council. That ended when the council expelled her.

In the meantime, the tricky and shifting relationship between Canada and the USSR continued to affect CCF–union relations. At the July 1942 Trade Union Conference, convened by the CCF Ontario Section and held in Toronto, a motion was put to the floor asking unions to affiliate with the CCF as the political arm of the labour movement. Delegate Williamson of the U.A.W.A. in St. Catharines stood to speak against the motion, stating that if the CCF wished to be the voice of labour, then it must fight for labour. When asked to cite an instance when the CCF had not publicly spoken for labour, he cited the CCF's refusal to participate in the Salute to Russia meeting and the plebiscite campaign. Williamson was told that these were not precisely labour issues and had been organized by the communists, but the point was made and the argument was lost.[51]

The confusion regarding support for the Soviet Union, linked with opposition to communism, continued to wreak havoc with the CCF as the war progressed. In 1944, the Ontario CCF voted 470 to 2 against closer ties to and cooperation with the LPP. In BC, the vote was closer, at 68 to 44, but again ties to the LPP were rejected. Meanwhile, the splits in the party continued to hurt. Two CCF MLAs from Manitoba left to join the LPP, followed by an Ontario MLA. Tim Buck continued his attempts to exploit the breaches. He sent a message to the December 1944 CCF National Convention, and had it printed in the December 9 *Canadian Tribune*, reiterating his assertion that the CCF membership was not well served by the right wing CCF leadership and that the rank-and-file members should reject their leaders and join with the LPP. He wrote that CCF members should "reject the false and partisan policy of Coldwell and the CCF leadership."[52]

The increasing effectiveness of LPP activities in attacking and dividing the CCF can be seen in the letters exchanged between the national and provincial executives in late 1944 and early 1945. In January 1945, for instance, Manitoba Provincial Secretary Don Swailes wrote to Lewis asking for clarification on the national position regarding the communists, arguing that they were growing in strength in his province.[53] Lewis responded with an admission that the new attacks by the LPP were a genuine cause for concern, and that meetings would be held in Ottawa to develop a national response. He advised that the policy of ignoring the communists, which they had been following for some time, needed to change, especially in those parts of the country where the LPP was strong. Lewis wrote, "In those sections where the

LPP is of some importance we should hit them hard, but at all times make clear and distinct that our condemnation of the local Communists has nothing whatever to do with our policies regarding the Soviet Union in the international world." [54] He then promised a leaflet for the upcoming election.

Later that fall, the increasingly frustrated Lewis was told that the St. Boniface paper *La Liberté* expressed the old confusion about the CCF and communism and the CCF's position with respect to the war and the Soviet Union. Lewis responded:

> Roosevelt and Churchill found it entirely possible to co-operate fully with Stalin, and in fact to become very close friends. This shows clearly that co-operation with the Soviet Union does not necessarily mean approval of everything that goes on in that country or acceptance of Soviet philosophy... The essential and fundamental differences between the democratic socialism of the CCF and the objectives of communism remain. This is the reason why the CCF still refuses to make any alliance with the L.P.P. or the Communist Party of Canada. [55]

The LPP continued to argue that unions should be wary of the CCF, as it wanted socialism now rather than dealing with the immediate problems of the war; that the CCF would not support the no-strike policy that was necessary to win the war; that the CCF was critical of Mackenzie King, at a time when national unity was needed; and that the CCF opposed the war.

One of the CCF's most persuasive speakers and loyal members was British Columbia's Grace MacInnis. In the spring of 1944, David Lewis tried to arrange for her to travel east on a promotional speaking tour. Lewis explained to McInnis that part of the reason for trip was the need to address the threats to the party from the LPP:

> I am a little disturbed about the relative strength of the LPP group. I realize that they are definitely in a minority, but unless I am mistaken they are a fairly substantial minority. From the news, it is becoming daily more clear that they will nominate right across the country in almost

every constituency in the industrial centers. This may well increase pressure inside the C.C.F. for some arrangement because of the fear of our losing a number of seats by competing with them.[56]

MacInnis indicated her willingness to participate and acknowledged Lewis' concern about the LPP. She reported that it was growing in strength in British Columbia and had infiltrated many riding associations; in a tone revealing desperation, she conceded that many CCF members appeared unable to effectively fight back.[57] She also argued that an important part of the LPP's growing strength was its coalition with the Liberals. She wrote, "Our growing strength on the Coast is making it worth while for our enemies—old parties and the LPP to avail them of every possible means to split us. Some of our own people are showing more energy than sense in the situation."[58]

MacInnis was forced to cancel her eastern speaking tour due to the LPP stirring trouble in her husband Angus' riding. Lewis wrote to express his regret, but acknowledged again the serious problems presented by the LPP: "The LPP campaign against the CCF is more bitter now, and will be for some time, more than it has been for years... In view of their strength in the organized labor movement in BC. I appreciate fully the urgent need for organizational work that will destroy the effectiveness of their campaign before it is too late."[59]

Lewis then attempted to find a replacement but found that all CCF members who could be effective in a speaking tour felt they needed to stay in their ridings. Eventually, nationally known Clarie Gillis was engaged and toured, but even then the tour was short, for in her riding of Glace Bay, the communists were quite strong. Lewis wrote, "The situation in Glace Bay is also not good. The LPP have concentrated there too and Clarie will have to spend some time in her own part of the country."[60]

The year 1945 was a crucial and fascinating one in that it witnessed an election in Ontario on June 4 followed by a federal election on June 11. It also saw both the Liberal and Progressive Conservative parties take actions that clearly mirrored the tone of the arguments and language of the Murray and Trestrail campaigns, while the two old-line parties cooperated with each other and the LPP to defeat CCF candidates. Finally, the election revealed that the premier of Ontario acted against the CCF in ways that were unethical and illegal. In his memoirs, David Lewis was unambiguous in his assessment of how important those campaigns were to the party: "We did not realize it at the time but, in retrospect, it seems clear to me that 1945 was the year which decided the fate of the CCF."[61]

In the run-up to the 1945 federal election, the LPP publicly announced its intentions to cooperate with and support the Liberals to defeat the CCF. The December 16, 1944, *Canadian Tribune* contained an article that spoke of acting in concert with others and concluded that the LPP's goal in the upcoming election was the "CCF's resounding defeat at the polls."[62] The article promised that the LPP would attack all CCF candidates planning to run against Liberal candidates.

The LPP ran 67 candidates in the federal election, and 61 of these were in ridings where the CCF either already held a seat or had a chance of winning. The *Canadian Tribune* ran a series of articles urging supporters to vote for Independent Labour or Liberal candidates. Campaign brochures stated that the party remained dedicated to the establishment of a socialist state, but that its first goal was to "maintain a high level of production and purchasing power in accordance with the people's needs and economic interests."[63] Buck spoke throughout the country, and the party purchased radio time to advertise his speeches and to replay excerpts. The slogans he and the party promoted were "Liberal Labour Coalition" and "Make Labour a Partner in Government."

The Liberal-Communist attack on the CCF was especially harsh in Saskatchewan. A letter to CCF research director Stuart Jamieson from E.G McCullough of Manor Saskatchewan in February 1945 asked for more copies of the CCF's *News Comment* to help stem the tide of the anti-CCF campaign. McCullough wrote, "We here in Saskatchewan are going thru [sic] the crucial test. The forces of reaction have launched their worst against us. From malicious rumor to false statements and misrepresentation in high places comes the attack."[64]

In Chapter Three, it was made clear that the Progressive Conservative Party worked with and supported B.A. Trestrail's anti-CCF campaign. In 1945, it was suspected, though never proven, that the Liberal Party was also tied to Trestrail. This suggestion came from an article that appeared in the June 2, 1945, edition of the CCF's *Manitoba Commonwealth*. It had been expanded for the election and was crammed with pictures of candidates and articles extolling various CCF policy positions. The editorial addressed the devastating effect of the Trestrail attacks on the party and on individual Manitoba candidates, equating the effects of Trestrail's attacks on CCF members to those suffered by the Winnipeg strikers in 1919. It said:

> Today, when the real issue at stake is the need for replacing our chaotic, utterly discredited "free enterprise" economy with a democratically-planned economy of abundance, the opponents of social progress flood the country with such vicious nonsense as Trestrail's *Social Suicide.*[65]

The editorial continued, arguing that the Liberal Party was not only in agreement, but gave significant support to the Trestrail attack in the province. It quoted the May 30 edition of the Liberal Party's *Canadian Outlook*, which included anti-CCF cartoons reprinted from *Social Suicide*, while the editorial repeated much of Trestrail's arguments and phrasing, including the equating of the CCF with National Socialism. The edition of *Canadian Outlook* had been widely distributed by Liberal candidates in Winnipeg. The *Manitoba Commonwealth* editorial stated, "This type of slander proves the desperate lack of principle, let alone common decency which the old-line parties readily exhibit in their panicky effort to retain public office.[66]

Beyond the new tactic of allying itself with the communists, some Liberals found their fear of the CCF sufficient to resort to old-fashioned corruption. That the dirty tricks had been going on for some time was seen in a 1943 report to the National Council from Herb Sovergin in Halifax:

> We worked in one of the Halifax polling stations that Monday and in this and other polls were the original cells of corruption agents of the old line parties with a pocketful of money and a supply of liquor bringing reluctant voters to the polls in cars; voters' names left off the lists intentionally; ballots destroyed by presiding officers; presiding officers so ignorant they call on scrutineers for instruction—and the whole incredible gamut of pre-election promises, political patronage, corporation donations, Trestrailism, ignorance, slanders, lies and confusion.[67]

In terms of dirty tricks and corruption, one of the more interesting races of that year, due to the notoriety of the candidates and events that followed, was the August 9 by-election in Cartier, Quebec. David Lewis had run against candidates from the Bloc Populaire, the LPP's Fred Rose, and two Liberals: Lazarus Phillips ran under the banner of the Liberal Party, while city councilor W. V. Victor was nominated as an Independent Liberal. All attacked socialism, the CCF, and Lewis personally, while Rose never criticized his Liberal opponents. Eventually, Victor withdrew and told the press that two Liberal candidates in the race was causing too much confusion among his supporters.[68]

Shortly after the Cartier race began, it became evident that the Liberal Party had manipulated the voters list. Coldwell rose in the House to protest the corruption and produced affidavits from those who had witnessed the tampering being done. The RCMP investigated and Chief Crown Prosecutor Gerald Fauteux brought charges against the four Liberal-appointed enumerators who had prepared the fraudulent lists. The list had been padded with at least 400 names that should not have appeared.[69] The left was split, votes were stolen, votes were invented, and Lewis lost.

In the 1945 federal election, the Liberals won another majority. Besides a host of other factors—including the rantings of the anti-CCF propagandists from the right—the Liberal-LPP actions, anti-CCF advertisements, and the running of LPP-Labour candidates in swing ridings cost the CCF votes and possible victories. Political scientist Ivan Avakumovic and sociologist Walter Young both analyzed the election in their scholarly studies of the CCF and agreed that the LPP-Liberal actions cost the CCF ten ridings.[70]

The barrage from the left continued unabated at the provincial level. In the 1945 Ontario election, which saw the Gestapo Affair, the Ontario CCF had to contend with the Liberal-LPP alliance and related anti-CCF attacks from organized labour. There were four Liberal-Labour candidates: George Burt, who was regional director of the UAW; Arthur Reaume, the mayor of Windsor; Alex Parent, president of the Chrysler local of the UAW; and Paul Siren, who was a corporal in the army but on leave from the UAW. Of these candidates, only Parent won a seat. Ontario CCF party leader Ted Jolliffe was defeated in York South, and it is conceded that the LPP had taken enough votes from him to ensure his defeat.[71] Avakumovic and Young's independent analyses of the Ontario election led each to the conclusion that, taking into account other factors, the CCF lost five ridings due to the LPP working against them and with the Liberals, while political scientist Norman Penner believed the number was eight.[72]

Shortly after the 1945 Ontario and federal elections, the LPP and the Canadian communist movement suffered a devastating blow. In September, Igor Gouzenko, a Soviet intelligence officer, was finally able to persuade someone in Ottawa to listen to him: he defected and surrendered documents to Canadian authorities indicating that the Soviets had been spying in Canada and the United States. The scandal started the Cold War in earnest. Further, among the Gouzenko documents was an indication that many LPP members and leaders were part of an international espionage ring. Fred Rose and LPP Organizational Secretary Sam Carr were named specifically and were arrested and convicted of violating the Official Secrets Act. Carr fled to the USA, but was extradited to stand trial. Both were sentenced to six years in prison.

LPP membership numbers began to suffer, due not only to the Gouzenko affair and the increasing chilliness of the Cold War, but also to the bad press about the arrests of LPP leaders and disenchantment with the Liberal-LPP cooperation, which had caused many members to question the policies and principles of the party. The 1946 LPP convention set 10,000 new members as a goal, but the 1947 convention reported that only 2,000 new members had signed up and that, in fact, there had been a net loss.[73]

The LPP continued to seek ways to grow while still hurting the CCF, and one way to accomplish both was to use the infiltration tactics and its costs it had been using so effectively and for so long to quietly infiltrate organizations and causes with which the CCF was linked. The efficacy of this tactic and its costs was revealed in the minutes of a meeting of the Ontario CCF Women's Conference, held at Woodsworth House in Ottawa on May 30-31, 1947, that was chaired by Grace MacInnis. The minutes listed 17 reasons why women did not join the CCF. Reason 6 reflected the fear and confusion that the anti-CCF movement had helped to generate and exploit and the role of business in that movement. It contended that women would not join the party because they believed that CCF membership would jeopardize their jobs or the jobs of their husbands. Reason 7 was, "women are afraid of being called Communists. The only cure for fear caused by ignorance is education. When women learn that the CCF provides for control from the bottom, while Communists issue the orders from the top, they will be anxious to pass on their knowledge to others."[74]

The actions of consumer groups also illustrate the complexity of the CCF-LPP fight. The Ontario CCF Women's Committee stated in 1946 that, if a woman wished to join a consumer society, she should join the Canadian Association of Consumers and not the Housewives Consumers Association. The Committee declared that the HCA was a front for the LPP. It reported that women in many cities were aware that the LPP was behind the HCA and refused to join it or had left it. Only in Toronto and Sudbury, it was reported, was the HCA still strong and uncontrolled by the LPP. The Committee minutes stated, "We will not work with the LPP directly or through their 'front' organizations in other fields so we can not work with them in the consumer field."[75] In summary it was stated, "As I said at the beginning we have spent considerable time and thought on this whole subject. And the reason we have done that is because we are convinced that our attitude to the Housewives is another evidence of the contunuous [sic] tests we are faced with in the socialist struggle against communism."[76] These two instances of women acting in support of the party and against the forces aligned against it are two of many that demonstrate the significant role women played in that struggle.

Similar struggles against communist infiltration were seen in other provinces. In Manitoba, for example, the LPP was the driving force behind the creation of the People's Co-Operative Ltd. In September 1946, the cooperative supported a non-delivery farm strike that spread to Saskatchewan and Alberta. Meanwhile, in Manitoba it claimed 2,000 members and 10,000 customers. When asked for information on the cooperative, Manitoba CCF secretary-treasurer Don Swailes explained to David Lewis that the cooperative owned a modern creamery and a woodlot that provided the best firewood in the province, and, perhaps most surprisingly, that even he was a member. He wrote, "It is completely controlled by the Communist Party, and I have no doubt but that the LPP here, and the national movement, get substantial funds from this cooperative."[77] Lewis responded in a dejected-sounding and perfunctory note, which was rare for him: "Thank you for your letter of September 27 regarding the People's Co-Operative. The information is about what I expected."[78]

Despite these activities, the year 1948 began with LPP membership and support continuing to shrink and the party considering its very survival. Regardless of that trend, Buck continued to maneuver and, in a January 22 speech, announced another new LPP policy with respect to the CCF. He said that the party would drop its alliance with the Liberals and support the CCF. Buck was challenged by the LPP membership, which had not been consulted about the party's shift, but he argued there was really nothing new in asking the LPP to support the left-wing CCF in defiance of right-wing leaders, as it always had. According to scathing letters-to-the-editor in the *National Affairs Monthly* and *Canadian Tribune*, LPP supporters failed to see the distinction and decried the turnabout. The LPP placed a full page advertisement in *National Affairs Monthly*, declaring, "Unite at the Polls—Elect a CCF Government."[79]

Buck was again hurting the CCF by attempting to erase the years of effort the party had devoted to distancing itself from communism and the Communist Party. On the very day that Buck offered his olive leaf, Coldwell responded:

> The CCF will not collaborate with the Labour-Progressive party in any way, direct or indirect. It will not enter into any electoral arrangement with it or with any other party, whether on a national, provincial or constituency basis. …We know that at bottom the communists have not changed their views about the CCF and democratic socialism. They have always declared democratic socialist movements to be their principal enemy and their ultimate objective is to liquidate such movements as the CCF. The present communist policy is therefore just a maneuver. The CCF will have nothing to do with it.[80]

The CCF National Executive later voted unanimously to support Coldwell's statement. It released a statement from Coldwell that not only summarized the CCF's position but also betrayed the leaderships' exasperation. It deserves to be quoted at length:

> In the 1945 elections, Canada's communist party—the LPP—called on the Canadian people to support Mackenzie King and the Liberals. Today the party has switched its line again and is now declaring its support for the CCF. It is clear to me that the new switch in the

Communist line is an admission to the utter failure of the Labour-Progressive Party to make any progress in Canada and of its loss of support even in those trade unions in which the communists have had dominant control hitherto. They are apparently trying to halt their party's decline by seeking to identify themselves with the CCF... The CCF will not collaborate with the Labour-Progressive Party in any way, direct or indirect. It will not enter into any electoral arrangement with it or any other party, whether on a national, provincial, or constituency basis. There is a fundamental difference between the CCF methods and philosophy and those of the Communists. We have always opposed, and oppose today, every form of dictatorship, including Communist dictatorship. We abhor Communist methods in crushing political opposition whenever and wherever Communists become the dominant force in a country.[81]

The statement continued with a repetition of Coldwell's earlier press release. The February meeting of the executive council also discussed the fact that communists were organizing rallies, ostensibly to debate labour and other issues, and that CCF representatives were also being asked to speak. It was left to local clubs and provincial offices to respond to these invitations, but they were reminded to be wary of traps that would find Communists and CCF members sharing a platform. The advice to provincial executives, riding associations, and clubs was that "each such case should be considered on its merits, and that where there is definite indication of communist control, the CCF should abstain from sending speakers, and should state the reason frankly."[82]

Meanwhile, the problems posed by the communists continued to plague the party. This can be seen in a fascinating speech delivered by Tommy Douglas. On March 9, 1948, the CCF premier and Minister of Public Health rose in the Saskatchewan legislature as part of the annual budget debate. His speech was later published in a small booklet and made available to riding associations across the country. In the third paragraph, Douglas began to address accusations from a Liberal opposition member from Moosomin that certain CCF MLAs were communists. He stated that there were CCF members that had been investigated by the RCMP, but that those investigations did not mean that the members were communists. The investigations, he said, reflected the political purposes for which the RCMP was being used. Recalling Ontario's Gestapo Affair but making no specific allegations, Douglas said, "It is a reflection on those people who have tried to use the Mounted Police for political purposes to spy on their political opponents."[83]

Douglas then attacked the Liberals with evidence that it was they who were allied with the communists. He produced an article from the *Leader-Post* in which Tim Buck had encouraged support for the Liberal-Labour coalition. He quoted from the article, in which Buck had stated:

> While party reaction stirs up the smokescreen of State Socialism to obstruct reform and the CCF leadership flies in the face of reality with its Socialism and spreads defeatism and hopelessness with predictions of collapse at home and abroad after Hitler was smashed, the King Government has led our country's magnificent war effort and is playing an important part in strengthening the United Nations' unity. It can further strengthen national unity through Democratic Coalition with all patriotic forces.[84]

Douglas went on to quote from a LPP pamphlet that had been distributed during the previous election, entitled "A Call for a Liberal-Labour Coalition":

> It is the considered opinion of the Labour Progressive Party that only a coalition of the Liberal, Labour and farm forces can express in Government form the national unity of Canada. A Liberal-Labour coalition Government offers the only practical political path ahead by which to maintain and strengthen national unity to win the war and peace... The CCF leaders are among the chief critics and attackers of the United Nations and chiefly pounce on every war-time difficulty to win votes.[85]

Douglas pointed out that the LPP had offered a coalition with the Liberals and that the Liberals had agreed, while the CCF, when offered a similar deal, had declined. He concluded, "The only effective bulwark against Communism today lies in the forces of Social Democratic forces... The hope of stopping Communism lies not in reaction but in those who are prepared to make the necessary social and economic adjustments, to make them constitutionally and to make them quickly."[86] Only then did Douglas turn to defending his budget.

The pertinacity of the trouble posed by the LPP and communism at the national level is evidenced by the fact that the issue was discussed at length at the April 1948 meeting of the CCF National Executive Council with the parliamentary caucus. The discussion and motion that followed made it evident that the confusion between communism and socialism remained a major issue. It was decided that the party would organize an education campaign geared not only to voters but also to party members, in an attempt to remind everyone about the differences between communism and democratic socialism.[87]

Meanwhile, at the same meeting, it was decided that, with the Second World War over and the Cold War having begun, it was appropriate for the party to criticize not only communism, but also the Soviet Union. A statement of foreign policy allowed the CCF to begin to criticize the Soviet Union, communism, and capitalism at the same time. It said, "The CCF will resolutely resist any attempt either by the forces of communism or those of capitalism, to dominate the world. It will continue to fight against totalitarian dictatorship of every kind, whether it comes from the so-called Left or from the capitalist Right."[88] The transition from one war to the next had solved a particularly thorny issue for the party.

The CCF was not alone in attempting to address the confusion caused and exploited by winds blowing from the left and right twisting together communism and the CCF. The party, in fact, found a surprising and ironic ally. *The Canadian Register* was the official weekly newsletter from the Ontario Catholic Archdiocese. On June 19, 1948, it published an article entitled "Political Confusion and Religious Scandal," which acknowledged the Church's complicity in creating the confusion between communism and socialism, and the Communist and CCF parties. It also, rather disingenuously, criticized the

Liberal Party's audacity in feeding and exploiting that confusion. Nonetheless, the article is important, for the archdiocese sought to clarify the church's position with respect to the CCF: the Catholic Church stood in opposition to communism as an "atheistic philosophy" that worked against the goals of the church, but admitted that there remained many Catholics who continued to confuse the CCF with the communists. It listed three typical criticisms from the anti-CCF movements and referred accurately to the CCF responses to each:

> To the first of the foregoing arguments they reply that the Communist support of the CCF is purely tactical, as was the Communist support of the Liberal Party in the last federal general election. To the second argument they reply that every party has its individual extremists and bigots of various kinds. The third argument they dismiss as due to an irrational reaction from one extreme to the other, as if moving as far away as possible from what Communism stands for was the best method of resisting its advance. We ourselves do not decide between these arguments.[89]

In 1948, the LPP initiated a campaign in which it spoke repeatedly of the American influence on the Canadian economy as a new evil that was hurting working people in the country. Ignoring his own stand—that the LPP should no longer criticize the CCF—Buck found ways to blame the party for growing foreign ownership. He argued that the CCF had aided the US takeover of Canada by distracting workers with their criticism of Soviet totalitarianism, when American penetration of the businesses at which they worked was the real enemy.[90]

An international peace conference was held in Paris in April 1948, which offered the LPP a new weapon to use against the CCF. The LPP took the lead in creating a Canadian Peace Conference and worked to gather 448,000 signatures on a petition to ban the bomb and to support the Stockholm Appeal. Peace councils were created in a number of cities. At the 1950 CCF convention, it was declared that the Canadian Peace Conference was a front meant to promote a communist view of the world and to promote the LPP within Canada, and that the CCF would not support it. Many CCF members agreed with the movement's goals and tactics, however, and not only signed the nationally organized petition, but also actively supported the movement. Included among the high-profile CCF supporters of the movement were three CCF British Columbia MLAs. Many CCF clubs also voted to support the movement.[91] It was merely the latest split between the CCF leadership and membership, caused by yet another sly move by the communists.

In the 1949 federal election, the CCF National Executive recognized that the confusion regarding communism and the CCF remained sufficiently troublesome as to still represent a significant threat to CCF electoral support. At the same time, however, there was a growing sense that the tide had gone out on the allure of the Communist Party and its ideology. Both beliefs led to the creation of a nationally run quarter-page advertisement under the heading "THE CCF—the most effective force against Communism." The advertisement quoted an editorial from the June 19, 1948, edition of the *Canadian Register:*

> But we must affirm with all emphasis that it is false, unjust and dangerous to say that the CCF is Communist or to confound the CCF with Communism. The CCF has fought the Communist Party with all its strength both in the political field and in the labor unions, in the great industrial plants during the day-time and at lodge meetings in the evenings and week-ends.[92]

On May 27, 1949, in Windsor, Coldwell left his prepared speech to answer new charges, this time from Nova Scotia, claiming that the CCF was a communist party. Showing rare anger, Coldwell attacked the LPP, the Soviet system, and communism in general.[93] When he stepped off the plane in St. John's, Newfoundland, the first question from the assembled reporters was about the "Red" influence in the CCF. Coldwell snapped, "If you mean red-blooded, that's right. Where ever a party such as the CCF is found the Communists are weak."[94] Despite his quick-witted response, many people in the newest province remained unconvinced. At Coldwell's first speech in St. John's, a heckler yelled, "Any party that supports communism is not wanted in Newfoundland. We love our churches."[95]

The 1949 election saw unprecedented cooperation among the CCF's opponents, making strange bedfellows of not only the Liberals and Communists, as had happened before, but new cooperation between the

Liberals and the Progressive Conservatives. Many Progressive Conservative and Liberal candidates made it a point to exploit the fear and confusion about communism and the tactics of the LPP. Among them was future prime minister John Diefenbaker who on June 10, 1949, stated that his CCF opponent had the support of "100% of the communists in the riding."[96]

The two old-line parties combined forces in a number of ridings where the CCF appeared strong. Tommy Douglas made campaign speeches throughout the country and noted the new cooperation which, while it had been seen before in Saskatchewan, was new to the national political stage. On June 3, he spoke before an audience of 3,000 in Vancouver's Exhibition Gardens and said that the CCF victory in Saskatchewan had surprised the old-line parties, to the extent that they had formed coalitions in many ridings in the next election to defeat CCF candidates. He said, "In 1948 we faced a coalition of the two parties…not a consummated union, a behind-the-door arrangement where the parties have lived together."[97]

Despite growing ill health, Coldwell remained a tireless campaigner in the 1949 election, travelling throughout the country on a gruelling schedule, sometimes delivering as many as three speeches a day. On June 4, in Flin Flon, Manitoba, Coldwell took up the charges raised by Douglas and argued that he saw a day when the two old-line parties would merge into one and that the current election, in which the two were so closely cooperating to defeat his party, could be seen as evidence that they were taking steps toward that merger.[98]

Meanwhile, the Liberals and Progressive Conservatives continued to cooperate; for instance, the Liberals decided to refrain from nominating candidates in the strong CCF ridings of Yale and Kootenay West in British Columbia, leaving the PC candidates alone to oppose the CCF. In two other BC ridings, both held by CCF incumbents, the Progressive Conservatives reciprocated by not nominating candidates. Meanwhile, the Ontario Liberals did not nominate candidates in a number of by-elections, including Cochrane North, thereby allowing the Progressive Conservative candidate to face the strong CCF candidates with a better chance of success.[99]

On June 13, Douglas repeated his argument that the St. Laurent Liberals were less afraid of the Progressive Conservatives than they were of the CCF. It was this fear, he said, that had inspired the Liberals to form new alliances with their old rivals to defeat CCF candidates. Douglas said, "The Liberals in Canada are not afraid of the Conservatives one bit. If they were, why would both parties coalesce in BC, why would they run together in an effort to beat my government in Saskatchewan, and why would they unite their strength in Manitoba?"[100]

On the same day, in a Vancouver speech, Coldwell was forced to yet again answer charges that the CCF and Communists were allied, and he used the opportunity to remind listeners of the open cooperation between the Liberals, Progressive Conservatives and Communists. He contended, "The Communists in Ontario are instructing their followers to return the Tories to power. This would bring about chaos quicker than anything else."[101]

Angus MacInnis also addressed the issue of the unnatural coalitions that were affecting the election. He said, "If there is a secret deal, it is not with the CCF but with certain Independents who are supported in BC by coalition money. The Communists will support anyone from Hitler down."[102]

The 1949 campaign also saw the Progressive Conservative party run advertisements that echoed the same slander and rhetoric of Murray and Trestrail. One such advertisement had the bold and underlined title, "Don't LOSE your rights." The advertisement attacked the CCF as supporting the creation of a dictatorship in Canada and of creating concentration camps for those who opposed CCF policies. It concluded that one should vote PC "if you want your government to be your servant, not your master."[103]

During the 1953 federal campaign, Buck hurt the CCF by repeating his old canard that someday the CCF, and perhaps even the Social Credit Party, would form a coalition with the LPP. In a July 16, 1953, speech, attended by only 183 people in Toronto's 1,800-seat Exhibition Stadium, Buck said, "We will fight for that coalition of the new parties to defeat monopoly capitalism. It will be a national crusade and by the logic of history, it is also Canada's road to Socialism."[104]

The Toronto rally demonstrated, however, that by the 1953 election, the LPP was no longer an electoral threat. In that election, it earned a mere 59,622 votes to the CCF's 636,310.[105] The June 18, 1956 *Canadian Tribune* released Khrushchev's speech to the 20th Congress in Moscow in which he outlined Stalin's crimes. This led to more disillusionment among LPP members and sympathizers. In the October 1959 federal election, with the Cold War and anti-communist hysteria at its height, the LPP had changed its name back to the CPC, ran in only one riding, and earned less than 1,000 votes. It no longer mattered. What mattered, however, was the damage it had inflicted and helped to inflict on the CCF.

The slow death of the Communist Party of Canada in the early 1950s did not end the cooperation between the Liberals and Progressive Conservatives in their drive to defeat the CCF. On January 13, 1956, the national secretary to the CCF's National Council considered a report that reviewed recent elections, including the 1955 Ontario provincial election, and admitted that organization, while it could have been improved, was better than it had previously been. However, the report continued, at least some defeats were due to the alliance between the two mainline parties: "We lost veteran CCF MLA William Grummett, who lost to a candidate supported by both Liberals and Conservatives. In at least one other riding it was apparent that the collaboration of the Liberals and the Conservatives cost the CCF another seat when they combined to defeat C. C. 'Doc' Ames in the Temiskaming riding."[106]

It is perhaps appropriate to pause to consider that, while CCF leaders and candidates were not angels, they often heeded a call from their consciences that the many people who conspired against them did not. They somehow avoided making unscrupulous attacks. For example, in November 1944, in the middle of the anti-CCF hurricane, the party's Port Arthur, Ontario, candidate John A. Thompson was preparing to run against the formidable C.D. Howe, who was one of the most powerful cabinet ministers of all time. In desperation, Thompson wrote to Stuart Jamieson asking for dirt to throw at Howe during the campaign. Thompson wrote, "Since C.D. Howe is my opponent here, have you any evidence to show that C.D. Howe is (a) one of Canada's war millionaires (b) using his position as Minister of Munitions and Supply to give contracts to firms in which he has a financial interest?"[107] Jamieson was unequivocal in his reply, stating that the CCF did not operate in such a manner. Jamieson suggested several criticisms of government policy that Thompson could employ, but wrote, "I have no evidence regarding C.D. Howe along the lines you requested in your letter. So far as we know he has been a scrupulously honest administrator, and hasn't taken personal advantage of his position, financially speaking."[108] Such a reply, written, from the eye of a hurricane of hateful venom, is refreshing indeed.

The actions of the Communist and old-line parties must be seen in the political-electoral context of the day, and one must consider their perceived need to do all that they could to pursue their goal of increasing their popular support. But more important to this study is the degree to which they played a significant role in the anti-socialist/anti-CCF campaign and the degree to which they fed into, while benefiting from, the similar actions and discourse of the right. It must be seen as one campaign simultaneously buffeting the CCF from both ends of the political spectrum.

It is interesting to note that, in the letters and meeting minutes of CCF leaders at the time, and in later recollections, it was the actions of the left, including labour leaders, that were most difficult to watch. In his memoirs, David Lewis quipped that the CCF's failure to gain electoral ground in the 1940s was due partly to the "unholy alliance between the Liberals, who have no principles, and the communists, who have no ethics."[109] There is no escaping a hurricane.

6

CONCLUSION: THE WINDS BECALM

This study has suggested that, for the first half-century of its development, Canada was dominated by ideas inherent in liberal democracy and industrial capitalism. While there were challenges to that dominance, none was more significant than that presented by the Cooperative Commonwealth Federation. The CCF was born in the despair of the Depression and evolved during the horrors of the Second World War. Its founding manifesto promised to bring about a new society based on an ideological premise that was outside the Canadian mainstream. By 1943, the party seemed to have gathered political momentum. It had been winning electoral victories in municipal, provincial, and federal elections; it had come within four seats of forming the government in Ontario; it had won a Toronto by-election against a former prime minister; and it had stood first in a national party poll. The party's successes suggest that maybe, in the midst of difficult times, Canadians were considering the democratic socialist alternative being presented by the party and that an ideological turning point was perhaps at hand.

However, by the end of the decade, and despite success in Saskatchewan, where, in 1944, under the spirited leadership of Tommy Douglas, the party formed the government, the party's momentum was lost. The CCF's popular vote decreased with every federal election. Its party membership went from a high of 39, 273 in 1948 to only 18,273 in 1954, with a third of those members in Saskatchewan.[1] The trend can be seen most dramatically in Ontario, where, between 1948 and 1951, it lost 43% of its membership and many of its riding associations simply collapsed.[2] The party continued to influence Canadian social policy, but it failed as an electoral force. By 1959 it was gone.

A great deal of scholarship has addressed the reasons for the party's decline. Many important and valid ideas have been examined. This study has suggested, however, that the scholarship that has addressed the decline of the CCF as a party of electoral significance has afforded inadequate emphasis to the forces that acted against it. Its purpose was to address that gap in the scholarship.

The ideas of Italian Marxist Antonio Gramsci have provided a useful theoretical structure for the analysis of those forces. Gramsci wrestled with understanding the processes through which those with power attain, maintain, and enhance their dominance. His concept of hegemony offered a way to understand that effort.[3] The drive for power, he suggested, involves a constant struggle in the civil society in which the dominant group attempts to control the ideas and discourse of political discussions. If the struggle is successful, Gramsci argued, the material needs of both the dominant and subaltern groups are addressed. But more importantly, the dominant group's ideology is accepted by the subaltern group, not as one of many competing ideologies, but rather, as common sense.[4] Alternative ideologies are rejected as dangerous. Gramsci argued that this struggle for hegemony involves symbols and emotionally charged words. It occurs in professional and social clubs, and in newspapers. It occurs at church, at work, and at home.[5] Gramsci's ideas suggest that an examination of those attacking socialism and the CCF necessitates an exploration of the struggle that occurred in those areas of the civil society. It invites an exploration of the people who undertook the struggle, and of the words, images, and tactics they used.

With Gramsci as a guide, this study has explored the ideological debate that took place in Canada in the 1940s by examining the anti-socialist/anti-CCF campaign that worked to destroy the party and the ideas upon which it was based. It looked at the instrumental role Canada's business community played in the campaign. Its involvement was seen through the actions of insurance companies, the Canadian Chamber of Commerce, and newspapers. The business community's commitment to the campaign was also seen in the activities of Gladstone Murray and Burdick Trestrail. The study noted that the Progressive Conservative Party also played an assertive role. It explored how the campaign was assisted by the Catholic Church, certain Protestant clergymen, and all who brought religion to the debate. It then looked briefly at the attacks on socialism and communism from the left by exploring the roles played by the Communist Party and, to a lesser extent, the Liberal Party and organized labour.

The study has demonstrated that the anti-socialist/anti-CCF campaign exploited Canadians' memories of the Depression and thoughts about the Second World War. It also used the fears and uncertainties aroused in a society that celebrated winning the war against fascism, but also worried about communism and the challenge of rebuilding a post-war Canada. The campaign encouraged concern and confusion as it contended that socialism was the same as communism, or allied with it, or a precursor to a communist, fascist, or perhaps totalitarian state. The CCF was portrayed as deviously disguising a plan to create a society based on the models of Hitler, Stalin, and Mussolini. The campaign tried to persuade Canadians that the election of a CCF government in Ottawa would lead to the end of economic prosperity, land ownership, and private property. A CCF government, it warned, would also end freedom of the press, freedom of expression, and freedom of worship. It would end democracy. A social-democratic CCF government, it promised, would destroy all that Canada's reliance upon the values of liberal democracy, industrial capitalism, and Christianity had brought to the country and its people. Even if some of the ends were agreed upon, those attacking from the right argued that the CCF wanted to move too quickly, and those from the left that it lacked the courage to move quickly enough.

The study has established that the campaign effectively brought its message, words, and images to events and activities in people's everyday lives. Its written communications arrived in people's homes and included pamphlets, company newsletters, party documents, and pay-packet inserts. These documents were supported by newspaper articles, editorials, cartoons, and advertisements. Short films were created and shown before features in movie theatres. Speeches were made by political candidates, including a future prime minister and Ontario premier, which echoed the campaign's themes and discourse. Other speeches were made by business leaders who acted on their own or through their chamber of commerce. Numerous speeches were made by Gladstone Murray. Having heard these speeches at political rallies, and professional and social club meetings, many Canadians heard similar messages in their churches on Sunday mornings, from their living room radios in the evenings, and in conversations with their insurance agents around their kitchen tables. For those not convinced by the political right that the CCF represented a dangerous, and perhaps communist, threat, the Communists, with their Liberal and sometimes Conservative co-conspirators, helped to spin confusion and thus advance the case. It has thus been shown that the efficacy of the campaign, from the right and the left, rested on the consistency and pervasiveness of its message, words, and images, on the status of its messengers, and on the power of sheer repetition in the civil society.

It has been shown that the CCF attempted to respond to the campaign that sought to destroy it. However, the party was no match for its enemies. In 1945-46, the CCF's national office had only two full-time employees and an income of $38,166. By 1950-51, one of those employees had been reduced to part-time and the party's income was only $25,679.[6] Meanwhile, the anti-socialist/anti-CCF campaign had access to funds from business leaders, and to the benefits of business donations-in-kind. Different facets of the campaign also collected donations from individuals and groups across the country. Moreover, the campaign drew strength from the many personal and professional ties among its many supporters. These ties were seen most explicitly in the connections between business leaders, Gladstone Murray, and the Progressive Conservative Party. These links, the campaign's money, and the support it enjoyed from many newspapers and clergy, rendered the campaign too powerful and too elusive a target for the CCF to hit. It could only become defensive and reactive. CCF members and leaders recognized the significance of the campaign being waged against the party, and that it was losing.

This study has suggested that, at a point in Canada's history when Canadians appeared willing to consider the CCF and the ideological alternative it offered, a multi-faceted, well-financed, brilliantly orchestrated, and ruthlessly executed campaign was undertaken to destroy the party and its ideology. Any assessment of the decline of the CCF must consider the power and influence of that campaign. One must not ignore the hurricane.

APPENDIX 1
CCF FEDERAL ELECTION STATISTICS 1935–1958

Year	Votes	Seats	Popular Vote
1935	387,056	7	8.7%
1940	393,230	8	8.5%
1945	816,259	28	15.6%
1949	782,410	13	13.4%
1953	636,310	23	11.3%
1957	707,659	2	10.7%
1958	692,398	8	9.5%

(Adapted from a number of sources.)

APPENDIX 2
PARTIAL LIST OF MURRAY'S RESPONSIBLE ENTERPRISE PARTICIPANTS

Imperial Oil (G. Harrison Smith)
Stovin and Wright
Rogers Radio
Western Broadcasting
Buckerfields
International Nickel
Massey-Harris
Ontario Paper
McIntyre-Porcupine (J. P. Bickell)
Noranda (J. Y. Murdoch)
Canadian Oils (John Irwin)
Montreal Light Heat & Power
Coniagas Mines
National Breweries
Nesbitt Thomson
Hollinger Consolidated Mines
Imperial Tobacco
Toronto Elevators
National Steel Car
Upper Lakes and St. Lawrence Transportation Company

(Murray to Drew, 9 September 1943. National Archives of Canada, George Drew Papers, file 11, Vol. 96.)

APPENDIX 3
SPEECHES BY GLADSTONE MURRAY

1943

Toronto: Women's Art Association
                   Military Institute
                   Salvation Army
                   Rotary Club
                   Lions Club
                   Empire Club
                   Kiwanis Club of West Toronto and East York
                   Canadian Corps Association
                   Queen's Alumni
                   Conservative Progress Club
Forest Hill Village:Legion
Kitchener: Rotary Club
Morrisburg: Canadian Club

1944

Toronto: Foreman's Club of West Toronto
                   Men's Club—Grace Church-on the-Hill
                   Accountants' Club
                   Young Men's Advertising Club
                   Toronto Graphic Arts Association
                   Trinity Forum—In debate with Leslie Morris
                   Canadian Retail Federation
                   Board of Trade

	Canada Lodge
	Canadian Fraternal Association
	Ontario Property Owners Association
	Reunion dinner of the Third Battalion and Toronto
	Regiment Club
	Aesculpaian Club
	Bathurst United Church Sunday Evening Forum
	Ontario Property Owners Association
Winnipeg:	Rotary Club
	Empire Club of Manitoba
London:	Kiwanis Club
Hamilton:	Rotary Club
Mimico:	Lake Shore Lions
New York:	Advertising Club of New York
Moose Jaw:	Rotary Club
Calgary:	Rotary Club
Yorkton:	Board of Trade
St. Catharines:	Life Underwriters'Association
Niagara Falls:	Paper Manufacturers
Kingston:	Kiwanis Club

1945

Toronto:	Northern Vocational School
	Association of Furniture Dealers Annual Dinner
	Toronto Secondary School Teachers Association
	Canadian Shorthorn Association Annual Dinner
Montreal:	Kiwanis Club
Bowmanville:	Canadian Club

1946

Toronto:	Hart House—University of Toronto—Debate against
	A. R. Mosher
	Kiwanis Club
	St. Andrew's Society
	Canadian Association of Contracting Painters
	and Decorators
	Albany Club

	CBC Broadcast
	Workers Educational Association—debate against
	George Grube (CCF) and Michael Freeman (LPP)
	The Keo Club of the Glenview Presbyterian Church
Montreal:	Montreal Forum
	Canadian Unity Alliance
Niagara Falls:	Ontario Carbonated Beverage Association
Islington:	St. George's Men's Club
Belleville:	Junior Board of Trade and Chamber of Commerce (Broadcast)
Port Arthur:	Chamber of Commerce (Broadcast)
Sherbrooke:	Rotary Club
New York:	Forum
Hamilton:	Purchasing Agents of Canada
Orillia:	Legion (Broadcast)

1947

Toronto:	Watsonian Club
	Conservative Progress Association
	Albany Club
	Ontario Hospital Association
	Junior Investment Dealers Association
Welland:	Welland Rotary Club
Ancaster:	Lions Club
Montreal:	Kiwanis Club
St. Catharines:	Rotary Club
Welland:	Lions Club
Oshawa:	Kiwanis Club
North Bay:	Rotary Club
Sherbrooke:	Rotary Club
Barrie:	Ontario Medical Association

1948

Toronto:	Masonic Hall—Harcourt Lodge
	American Men's Club
	Altrusa Club
	Honorable Order of Blue Goose

Niagara Falls:	Rotary Club (Broadcast)
	Lions Club
Stratford:	Rotary Club (Broadcast)
Brantford:	Scottish Rite Association (Broadcast)
Lakeland Florida:	Commencement Address Florida Southern College (Broadcast)

1949

Toronto:	Artillery Officers Association of Toronto
	Empire Club
	Kiwanis Club
	Overseas League
	University of Toronto Graduates Dinner
Orillia:	Presbyterian Church Hunters' Festival

1950

Toronto:	Canadian Legion
	Riverdale Kiwanis
	Empire Club
	Kiwanis Club
	Toronto Board of Trade
	Toilet Goods Manufacturers Association
	Current Events Club of Toronto
Kingston:	Kinsmen Club
Orillia:	Kiwanis Club

1951

Orillia:	Women's Canadian Club of Orillia
	Leacock Memorial Dinner
Toronto:	Leaside Foreman's Club
	Junior League of Toronto
Whitby:	The Men's Club
Oakville:	Rotary Club

1952

| Niagara Falls: | Canadian Ceramic Society |
| | Rotary Club |

Stratford:	Junior Chamber of Commerce
Wellington:	St. George's Society
Montreal:	First District International Altrusa Club
Boston:	Boston Conference on Distribution
Toronto:	Association of Ice Cream Manufacturers

1953

Toronto:	St. George's United Church Men's Club
	Heliconian Club
Waterloo:	Life Insurance Institute of Canada
Orillia:	Sons of England
Belleville:	Rotary Club
Trenton:	Rotary Club
Bowmanville:	Women's Canadian Club

1954

Toronto:	Pen Guild of Toronto
	Zonta Club of Toronto
	Deer Park United Church Men's Association

1955

Toronto:	Chartered Institute of Secretaries
	Property Owners Association
Bowmanville:	Canadian Club of Bowmanville
Elmville:	North Simcoe Soil and Crop Improvement Association
Montreal:	Canadian Industrial Trainers Association

1956

Chatham:	Rotary Club
Toronto:	Annual Dominion Convention

1957

London:	Canadian Club
Vancouver:	Canadian Club
Victoria:	Canadian Club

1958
Toronto: Board of Trade
                Canadian Roofing Contractors Association
Montreal: Royal Empire Society

1962
Toronto: Halconian Club

(National Archives of Canada, Gladstone Murray Papers, Vol.6.)

BIBLIOGRAPHY

Archival Sources

National Archives of Canada (NAC)

- Canadian Chamber of Commerce Papers (CCC)

- Federal CCF Papers (CCF)

- George Drew Papers (GD)

- Gladstone Murray Papers (GM)

Trent University Archives (TU)

- *Peterborough Examiner* Collection (PE)

- Harry Robbins Fonds (HR)

Secondary Sources

Adamson, Walter. *Hegemony and Revolution: A Study of Antonio Gramsci's Political and Cultural Theory.* Berkeley: University of California Press, 1980.

Allen, Richard. *The Social Passion: Religion and Social Reform in Canada, 1914-1928.* Toronto: University of Toronto Press, 1971.

Avakumovic, Ivan. *Socialism in Canada: A Study of the CCF-NDP in Federal and Provincial Politics.* Toronto: McClelland and Stewart, 1978.

———. *The Communist Party in Canada: A History.* Toronto: McClelland and Stewart, 1975.

Azoulay, Dan. "The Cold War Within: The Ginger Group, The Woodsworth Foundation, and the Ontario CCF, 1944-1953." *Ontario History.* Vol. 84, No. 2, June 1992.

———, ed. *Canadian Political Parties.* Toronto: Irwin Publishing, 1999.

———. *Keeping the Dream Alive: The Survival of the Ontario CCF/NDP, 1950-1963.* Montreal and Kingston: McGill-Queen's University Press, 1997.

———. "Ruthless in a Ladylike Way: CCF Women Confront the Postwar Communist Menace." *Ontario History.* Vol. 89. No. 1, March 1997.

Bell, Daniel. *Marxian Socialism in the United States.* Princeton: Princeton University Press, 1967.

Bennett, John and Cynthia Kruger. "Agrarian Pragmatism and Radical Politics." Seymore Lipset, ed. *Agrarian Socialism: The Cooperative Commonwealth Federation in Saskatchewan—A Study in Political Sociology.* Berkeley: University of California Press, 1950. 347-363.

Blaazer, David. *The Popular Front and the Progressive Tradition: Socialists, Liberals, and the Quest for Unity, 1884-1939.* Cambridge: Oxford University Press. 1992.

Brennan, J. William, ed. *Building The Co-Operative Commonwealth- Essays on the Democratic Socialist Tradition in Canada.* Regina: University of Regina, 1983.

Brodie, Janine. *Women and Politics in Canada.* Toronto: McGraw Hill Ryerson Ltd., 1985.

Brodie, Janine and Jane Jenson. "Piercing the Smokescreen: Brokerage Parties and Class Politics." Alain G. Gagnon and A. Brien Tanguay, eds. *Canadian Parties in Transition: Discourse, Organization and Representation.* Scarborough: Nelson Canada, 1989. 24-44.

———. *Crisis, Challenge and Change: Party and Class in Canada.* Toronto: Methuen, 1980.

Campbell, Peter. *Canadian Marxists and the Search for a Third Way.* Montreal: McGill-Queens Press, 1999.

Caplan, Gerald. *The Dilemma of Canadian Socialism.* Toronto: McClelland and Stewart Ltd., 1973.

Careless, J.M.S. and Craig Brown, eds. *The Canadians, 1867-1967.* Toronto: MacMillan, 1967.

Carroll, William. "Restructuring Capital, Reorganizing Consent: Gramsci, Political Economy and Canada." *Canadian Review of Sociology and Anthropology.* 27: 3, 1990.

Chi, N.H. "Class Cleavage." Conrad Winn and John Menemy, eds. *Political Parties in Canada.* Toronto: McGraw-Hill Ryerson, 1976.

Christian, William and Colin Campbell. *Political Ideologies in Canada: Liberals, Conservatives, Socialists, Nationalists.* Toronto: McGraw-Hill Ryerson, 1974.

Cross, Michael. *Decline and Fall of a Good Idea.* Toronto: New Hogtown Press, 1974.

Crowley, Terry. *Agnes Macphail and the Politics of Equality.* Toronto: James Lorimer and Company Publishers, 1990.

Dworkin, Dennis. *Cultural Marxism in Post War Britain: History, The New Left and The Origins of Cultural Studies.* London: Duke University Press, 1997.

Dunn, Christopher. *Canadian Political Debates: Opposing Views on Issues that Divide Canadians.* Toronto: McClelland and Stewart. 1995.

Eagleton, Terry. *Criticism of Ideology: A Study in Marxist Literacy Theory.* London: New Left Books, 1976.

———. *The Significance of Theory.* Cambridge: Basil Blackwell. 1990.

———. *Ideology: An Introduction.* London/New York: Verso, 1991.

Fink, Leon. *Working Man's Democracy: The Knights of Labour and American Politics.* Urbana: University of Illinois Press, 1983.

Fisk, John. *Television Culture.* London: Methuen and Company, 1982.

Fontana, Benedetto. *Hegemony and Power: On the Relation between Gramsci and Power.* Minneapolis: University of Minneapolis Press, 1993.

172

Foote, Geoffrey. *The Labour Party's Political Thought—A New History*. London: Croom Helm, 1985.

Forgacs, David, ed. *Antonio Gramsci Reader*. New York: Schocken Books, 1988.

Gagnon, A. and A. Tanguay. *Canadian Parties in Transition: Discourse, Organization and Representation*. Scarborough: Nelson Canada, 1989.

Golding, Sue. *Gramsci's Democratic Theory: Contributions to a Post-Liberal Democracy*. Toronto: University of Toronto Press, 1992.

Gramsci, Antonio. *Selections From the Prison Notebook*. Quintin Hoare and Geoffry Nowel Smith, eds. London: Lawrence and Wishart, 1971.

Granatstein, Jack. "The York South By-election of February 9, 1942: A Turning Point in Canadian History." *Canadian Historical Review*. 48:2, 1967.

Hartz, Louis. *The Liberal Tradition in America: An Interpretation of American Political Thought Since the Revolution*. New York: Harcourt, Brace and World, 1955.

————. *The Structure of Canadian History*. New York: Harcourt, Brace and World, 1966.

Heron, Craig. *The Canadian Labour Movement: A Short History*. Toronto: James Lorimer and Company Publishers, 1989.

Hoffman, John. *The Gramscian Challenge: Coercion and Consent in Marxist Political Theory*. New York: Basil Blackwell Publishers, 1984.

Horowitz, Gad. *Canadian Labour in Politics*. Toronto: University of Toronto Press, 1968.

Howe, Irving. *Socialism in America*. San Diego: Harcourt Brace Jovanovich Publishers, 1985.

Hutchison, Bruce. *The Incredible Canadian*. Toronto: Longmans, Green and Company, 1953.

Irvine, William. *The Farmers in Politics*. Toronto: McClelland and Stewart, 1920.

Kealey, Linda and Joan Sangster, eds. *Beyond the Vote: Canadian Women and Politics*. Toronto: University of Toronto Press, 1989.

Laslett, J.H.M. and S.M. Lipset, eds. *Failure of a Dream: Essays on the History of American Socialism.* Berkeley: University of California Press, 1974.

Laycock, David. *Populism and Democratic Thought in the Canadian Prairies, 1910 to 1945.* Toronto: University of Toronto Press, 1990.

Lears, T.J. "The Concept of Cultural Hegemony: Problems and Possibilities." *American Historical Review.* 90, 1985: 567-593.

Lewis, David. *A Good Fight: Political Memoirs, 1909-1958.* Toronto: MacMillan of Canada, 1981.

Lipset, Seymour. *Agrarian Socialism: The Cooperative Commonwealth Federation in Saskatchewan—A Study in Political Sociology.* Berkeley: University of California Press, 1950.

Logan, H.A. *Trade Unions in Canada.* Toronto: Macmillan, 1948.

Macdonald, Donald. *The Happy Warrior: Political Memoirs.* Markham: Fitzhenry and Whiteside, 1988.

MacPherson, C.B. *The Real World of Democracy.* Toronto: CBC Publications, 1965.

Mann, Michael. *Consciousness and Action Among the Western Working Class.* Toronto: Macmillan, 1973.

McHenry, Dean E. *The Third Force in Canada: The Cooperative Commonwealth Federation 1932-1948.* Berkeley and Los Angeles: University of California Press, 1950.

Melnyk, Olenka. *No Bankers in Heaven: Remembering the CCF.* Toronto: McGraw-Hill Ryerson, 1989.

Michels, Robert. *Political Parties: A Sociological Study of the Oligarchic Tendencies of Modern Democracy.* Glencoe: Free Press (1915), 1955.

Miesel, M., ed. *Papers on the 1962 Election.* Toronto: University of Toronto Press, 1964.

Mills, Allen. *Fool for Christ: The Political Thought of J. S. Woodsworth.* Toronto: University of Toronto Press, 1991.

Morley, J. Terence. *Secular Socialists: The CCF/NDP in Ontario—A Biography.* Kingston and Montreal: McGill-Queens University Press, 1984.

Morton, Desmond. *NDP: Social Democracy in Canada, 3rd ed.* Toronto: Samuel Stevens Hakkert and Company, 1977.

Palmer, Bryan. *Culture and Conflict: Skilled Workers and Industrial Capitalism in Hamilton Ontario, 1860-1914.* Montreal: McGill-Queens University Press, 1979.

Penner, Norman. *From Protest to Power: Social Democracy in Canada: 1900– Present.* Toronto: James Lorimer and Company Publishers, 1992.

————. *Canadian Communism: The Stalin Years and Beyond.* Toronto: Methuen, 1988.

Phillips, Gordon. *The Rise of The Labour Party, 1893–1931.* London/New York: Routledge, 1992.

Pickersgill, Jack. *The Mackenzie King Record I: 1939-1944.* Toronto: University of Toronto Press, 1960.

Ransome, P. *Antonio Gramsci: An Introduction.* New York and London: Harvester and Wheatsheaf, 1995.

Sangster, Joan. *Dreams of Equality: Women On The Canadian Left, 1920-1950.* Toronto: McClelland and Stewart, 1989.

Silverstein, Sanford. "Occupation, Class and Voting Behaviour: Electoral support of a Left Wing Protest Movement in a Period of Prosperity." *Agrarian Socialism: The Cooperative Commonwealth Federation in Saskatchewan—A Study in Political Sociology.* Seymour Lipset, ed. Berkeley: University of California Press, 1970. 435-379.

Simon, Roger. *Gramsci's Political Thought: An Introduction.* London: Lawrence and Wishart, 1982.

Sombart, Werner. *Why is there No Socialism in the United States?* White Plains: International Arts and Sciences Press, (1905) 1976.

Stewart, M. and D. French. *Ask No Quarter.* Toronto: Longmans, Green, 1959.

Stewart, Walter. *MJ: The Life and Times of M.J. Coldwell.* Toronto: Stoddart, 2000.

Strinati, Dominic. *An Introduction to Theories of Popular Culture,* London and New York: Routledge, 1995.

Trestrail, B.A. *Stand Up and Be Counted*. Toronto: McClelland and Stewart, 1944.

Tyne, Robert. *Douglas in Saskatchewan: The Story of a Socialist Experiment.* Vancouver: Mitchell Press, 1962.

Wearing, Joseph. *Strained Relations: Canadian Parties and Voters.* Toronto: McClelland and Stewart, 1988.

Whitehorn, Alan. *Canadian Socialism: Essays on the CCF/NDP.* Toronto: Oxford University Press, 1992.

Williams, Paul, David Bates, Michael Ornstein, and Michael Stevenson. *Class, Ideology and Partisanship in Canada.* Toronto: York University, 1982.

Wrong, Dennis. "Ontario Provincial Elections 1934-1955, A Preliminary Survey of Voting." *Canadian Journal of Economics and Political Science.* 24:2 (May 1958).

Young, Walter. *Anatomy of a Party: The National CCF, 1932-1961.* Toronto: University of Toronto Press, 1969.

———. "Ideology, Personality and the Origins of the CCF in BC." *BC Studies.* (Winter 1976-77): 139-162.

Zakuta, Leo. *A Protest Movement Becalmed: A Study of Change in the CCF.* Toronto: McClelland and Stewart, 1964.

...Socialism and the CCF. Montreal: Contemporary Publishers, 1934.

...Program of the Labour-Progressive Party. Toronto: Ever Ready Printers Ltd, 1943.

NOTES

CHAPTER ONE

1. T. Eagleton, *Ideology: An Introduction*. London/New York: Verso, 1991. 29-30.

2. S. Lipset, *Agrarian Socialism: The Cooperative Commonwealth Federation in Saskatchewan: A Study in Political Sociology*. Berkeley: University of California Press, 1950. xiv.

3. C.B. Macpherson, *The Real World of Democracy*. Toronto: CBC Publications, 1965. 7-8. See also M. Robin, *Radical Politics and Canadian Labour 1880-1930*. Kingston: International Relations Centre, 1968. 5-12.

4. L. Fink, *Working Man's Democracy: The Knights of Labour and American Politics*. Urbana: University of Illinois Press, 1983. 221.

5. The Regina Manifesto. Cited in M.Cross, *Decline and Fall of a Good Idea*. Toronto: New Hogtown Press, 1974. 23.

6. W. Young, *Anatomy of a Party: The National CCF, 1932-61*. Toronto: University of Toronto Press, 1969. 295. See also F. Underhill, *In Search of Canadian Liberalism*. Toronto: Toronto University Press, 1960. 198.

7. J. Pickersgill, *The Mackenzie Record: 1939-1944*. Toronto: University of Toronto Press, 1960. 571.

8. W. Young, *Anatomy of a Party: The National CCF, 1932-61*. Toronto: University of Toronto Press, 1969. 298. For a more substantive examination of the idea see A. Gramsci, *Selections From The Prison Notebooks of Antonio Gramsci*. Hoare and Nowel Smith (ed.), London: Lawrence and Wishart, 1971. 161.

9. D. Lewis, *The Good Fight: Political Memoirs 1909-1958*. Toronto: Macmillan of Canada, 1981. 319.

10. D. Dworkin, *Cultural Marxism in Post War Britain: History, The New Left and The Origins of Cultural Studies*. London: Duke University Press, 1997. 19.

11. G. Phillips, *The Rise of The Labour Party, 1893–1931*. London/New York: Routledge, 1992. 25.

12. D. Laycock, *Populism and Democratic Thought in the Canadian Prairies, 1910 to 1945*. Toronto: University of Toronto Press, 1990. 142-143. See also W. Irvine, *The Farmers in Politics*. Toronto: McClelland and Stewart, 1920. Chapter 1.

13. S. Lipset, *Agrarian Socialism: The Cooperative Commonwealth Federation in Saskatchewan: A Study in Political Sociology* Berkeley: University of California Press, 1950. 70.

14. P. Campbell, *Canadian Marxists and the Search for a Third Way*, Montreal: McGill-Queens Press, 1999. Introduction.

15. M. Mann, *Consciousness and Action Among the Western Working Class.* Toronto: Macmillan, 1973. 70.

16. J. Brodie and J. Jenson, *Crisis, Challenge and Change: Party and Class in Canada.* Toronto: Methuen, 1980. 39. See also D. Morton, *NDP: Social Democracy in Canada, New and Revised 3rd Edition.* Toronto: Samuel Stevens Hakkert and Company, 1977. 7. For an international perspective, see also R. Alford, *Party and Society: The Anglo-American Democracies,* Chicago: Rand-McNally, 1963. 256.

17. I. Avakumovic, *Socialism in Canada: A Study of the CCF-NDP in Federal and Provincial Politics.* Toronto: McClelland and Stewart, 1978. See also J. Brodie, and J. Jenson, *Crisis, Challenge and Change: Party and Class in Canada.* Toronto: Methuen, 1980. See also J. Sangster, *Dreams of Equality: Women On The Canadian Left, 1920-1950.* Toronto: McClelland and Stewart, 1989.

18. M. Cross, *Decline and Fall of a Good Idea.* Toronto: New Hogtown Press, 1974. 8-9.

19. I. Avakumovic, *Socialism in Canada: A Study of the CCF-NDP in Federal and Provincial Politics.* Toronto: McClelland and Stewart, 1978. 286.

20. Ibid. 70-71.

21. Ibid. 157.

22. R. Michels, *Political Parties: A Sociological Study of the Oligarchical Tendencies of Modern Democracy.* Translated by Eden and Cedar Paul. Hearst's International Library, 1915; reprint, New York: Dover Publications, 1959. 25-26.

23. L. Zakuta, *A Protest Movement Becalmed: A Study of Change in the CCF.* Toronto: University of Toronto Press, 1964. 68.

24. W. Young, *Anatomy of a Party: The National CCF, 1932-61.* Toronto: University of Toronto Press, 1969. 301-302.

25. D. Azoulay, *Keeping the Dream Alive: The Survival of the Ontario CCF/NDP, 1950-1963.* 1997. 237.

26. W. Young, *Anatomy of a Party: The National CCF, 1932-61.* Toronto: University of Toronto Press, 1969. 200.

27. D. Lewis, *The Good Fight: Political Memoirs 1909-1958.* Toronto: Macmillan of Canada, 1981. 304.

28. J. Hoffman, *The Gramscian Challenge: Coercion and Consent in Marxist Political Theory.* New York: Basil Blackwell Publishers, 1984. 9.

29. T. Eagleton, *Ideology: An Introduction.* London/New York: Verso, 1991. 58.

30. A. Gramsci, *Selections From The Prison Notebooks of Antonio Gramsci.* Hoare and Nowel Smith (ed.), London: Lawrence and Wishart, 1971. 160.

CHAPTER TWO

1. *Reader's Digest.* April 1945. "The Road To Serfdom" 20. National Archives of Canada (hereafter NAC), Cooperative Commonwealth Federation Papers (hereafter CCF) file 5, Vol. 361.

2. *Harper's.* April 1945. "Hayek's Hayride" 46-47. NAC, CCF, file 5, Vol. 361.

3. Canadian Chamber of Commerce Report to Its Members, 21 November 1945. 16. NAC, Canadian Chamber of Commerce Papers (hereafter CCC), file 1, Vol. 5.

4. NAC, CCF, file 5, Vol. 361.

5. Ibid.

6. D. Lewis, *A Good Fight: Political Memoirs, 1909-1958.* Toronto: Macmillan of Canada, 1981. 304-305.

7. Shultz to Ingle, 9 December 1952. NAC, CCF, file 2, Vol. 125.

8. NAC, CCF, file 2, Vol. 163.

9. Ibid.

10. Ibid.

11. NAC, CCF, file 1, Vol. 163.

12. NAC, CCF, file 2, Vol. 163.

13. Ibid.

14. NAC, CCF, file 3, Vol. 163.

15. Ibid.

16. Ibid.

17. Ibid.

18. Ibid.

19. NAC, CCF, file 2, Vol. 163.

20. Ibid.

21. Ibid.

22. NAC, CCF, file 3, Vol. 163.

23. NAC, CCF, file 2, Vol. 163.

24. NAC, CCF, file 3, Vol. 163.

25. NAC, CCF, file 2, Vol. 163.

26. Ibid.

27. *CCF News*, 13 April 1944. NAC, CCF, file 2, Vol. 163.

28. NAC, CCF, file 2, Vol. 163.

29. NAC, CCF, file 3, Vol. 163.

30. NAC, CCF, file 2, Vol. 163

31. Ibid.

32. *Bulletin of the Canadian Life Insurance Officers Association,* 4. NAC, CCF, file 3, Vol. 163.

33. *Bulletin of the Canadian Life Insurance Officers Association,* 5. NAC, CCF, file 3, Vol. 163.

34. NAC, CCF, file 3, Vol. 163.

35. NAC, CCF, file 2, Vol. 163.

36. NAC, CCF, file 3, Vol. 163.

37. Ibid.

38. Hiltz to Lewis, 22 January 1947. NAC, CCF, file 1, Vol. 361.

39. *Let's All Join the CCF!* NAC, CCF, file 3, Vol. 361.

40. Lewis to Hiltz, 30 January 1948. NAC, CCF, file 3, Vol. 361.

41. *Saskatchewan Government Insurance,* 1. NAC, CCF, file 3, Vol. 163.

JOHN BOYKO

42. NAC, CCF, file 3, Vol. 163.

43. *Let There Be Light,* 1. NAC, CCF, file 3, Vol. 163.

44. *Let There Be Light,* back cover. NAC, CCF, Vol. 163.

45. NAC, CCF, file 3, Vol. 163.

46. *Nation's Business Address by M. J. Coldwell,* 1. NAC, CCF, file 3 Vol. 163.

47. *Nation's Business Address by M. J. Coldwell,* 3. NAC, CCF, file 3, Vol. 163.

48. NAC, CCF, file 3 Vol. 163.

49. Ibid.

50. Ibid.

51. Ibid.

52. NAC, CCF, file 6 Vol. 406.

53. *Canadian Chamber of Commerce Annual Report 1943,* 12-13. NAC, CCF, file 6, Vol. 361.

54. *Canadian Business.* April 1943. "This is the CCF", 52. NAC, CCF, file 2, Vol. 361

55. *Canadian Business.* April 1943. "This is the CCF", 54. NAC, CCF, file 2, Vol. 361.

56. *Canadian Chamber of Commerce Reports to Its Members 1945,* 16-18, 29. NAC, CCC, file 1, Vol. 5.

57. *Canadian Chamber of Commerce Reports to Its Members 1946,* 14. NAC, CCC, file 1, Vol. 5.

58. *Canadian Chamber of Commerce Reports to Its Members 1946,* 15. NAC, CCC, file 1, Vol. 5.

59. Ibid.

60. *Canadian Chamber of Commerce Reports to Its Members 1948-1949,* 11. NAC, CCC, file 1, Vol. 5.

61. National Affairs Committee, London Chamber of Commerce to members, 20 November 1947. NAC, CCF, file 1, Vol. 361.

62. *London Free Press,* 31 January 1948. NAC, CCF, file 1, Vol. 361.

63. *Canadian Chamber of Commerce Newsletter,* No. 64, January 1948. 1. NAC, CCC, file 3, Vol. 36.

64. *Canadian Chamber of Commerce Newsletter,* No. 64, January 1948. 3. NAC, CCC, file 3, Vol. 36.

65. *Canadian Chamber of Commerce Newsletter,* No. 70, April 1948. 1. NAC, CCC, file 3, Vol. 36.

66. *Canadian Chamber of Commerce Newsletter,* No. 71, April 1948. 1. NAC, CCC, file 3, Vol. 36.

67. *Canadian Chamber of Commerce Newsletter,* No. 75, July 1948. 1. NAC, CCC, file 3. Vol. 36.

68. *Regina Leader Post,* 18 June 1949. NAC, CCF, file 6, Vol. 406.

69. *Vancouver Sunday,* 18 June 1949. NAC, CCF, file 6, Vol. 406.

70. *The Globe and Mail,* 13 June 1945. NAC, CCF, file 5, Vol. 406.

71. *Canadian Chamber of Commerce Report to the Twentieth-Fourth Annual Meeting, 1953,* 9. NAC, CCC, file 3, Vol. 62.

72. Hamilton to Macdonald, 2 May 1959. NAC, CCF, file 1, Vol. 427.

73. *Canadian Chamber of Commerce Reports to Its Members 1959,* 10-11. NAC, CCC, file 1, Vol. 5.

INTO THE HURRICANE

74   Gramsci, Antonio. *Selections From the Prison Notebook.* Quintin Hoare and Geoffry Nowel Smith. (ed.) London: Lawrence and Wishart, 1971.148.

75.   *New Commonwealth,* 13 March 1944. NAC, CCF, file 2, Vol. 163.

76.   NAC, CCF, file 2, Vol. 163.

77.   Mugridge to Lewis, 16 April 1944. NAC, CCF, file 3, Vol.102.

78.   Mugridge to Lewis, 6 March 1944. NAC, CCF, file 3, Vol.102.

79.   Stinson to Lewis, 6 October 1944. NAC, CCF, file 3, Vol. 61.

80.   *Winnipeg Free Press,* 12 October 1944. NAC, CCF, file 4, Vol. 361.

81.   *Winnipeg Free Press,* 16 October 1944. NAC, CCF, file 4, Vol. 361.

82.   *Winnipeg Free Press,* 15 April 1945. NAC, CCF, file 4, Vol. 361.

83.   *Winnipeg Free Press,* 23 May 1945. NAC, CCF, file 4, Vol. 361.

84.   Ibid.

85.   *Winnipeg Free Press,* 27 May 1945. NAC, CCF, file 4, Vol. 361.

86.   *Winnipeg Free Press,* 11 June 1945. NAC, CCF, file 4, Vol. 361.

87.   Forsey to the *Economist,* 23 February 1945. NAC, CCF, file 5 Vol. 361.

88.   *Ottawa Journal,* 12 January 1944. NAC, CCF, file 4, Vol. 361.

89.   *Ottawa Journal,* 11 April 1944. NAC, CCF, file 4, Vol. 361.

90.   Ibid.

91.   Ibid.

92.   *Ottawa Journal,* 13 June 1945. NAC, CCF, file 11, Vol. 406.

93.   *Ottawa Journal,* 15 June 1945. NAC, CCF, file 11, Vol. 406.

94.   Ibid.

95.   D. Lewis, *A Good Fight: Political Memoirs, 1909-1958.* Toronto: MacMillan of Canada, 1981. 305.

96.   *Evening Citizen,* 15 June 1949. NAC, CCF, file 7, Vol. 406.

97.   *Toronto Daily Star,* 27 May 1949. NAC, CCF, file 7, Vol. 406.

98.   Forsey to Gibson, 22 February 1943. NAC, CCF, file 4, Vol. 361.

99.   D. Lewis, *A Good Fight: Political Memoirs, 1909-1958.* Toronto: MacMillan of Canada, 1981. 316.

100. MacLean, *Reflections of a Wicked Capitalist,* 1. NAC, CCF, file 6, Vol. 361.

101. MacLean, *Reflections of a Wicked Capitalist,* 16. NAC, CCF, file 6, Vol. 361.

102. *Pie in the Sky Socialism,* 1. NAC, CCF, file 6, Vol. 361.

103. *Pie in the Sky Socialism,* 2. NAC, CCF, file 6 Vol. 361.

104. *Pie in the Sky Socialism,* 13. NAC, CCF, file 6, Vol. 361.

105. *Peterborough Examiner,* 18 May 1945. Trent University (hereafter TU) *Peterborough Examiner* Collection (hereafter PE), box 228.

106. Ibid.

107. Ibid.

108. *Peterborough Examiner,* 19 May 1945. TU, PE, box 228.

109. *Peterborough Examiner,* 25 May 1945. TU, PE, box 228.

110. *Peterborough Examiner,* 28 May 1945. TU, PE, box 228.

111. Ibid.

112. Ibid.

113. *Peterborough Examiner,* 29 May 1945. TU, PE, box 228.
114. Ibid.
115. *Peterborough Examiner,* 1 June 1945. TU, PE, Box 229.
116. Ibid.
117. *Peterborough Examiner,* 2 June 1945. TU, PE, box 229.
118. *Peterborough Examiner,* 14 June 1945. TU, PE, box 229.

NOTES – CHAPTER THREE

1. Policy Council Report Memorandum D9, September 1943. 2. National Archives of Canada (hereafter NAC), George Drew Papers (hereafter GD), file 11, Vol. 96.
2. Policy Council Report Memorandum D7, Murray to R. R. Bongard 11 August 1943. NAC, GD, file 11, Vol. 96.
3. Ibid.
4. Crump to Murray, 6 November 1956. NAC, Gladstone Murray Papers (hereafter GM) Vol. 10.
5. One of many examples is the October 1952 letter from Joanne Flintoft to Murray in which she stated, "…I am writing you on behalf of the Junior League Board who wish to express to you their gratefulness for allowing us to select a suitable charity to which we might donate your speaker's fee. The decision reached by the Board was to include your cheque in our contribution to the paper, *Canadian Scene.* Realizing that a great deal of your time is spent in fighting communism, and since the League this year is contributing to that cause by helping support *Canadian Scene,* they thought you would be agreeable to having your fee forwarded to them." Flintoft to Murray, 25 October 25 1952. NAC, GM, Vol.10.
6. Murray to Drew, 9 September 1943. NAC, GD, Vol. 96, file 11.
7. Gladstone Murray, *The Social Conscience in the Future of Canada,* 5. NAC, GM, Vol. 6.
8. Gladstone Murray, *Canada's Future: A Vital Decision,* copy of a speech to Canadian Shorthorn Annual Dinner, 13 February 1945. 5. NAC, GM, Vol. 6.
9. Gladstone Murray, *Problems of The Canadian Economy,* copy of a speech to Purchasing Agents of Canada, 12 November 1944, 10-11. NAC, GM, Vol. 7.
10. Gladstone Murray, *The Population Factor in the Future of Canada,* copy of a speech to the Canadian Corps Association, 16 November 1943. 4. NAC, GM, Vol. 6.
11. Gladstone Murray, *Common Sense About the Future of Canada,* copy of a speech to the Kiwanis Club of London, 4 February 1944. 1. NAC, GM, Vol. 6.
12. Gladstone Murray, *Common Sense About the Future of Canada,,* copy of a speech to the Kiwanis Club of London, 4 February 1944. 7. NAC, GM, Vol. 6.
13. Gladstone Murray, *Some Aspects Of the Future,* copy of a speech to Grace Church on the Hill, 14 February 1944. 1. NAC, GM, Vol. 6.
14. Gladstone Murray, *Common Sense About the Future of Canada,* copy of a speech to the Kiwanis Club of London, 4 February 1944. 2-4. NAC, GM, Vol. 6.
15. Gladstone Murray, *Common Sense About the Future of Canada,* copy of a speech to the Kiwanis Club of London, 4 February 1944. 5. NAC, GM, Vol. 6.
16. Gladstone Murray, *How to Save Freedom,* copy of a speech to the Conservative Progress Association, 12 March 1947. 9. NAC, GM, Vol. 8.

17. Gladstone Murray, *How to Save Freedom,* copy of a speech to the Conservative Progress Association, 12 March 1947. 10. NAC, GM, Vol. 8.

18. Gladstone Murray, *Is the Profit Motive Anti-Social?* copy of a speech to Toronto Sunday Evening Forum, 22 October 1944. NAC, CCF Vol. file 1, 361.

19. Johnston to Murray, 8 March 1944. NAC, GM, Vol. 6.

20. Soden to Murray, 28 April 28 1947. Ridell to Murray, 15 May 1947. McNab to Murray, 20 May 1947. Murray to Dr. Turnbull, 18 September 1947. Clark to Murray, ? December 1947. NAC, GM, Vol.8.

21. NAC, GM, Vol. 10.

22. Fraser to Murray, 9 April 1946. NAC, GM, Vol. 6.

23. *Canadian Dairy and Ice Cream Journal,* January 1953. NAC, GM, Vol. 10.

24. *The Canadian Banker,* Vol. 60, No. 3, Autumn, 1953. NAC, GM, Vol. 10.

25. Gray to Murray, 14 June 1944. NAC, GM, Vol. 6.

26. Gray to Murray, 16 June 1944. NAC, GM, Vol. 6.

27. Toronto Board of Trade Newsletter, January 1944. NAC, GM, Vol. 10.

28. Prittie to Murray, 7 December 1944. NAC, GM, Vol. 7.

29. Clark to Murray, 13 February 1947. NAC, GM, Vol. 8.

30. F. C. Murray to Gladstone Murray, 16 July 1953. NAC, GM, Vol. 6.

31. NAC, GM, Vol. 10

32. Murray to Stewart, 1 December 1943. NAC, GM, Vol. 6.

33. letter to editor, December, 1943. NAC, GM, Vol. 6.

34. David _____ to Fraser, 19 November 1946. NAC, GM, Vol. 8.

35. *New Commonwealth.* 9 December 1944. NAC, CCF, file 1, Vol. 361.

36. *Vancouver Sun,* 9 June 1949. NAC, CCF, file 3, Vol. 406.

37. Murray to Robbins, 9 August 1955. Trent University Archives (hereafter TU) Harry Robbins fonds (hereafter HR), file 27, Box 5.

38. D. Lewis, *A Good Fight: Political Memoirs, 1909-1958.* Toronto: MacMillan of Canada, 1981. 317.

39. CCF bulletin to candidates, 18 May 1945. NAC, CCF, file 5, Vol. 361.

40. B. A. Trestrail, *Stand Up and Be Counted.* Toronto: McClelland and Stewart, 1944. 10.

41. Ibid. 25-26.

42. Ibid. 81-82.

43. B. A Trestrail, *Social Suicide*, front and back cover, NAC, CCF, file 2, Vol. 361.

44. Ibid. 8. NAC, CCF, file 2, Vol. 361.

45. Ibid. 3. NAC, CCF, file 2, Vol. 361.

46. Ibid. 5. NAC, CCF, file 2, Vol. 361.

47. Ibid. 23. NAC, CCF, file 2, Vol. 361.

48. Millar to employees, 5 June 1945. NAC, CCF, file 2, Vol. 361.

49. Ibid.

50. D. Lewis, *A Good Fight: Political Memoirs, 1909-1958.* Toronto: MacMillan of Canada, 1981. 319.

51. Thorne to Andrew and referred to Jamieson, 20 May 1945. NAC, CCF, file 2, Vol. 361.

52. Wilks to Lewis, 7 May 1945. NAC, CCF, file 5, Vol. 361.

53. Lewis to Coolican, 9 May 1945. NAC, CCF, file 5, Vol. 361.

54. Lewis to P. T. Coolican, Assistant Postmaster General, 10 May 1945. NAC, CCF, file 5, Vol. 361.

55. Baldwin to Jamieson 18 May 18, 1945. NAC, CCF, file 5, Vol. 361.

56. Bristow to Lewis, 27 June 1945. NAC, CCF, file 2, Vol. 361.

57. *Who Paid For the Lies They Told,* 1. NAC, CCF, file 2, Vol. 361.

58. *Who Paid For the Lies They Told,* 5. NAC, CCF, file 2, Vol. 361.

59. *Who Paid For the Lies They Told,* 8. NAC, CCF, file 2, Vol. 361.

60. *Vancouver Sun,* 3 July 1945. NAC, CCF, file 5, Vol. 361.

61. NAC, CCF, file 11, Vol. 406.

62. NAC, CCF, file 5, Vol. 361.

63. D. Lewis, *A Good Fight: Political Memoirs, 1909-1958.* Toronto: MacMillan of Canada, 1981. 315.

64. NAC, CCF, file 11, Vol. 406.

65. *Ottawa Citizen,* 18 May 1945. NAC, CCF, file 11, Vol. 406.

66. Ibid.

67. NAC, CCF, file 11, Vol. 406.

68. Ibid.

69. Ibid.

70. Ibid.

71. NAC, CCF, file 2, Vol. 361.

72. I. Avakumovic, *Socialism in Canada: A Study of the CCF-NDP in Federal and Provincial Politics.* Toronto: McClelland and Stewart, 1978. 131.

73. D. Lewis, *A Good Fight: Political Memoirs, 1909-1958.* Toronto: MacMillan of Canada, 1981. 318.

74. *Peterborough Examiner,* 3 June 1945. TU, PE., box 229.

75. *Peterborough Examiner,* 4 June 1945. TU, PE., box 229.

76. *Proposed Educational Campaign By the Public Information Association.* NAC, CCF, file 2, Vol. 361.

77. *General Outline of the 7 Point Educational Program to be conducted by the Public Information Association,* 1. NAC, CCF, file 2, Vol. 361.

78. Ibid.

79. Trestrail to subscribers, 19 May 1949. NAC, CCF, file 2, Vol. 361.

80. *Is Democracy in Canada Doomed?* Cover. NAC, CCF, file 2, Vol. 361.

81. *Is Democracy in Canada Doomed?* 1. NAC, CCF, file 2, Vol. 361.

82. Ibid.

83. *Is Democracy in Canada Doomed?* 2. NAC, CCF, file 2, Vol. 361.

84. *Is Democracy in Canada Doomed?* 18. NAC, CCF, file 2, Vol. 361.

85. Ibid.

86. *Is Democracy in Canada Doomed?* 19. NAC, CCF, file 2, Vol. 361.

87. Lewis to Brewin, 22 July 1949. NAC, CCF, file 2, Vol. 361.

88. Jamieson to Thorne, ? July 1945. NAC, CCF, file 2, Vol. 361.

89. Lewis from Forsey, 30 May 1945. NAC, CCF, file 5, Vol. 361.

90. Ibid.

91. Forsey draft of response to *Social Suicide*, undated, 1945. NAC, CCF, file 5, Vol. 361.

92. *Montreal Gazette*, 8 June 1945. NAC, CCF, file 11, Vol. 406.

93. *Who Paid For the Lies They Told*, 10. NAC, CCF, file 2, Vol. 361.

94. *Montreal Gazette*, 8 June 1945. NAC, CCF, file 11, Vol. 406.

95. NAC, CCF, file 11, Vol. 406, file 11.

96. Montreal Gazette, 8 June 1945. NAC, CCF, file 11, Vol. 406.

97. NAC, CCF, file 11, Vol. 406.

98. Ibid.

99. Trestrail to _____President, _____ Ltd. St Catharines, 1 May 1949. NAC, CCF, file 2, Vol. 361.

100. Ibid.

101. DAB Murray to Friends, 2 March 1949. NAC, CCF, file 2, Vol. 361.

102. Ibid.

103. General Relations Service Limited retainer, NAC, CCF, file 2 Vol. 361.

104. Trestrail form letter, 19 May 1949. NAC, CCF, file 2, Vol. 361.

105. *Evening Citizen*, 28 May 1949. NAC, CCF, file 6, Vol. 406.

106. Ibid.

107. G. Caplan, *The Dilemma of Canadian Socialism.* Toronto: McClelland and Stewart Ltd., 1973. 159.

108. D. Lewis, *A Good Fight: Political Memoirs, 1909-1958.* Toronto: MacMillan of Canada, 1981. 319.

NOTES – CHAPTER FOUR

1. I. Avakumovic, *Socialism in Canada: A Study of the CCF-NDP in Federal and Provincial Politics.* Toronto: McClelland and Stewart, 1978. 14.

2. T. Eagleton, *Ideology: An Introduction.* London/New York: Verso, 1991. 113.

3. See J. Brodie, and J. Jenson, "Piercing the Smokescreen: Brokerage Parties and Class Politics." in Alain G. Gagnon and A. Brien Tanguay *Canadian Parties in Transition: Discourse, Organization and Representation.* Scarborough: Nelson Canada, 1989. 24-44.

4. N. Penner, *Canadian Communism: The Stalin Years and Beyond.* Toronto: Methuen, 1988. 113.

5. J. George, *The Menace to Canada.* 3. NAC, CCF, file 6, Vol. 361.

6. Forsey response to *The Menace to Canada*, undated, NAC, CCF, file 6, Vol. 361.

7. J. Paynter, *Masters of Misjudgment-The CCF's Record in War.* 3. NAC, CCF, file 6, Vol. 361.

8. J. Paynter, *We Can Learn a Lot from Russia.* 4-5. NAC, CCF, file 6, Vol. 361.

9. McKenzie to Ingle, 20 December 1946. NAC, CCF, file 6, Vol. 361.

10. Robbins to MacDonald, 17 December, 1946. NAC, CCF, file 6, Vol. 361.

11. Young to MacDonald, 3 January 1947 and McKenzie to MacDonald, 23 November 1946. NAC, CCF, file 6, Vol. 361.

12. Winch to Ingle, 20 December 1946. NAC, CCF, Vol. 361, file 6.

13. Winch to Ingle,31 December 1946. NAC, CCF, file 6, Vol. 361, file 6.

14. Diefenbaker to Murray, 29 January 1945. NAC, Gladstone Murray Papers (hereafter GM, Vol. 114.

15. Diefenbaker to Murray, 6 February 1945. NAC, GM, Vol. 114.

16. Diefenbaker to Lamb, 4 June 1945. NAC, GM, Vol. 114.

17. Diefenbaker to Murray, 23 March 1946. NAC, GM, Vol. 114.

18. Murray to Diefenbaker, 28 August 1948. NAC, GM, Vol. 114.

19. Diefenbaker to Murray, 25 August 1948. NAC, GM, Vol. 114.

20. Diefenbaker to Murray, 21 May 1949. NAC, GM, Vol. 114.

21. Murray to Diefenbaker, 23 May 1949. NAC, GM, Vol. 114.

22. Elmer Diefenbaker to Murray, 3 June 1949. NAC, GM, Vol. 114.

23. Diefenbaker to Murray, 18 July 1949. NAC, GM, Vol. 114.

24. Diefenbaker to Murray, 24 September 1957. NAC, GM, Vol. 114.

25. Murray to Drew, ? February 1941. NAC, George Drew Papers (hereafter GD), file 11, Vol. 96.

26. Letter from Murray to Drew, March 25, 1941. NAC, GD, file 11, Vol. 96.

27. Drew to Murray, 27 February 1943. NAC, GD, file 11, Vol. 96.

28. Cited in T. Crowley, *Agnes Macphail and the Politics of Equality* Toronto: James Lorimer and Company Publishers, 1990. 189.

29. Murray to Drew, ? November 1943. and 7 November 7, 1943. NAC, GD, file 11, Vol. 96.

30. Drew to Murray, 2 November 1943. NAC, GD, file 11, Vol. 96.

31. NAC, CCF, file 3, Vol. 126.

32. *Manitoba Commonwealth*, 2 June 1945. 5. NAC, CCF, file 10, Vol. 126.

33. Ibid. 8. NAC, CCF, file 10, Vol. 126.

34. *Winnipeg Free Press*, 25 May 1945. NAC, CCF, file 11, Vol. 406.

35. Ibid.

36. *Peterborough Examiner*, 26 May 1945. Trent University (hereafter TU) Peterborough Examination Collection (hereafter PE), box 228.

37. Ibid.

38. *Peterborough Examiner*, 28 May 1945. TU, PE, box 228.

39. *Peterborough Examiner*, 1 June 1945. TU, PE, box 229.

40. *Peterborough Examiner*, 12 June 1945. TU, PE, box 229.

41. D.208 to Drew, 13 May 1944. NAC, GD, file 11, Vol. 96.

42. Murray to Drew, 7 November 1943. NAC, GD, file 11, Vol. 96.

43. *Toronto Star*, 6 July 1945. NAC, GD, file 11, Vol. 96.

44. *Montreal Gazette*, 10 July 1945. NAC, GD, file 11, Vol. 96.

45. *The Globe and Mail*, 2 June 1949. NAC, CCF, file 6, Vol. 406.

46. *The Outlook*, 20 April 1948. 2. NAC, GM, Vol. 12.

47. *The Outlook*, 9 August 1948. 2. NAC, GM, Vol. 12.

48. Frank Murray to Gladstone Murray, 5 June 1953. NAC, GM, Vol. 6.

49. Murray to Robbins, undated. TU, Harry Robbins Papers (hereafter HR), file 27, Box 5.

50. Robbins to Murray, 1 June 1961. TU, HR, file 27, Box 5.
51. Ibid.
52. S. M. Lipset, *Agrarian Socialism: The Cooperative Commonwealth Federation in Saskatchewan—A Study in Political Sociology.* Berkeley: University of California Press, 1950. 161.
53. Brodie, Janine and Jenson, Jane. "Piercing the Smokescreen: Brokerage Parties and Class Politics." In Alain G. Gagnon and A. Brien Tanguay, *Canadian Parties in Transition: Discourse, Organization and Representation.* Scarborough: Nelson Canada, 1989. 25.
54. S. Lipset, *Agrarian Socialism: The Cooperative Commonwealth Federation in Saskatchewan—A Study in Political Sociology.* Berkeley: University of California Press, 1950. 170.
55. J. E. Branch to _____, undated, NAC, CCF, file 6, Vol. 361.
56. J. E. Branch circular, undated, NAC, CCF, file 6, Vol. 361.
57. *Our Way of Life,* subscription flyer, NAC, CCF, file 6, Vol. 361.
58. *Our Way of Life,* November 1948, Vol. IV, No. 1. NAC, CCF, file 6, Vol. 361.
59. B. A. Trestrail *Stand Up and Be Counted.* Toronto: McClelland and Stewart, 1944. 77.
60. *The Globe and Mail,* 29 July 1943. NAC, CCF, file 3, Vol. 361.
61. *The Globe and Mail,* 1 January 1944. NAC, CCF, file 3, Vol. 361.
62. G. Murray, *Thoughts on Effective Living,* copy of a speech to St. George's Men's Club, 26 March 1946. 3. NAC, GM, Vol. 6.
63. G. Murray, *Thoughts on Effective Living,* copy of a speech to St. George's Men's Club, 26 March 1946. 4-5. NAC, GM, Vol. 6.
64. G. Murray, *Is Individual Freedom Worth Keeping?* copy of a speech to Toronto's Keo Club, 18 November 1946. 5-6. NAC, GM, Vol. 8.
65. G. Murray, *The Message of Responsible Enterprise,* speech to Welland Rotary Club, 10 February 1946. 8. NAC, GM, Vol. 6.
66. Hamilton, *Things To Know About the CCF.* 1. NAC, CCF, file 6, Vol. 361.
67. Hamilton, *Things To Know About the CCF.* 14-15. NAC, CCF, file 6, Vol. 361.
68. Ibid.
69. M. Karson, "Catholic Anti-Socialism" in Lipset (ed.) *Failure of a Dream: Essays on the History of American Socialism.* Berkley: University of California Press, 1974. 84
70. S. Lipset,*Agrarian Socialism: The Cooperative Commonwealth Federation in Saskatchewan—A Study in Political Sociology.* Berkeley: University of California Press, 1950. 138.
71. Ibid.
72. Lewis to Mugridge, 4 April 1944. NAC, CCF, file 5, Vol. 102.
73. Progressive Conservative campaign poster, June 1945. TU, HR, file 5, Box 27.
74. NAC, CCF, file 1, Vol. 364.
75. NAC, CCF, file 1, Vol. 60.
76. Minutes, 27 January 1948. Minutes of the National Executive and Council from January 19, 1947 to August 31, 1948. NAC, CCF, file 4, Vol. 364.
77. *Canadian Churchman,* 16 June 1949. NAC, CCF, file 4, Vol. 406.
78. *Canadian Register,* 18 June 1949. NAC, CCF, file 3, Vol. 406.

79. CCF Council and Executive Minutes, February 1954—January 1956. NAC, CCF, file 1, Vol. 645.

NOTES – CHAPTER FIVE

1. I. Avakumovic, *Socialism in Canada: A Study of the CCF-NDP in Federal and Provincial Politics.* Toronto: McClelland and Stewart, 1978. 31.
2. Ibid. 54.
3. N. Penner, *Canadian Communism: The Stalin Years and Beyond.* Toronto: Methuen, 1988.128 -129. Wearing 1988 p 14
4. Ibid. 124.
5. Ibid. 113.
6. I. Avakumovic, *Socialism in Canada: A Study of the CCF-NDP in Federal and Provincial Politics.* Toronto: McClelland and Stewart, 1978. 68.
7. *The Worker.* 9 March 1929. NAC, CCF, file 1, Vol. 65.
8. I. Avakumovic, *Socialism in Canada: A Study of the CCF-NDP in Federal and Provincial Politics.* Toronto: McClelland and Stewart, 1978. 68.
9. Ibid. 67.
10. N. Penner, *Canadian Communism: The Stalin Years and Beyond.* Toronto: Methuen, 1988. 122.
11. Ibid. 148.
12. I. Avakumovic, *Socialism in Canada: A Study of the CCF-NDP in Federal and Provincial Politics.* Toronto: McClelland and Stewart, 1978. 101.
13. N. Penner, *Canadian Communism: The Stalin Years and Beyond.* Toronto: Methuen, 1988. 147.
14. Ibid.114.
15. Ibid.115.
16. I. Avakumovic, *Socialism in Canada: A Study of the CCF-NDP in Federal and Provincial Politics.* Toronto: McClelland and Stewart, 1978.101.
18. Ibid. 70-71.
19. H. Logan, *Trade Unions in Canada.* Toronto: MacMillan, 1948. 84.
20. N. Penner, *Canadian Communism: The Stalin Years and Beyond.* Toronto: Methuen, 1988. 144.
21. I. Avakumovic, *Socialism in Canada: A Study of the CCF-NDP in Federal and Provincial Politics.* Toronto: McClelland and Stewart, 1978.157.
22. See D. Lewis, *A Good Fight: Political Memoirs, 1909-1958.* Toronto: MacMillan of Canada, 1981. Chapter 6.
23. See W. Young, *Anatomy of a Party: The National CCF, 1932-1961.* Chapter 5. and G. Caplan, *Dilemma of Canadian Socialism.* Toronto: McClelland and Stewart, 1973. Chapter 7
24. I. Avakumovic, *Socialism in Canada: A Study of the CCF-NDP in Federal and Provincial Politics.* Toronto: McClelland and Stewart, 1978. 103.
25. Ibid. 105.

26. G.Caplan, *Dilemma of Canadian Socialism.* Toronto: McClelland and Stewart, 1973. 50.

27. NAC, CCF, file 1, Vol. 60.

28. Ibid.

29. I. Avakumovic, *Socialism in Canada: A Study of the CCF-NDP in Federal and Provincial Politics.* Toronto: McClelland and Stewart, 1978.137.

30. MacNeil to Lewis, 2 April 1941. NAC, CCF, file 2, Vol.102.

31. Stewart to Lewis, 17 March 1942. NAC, CCF, file 4, Vol. 60.

32. I. Avakumovic, *Socialism in Canada: A Study of the CCF-NDP in Federal and Provincial Politics.* Toronto: McClelland and Stewart, 1978.106.

33. G. Caplan, *Dilemma of Canadian Socialism.* Toronto: McClelland and Stewart., 1973.135.

34. NAC, CCF, file 5, Vol. 61.

35. MacInnis to Lewis, undated. NAC, CCF, file 5, Vol. 61.

36. Scott to Lewis, 15 August 1940. NAC, CCF, file Vol. 61.

37. N. Penner, *Canadian Communism: The Stalin Years and Beyond.* Toronto: Methuen, 1988.146.

38. *The Globe and Mail.* 26 July 1943. NAC, CCF, file 3, Vol. 361.

39. *The Globe and Mail.* 28 July 1943 NAC, CCF, file 3, Vol. 361.

40. *The Globe and Mail.* 28 July 1943. NAC, CCF, file Vol. 361.

41. NAC, CCF, file 1, Vol. 60.

42. Program of the Labour-Progressive Party Toronto: Ever Ready Printers Ltd, 1943. 20.

43. H. A. Logan, *Trade Unions in Canada.* Toronto: Macmillan, 1948. 559.

44. N. Penner, *Canadian Communism: The Stalin Years and Beyond.* Toronto: Methuen, 1988.196.

45. I. Avakumovic, *Socialism in Canada: A Study of the CCF-NDP in Federal and Provincial Politics.* Toronto: McClelland and Stewart, 1978.158.

46. N. Penner, *Canadian Communism: The Stalin Years and Beyond.* Toronto: Methuen, 1988. 197.

47. I. Avakumovic, *Socialism in Canada: A Study of the CCF-NDP in Federal and Provincial Politics.* Toronto: McClelland and Stewart, 1978.163.

48. D. Lewis, *A Good Fight: Political Memoirs, 1909-1958.* Toronto: MacMillan of Canada, 1981.263.

44. I. Avakumovic, *Socialism in Canada: A Study of the CCF-NDP in Federal and Provincial Politics.* Toronto: McClelland and Stewart, 1978.163.

50. N. Penner, *Canadian Communism: The Stalin Years and Beyond.* Toronto: Methuen, 1988. 201.

51. Proceedings Trade Union Conference, Toronto July 25, 1942. Convened by the Trade Union Committee CCF, Ontario Section.13. NAC, CCF, file 1, Vol. 60.

52. I. Avakumovic, *Socialism in Canada: A Study of the CCF-NDP in Federal and Provincial Politics.* Toronto: McClelland and Stewart, 1978.163.

53. Swailes to Lewis, 13 January 1945. NAC, CCF, file 3, Vol. 61.

54. Lewis to Swailes, 16 January 1945. NAC, CCF, file 3, Vol.61.

55. Lewis to Gagnon, 20 October 1945. NAC, CCF, file 4, Vol. 60.

56. Lewis to MacInnis, 5 May 1944. NAC, CCF, file 1, Vol.102.

57. MacInnis to Lewis, 15 May 1944. NAC, CCF, file 1, Vol.102.

58. MacInnis to Lewis, 25 May 1944. NAC, CCF, file 1, Vol.102.

59. Lewis to MacInnis, 21 June 1944. NAC, CCF, file 1, Vol. 102.

60. Lewis to MacInnis, 23 June 1944. NAC, CCF, file 1, Vol. 102.

61. D. Lewis, *A Good Fight: Political Memoirs, 1909-1958.* Toronto: MacMillan of Canada, 1981. 261.

62. I. Avakumovic, *Socialism in Canada: A Study of the CCF-NDP in Federal and Provincial Politics.* Toronto: McClelland and Stewart, 1978.163.

63. Ibid. 168.

64. Manor to Jamieson, 26 February 1945. NAC, CCF, file 6, Vol. 125.

65. *Manitoba Commonwealth. 2* June 1945. 3. NAC, CCF, file 10, Vol. 126.

66. *Manitoba Commonwealth. 2* June 1945. 4. NAC, CCF, file 10, Vol. 126.

67. NAC, CCF, file 5, Vol. 126.

68. *Montreal Gazette.* 26 July 1943. NAC, CCF, file 11,Vol. 406.

69. *Montreal Gazette.* 28 July 1943. NAC, CCF, file 11, Vol. 406.

70. Walter Young, *Anatomy of a Party: The National CCF, 1932-1961.* Toronto University of Toronto Press, 1969. 276-277.

71. N. Penner, *Canadian Communism: The Stalin Years and Beyond.* Toronto: Methuen, 1988. 204.

72. Walter Young, *Anatomy of a Party: The National CCF, 1932-1961.* Toronto University of Toronto Press, 1969. 276-277.

73. I. Avakumovic, S*ocialism in Canada: A Study of the CCF-NDP in Federal and Provincial Politics.* Toronto: McClelland and Stewart, 1978.176.

74. NAC, CCF, file 3, Vol. 60.

75. Ibid.

76. Ibid.

77. Swailes to Lewis, 27 September 1946. NAC, CCF, file 3, Vol. 61.

78. Lewis to Swailes, 29 September 1946. file 3, Vol. 60.

79   I. Avakumovic, *Socialism in Canada: A Study of the CCF-NDP in Federal and Provincial Politics.* Toronto: McClelland and Stewart, 1978.177.

80. CCF Speaker Notes, 1948. file 4, Vol. 364.

81. Minutes of the National Executive and Council, February 15, 1948. *Minutes of the National Executive and Council. from January 19, 1947 to August 31, 1948.* NAC, CCF, file 4, Vol. 364.

82. Minutes of the National Executive and Council, February 15, 1948. *Minutes of the National Executive and Council from January 19, 1947 to August 31, 1948.* NAC, CCF, file 6, Vol. 364.

83. NAC, CCF, file 1, Vol. 60.

84. Ibid.

85. Ibid.

86. Ibid.

87. Minutes of the National Executive and Council, April 16 1948. *Minutes of the National Executive and Council from January 19, 1947 to August 31, 1948.* NAC, CCF,file 6, Vol. 364.

INTO THE HURRICANE

88. Minutes of the National Executive and Council, April 17 1948. *Minutes of the National Executive and Council from January 19, 1947 to August 31, 1948.* NAC, CCF, file 6, Vol. 364.

89. NAC, CCF, file 1, Vol. 60.

90. I. Avakumovic, *Socialism in Canada: A Study of the CCF-NDP in Federal and Provincial Politics.* Toronto: McClelland and Stewart, 1978.183.

91. Ibid.185.

92. *The Canadian Register.* June 18, 1949. NAC, CCF, file 3, Vol. 406.

93. *Toronto Daily Star.* May 28, 1949. NAC, CCF, file 6, Vol.406.

94. *The Globe and Mail.* May 21, 1949. NAC, CCF, file 6, Vol.406.

95. *Toronto Daily Star.* May 21, 1949. NAC, CCF, file 6. Vol. 406.

96. *Leader-Post.* June 10, 1949. NAC, CCF, file 6, Vol. 406.

97. *Vancouver Sun.* June 3, 1949. NAC, CCF, file 6, Vol. 406.

98. *Montreal Gazette.* June 4, 1949. NAC, CCF, file Vol. 406.

99. *Montreal Gazette.* June 4, 1949. NAC, CCF, file 5, Vol. 406.

100. *Toronto Daily Star.* June 13, 1949. NAC, CCF, file 5, Vol. 406.

101. *Toronto Daily Star.* June 13, 1949. NAC, CCF, file 6, Vol. 406.

102. *Toronto Daily Star.* June 17, 1949. NAC, CCF, file 5, Vol. 406.

103. *The Canadian Register.* June 18, 1949. NAC, CCF, file 5, Vol. 406.

104. *Leader Post.* June 16, 1949. NAC, CCF, file 8, Vol.406.

105. I. Avakumovic, *Socialism in Canada: A Study of the CCF-NDP in Federal and Provincial Politics.* Toronto: McClelland and Stewart, 1978.180.

106. Council and Executive Minutes, January 21, 1956. Council and Executive Minutes January 1954–January 1956. NAC, CCF, file 1, Vol. 365.

107. Thompson to Jamieson, November 1944. NAC, CCF, file 6, Vol. 125.

108. Jamieson to Thompson, November 1944. NAC, CCF, file 6, Vol. 125.

109. D. Lewis, *A Good Fight: Political Memoirs, 1909-1958.* Toronto: MacMillan of Canada, 1981. 296.

NOTES – CHAPTER SIX

1. I. Avakumovic, *Socialism in Canada: A Study of the CCF-NDP in Federal and Provincial Politics.* Toronto: McClelland and Stewart, 1978. 143.

2. D. Azoulay, *Keeping the Dream Alive: The Survival of the Ontario CCF/NDP, 1950-1963.* Montreal and Kingston: McGill-Queen's University Press, 1997. 19.

3. T.J. Jackson Lears. "The Concept of Cultural Hegemony: Problems and Possibilities," *American Historical Review.* Vol. 90, 1985. 568.

4. A. Gramsci. *Selections From the Prison Notebook.* Quintin Hoare and Geoffry Nowel Smith. (ed.) London: Lawrence and Wishart, 1971. 55-60.

5. Ibid. 149-155.

6. I. Avakumovic, S*ocialism in Canada: A Study of the CCF-NDP in Federal and Provincial Politics.* Toronto: McClelland and Stewart, 1978. 155.

INDEX

Burton, E.G., 86
business leaders, vs. CCF, 16–17, 22–23

Cacic, Tom, 121
Cairns, Alan, 9
Campbell, Austin, 98
Campbell, Peter, 10
Canada, 1900–1950, 2–3
Canada election 1945, 55, 72
    anti-CCF cooperation, 138
Canada Faces Dangerous Political Program,
95–96.
    See also Menace to Canada, The
Canada Life Assurance Company, 67
Canada Permanent Mortgage Corporation, 65
Canada's Future Belongs to Free Canadians
(CCC, 1945), 37
Canada's Future Belongs to Free Canadians", 22
Canada–USSR relations, 136
Canadian Association of Consumers, 143
Canadian Banker (magazine), 66
Canadian Bankers Association, 86
Canadian Banking Association, 66
Canadian Breweries, 86
Canadian Business (magazine), as promoting
CCC's views, 37
*Canadian Capitalism and the Menace of a Fifth
Column* (CCC, 1946), 38
Canadian Chamber of Commerce, vs. CCF, 17, 18,
24, 36–41
    1944 articles, 22
    1946, 36–37
    1950s, 40–41
    ads, 39–40
    linking CCF and communists (1948), 39
Canadian Club (Morrisburg), 67–68
Canadian Congress of Labour, 124
    and Forsey, 49
Canadian Corps Association of Toronto, 62
Canadian Dairy and Ice Cream Journal, 66
Canadian Forum (1936), 126–27
Canadian General Electric, 65
Canadian Labor Press, 131
Canadian Labour Party, 124
Canadian League Against War and Fascism,
122, 123
Canadian Life Assurance Company, 28
Canadian Life Insurance Officers Association, 30
Canadian Life Underwriters Association, 28
Canadian Manufacturers' Association, 40
Canadian Outlook, 140
Canadian Peace Conference (1948), 149

Canadian Register, 147–48, 149
    vs. CCF, 113–14
Canadian Roofing Contractors Association, 65
Canadian Shorthorn Association, 60–61
Canadian Statesman, 95
Canadian Tribune, 124, 129, 134, 136, 139, 144, 151
    vs. CCF, 11
Canadian Underwriter, on CCF auto insurance,
33–34
Canadian Underwriters' Association, on CCF
insurance, 34, 35
Canadian unions. *See* unions in Canada
Canadian working class. *See* working class in
Canada
capitalism, 2, 12
Caplan, Gerald, 13, 14, 15, 91
Carr, Sam, 121, 142
Case, Garfield, 135
Cassidy, Harry, 45
Catholic Church, vs. CCF, 16–17, 93, 111–16, 147–
148, 156–57
    impact, 111
Catholic Church (Britain), 9
CCF News, on nationalized insurance, 28–29
CCL–CIO, attacked by Trestrail 1949, 85
churches, vs. CCF. *See* Catholic Church, vs.
CCF; Protestant clergymen, vs. CCF
Cities Service Oil Company, 65
Clark, George, 67
class-consciousness
    Britain, 8
    Canada, 9–10
clergy, vs. CCF. See Catholic Church, vs. CCF;
Protestant clergymen, vs. CCF
coalition government in Manitoba, 130
Cold War, 142
    effect on left wing, 13
Coldwell, M.J. (Major James), 136, 141
    1948 rejection of LPP, 144–45
    1949, attacked by CCC, 39
    1949 election, 150–51
    on anti-RC CCF comments, 111–12
    attacked in media, 44, 46–47, 51–52, 53, 54
    attacked by Trestrail 1949, 84
    and CCF insurance, 26, 27, 29–30, 34–35, 36
    as CCF leader, 3–4
    on media bias, 49
    on Public Information Association, 86–91
    on religious values, 114
Coldwell's Misleading Statement, 35
Comintern, 118
    Comintern VI (1928), confrontation track, 119

Responsible Enterprise (1961), 105
Responsible Enterprise, 58–70
Road to Serfdom, The (1944), 21–22, 23, 37
Robbins, Harry, 17, 105
Robbins, John, 97
Roberts, John, 13
Roebuck Arthur, 129
Roman Catholic Church. *See* Catholic Church, vs. CCF
Rose, Fred, 134, 141, 142
Ross, Phillip, 48
Rotary Club (Belleville), 67
Rotary Club (St. Catharines), 65
Rotary Club (Welland), 109–10
Rowe, John A., 101
Royal Bank, 86
Russian Revolution, 118

Salsberg, J.B., 131
Sanderson, M.A., 101–2, 108–9
Saskatchewan auto insurance 1951, 35
Saskatchewan Government Insurance Office, 34
Saskatchewan Industries, 39
Saskatchewan Story, The, 36
Saskatchewan Trade Union Act, 46
Scott, Frank, 77
    attacked in media 1944, 46
    on coalitions, 130
    defending CCF 1944, 42
Second International (1889), 6
Second National Congress Canadian League Against War and Fascism, 103
Second World War. *See* World War II
Shaw, Lloyd, 75
    on CCF and insurance, 25, 28
Shultz, A.G., 23
Siebert, Carl E., 35
Sifton, Clifford, 86
Sifton newspapers, 86
Silverwoods Dairies, 65
Simpson's, 86, 87
Sims, 135
Siren, Paul, 141
Sise committee, 37–38
Sise, Paul, 36–37
Smith, A.E., 122, 125
Smith, Adam, 2
Smith, Stewart, 122, 126, 129
Social Democracy Party of America, 6
Social Gospel movement, 10, 106
Social Planning for Canada, 95
Social Suicide, 50, 84, 86, 108, 140

and *Stand Up and be Counted*, 73
business funding, 86–87
contests, 79, 83
effectiveness, 74–83, 91
Lewis' response, 76
timed for elections, 72
Socialism and the CCF, 122
socialism
    early history, 6
    in U.S., 6–8
    international context, 6–9
    vs. communism, 119. *See also* communism
Socialist Labor Party, 6
Socialist Party of America, 6, 7

Society for Individual Freedom Against State Socialism (1943), 71.
    See also Public Information Association
Sombart, Werner, 6
Sons of England (Orillia), 67
Soverign, Herb, 140
Soviet Comintern, 118
Soviet Union, 136
Spanish Civil War, 120
Spencer, H.E., 125
Spirit of Enterprise, The, 72
Spry, Graham, 125
St. Catharines Standard, 66
St. George's United Men's Club, 65, 66, 109
St. Laurent, Louis, 49
Stalin, 21, 119, 151
    effect on Canadian communists, 134
Stand Up and be Counted (1944), 71–72, 87
Stewart, Alistair Labour Party (Canada), 129
Stewart, D.K., 67–68
Stinson, Lloyd, 43–44
Stockholm Appeal, 149
Sullivan, C.S., 135
Sullivan, Pat, 135
Sun Life, 31–32
Sun Oil Company, 65
Swailes, David, 143
Swailes, Don, 136

Taylor, Kenneth, 45
Telegram. See *Toronto Telegram*
Thatcherism, 8
The Anatomy of a Party: The National CCF 1932–1961, 14
The Good Fight: Political Memoirs, 1909–1958, 14
"The Only Path to Tomorrow", 72
"The Principles of Post-War Progress", 22

ABOUT THE AUTHOR

Into the Hurricane is John Boyko's third book. His first, *Politics: Conflict and Compromise* (Oxford University Press) quickly became the standard politics text in secondary schools across Canada. His second, *Last Steps to Freedom: The Evolution of Canadian Racism* (J. Gordon Shillingford Publishing) examines Canada's racist past and became widely read across the country and is now used by many groups struggling for a non-racist future and is on reading lists at a number of universities.

John is the History and Social Sciences Curriculum leader at Lakefield College School. He has earned a Masters of Arts degree in history, was elected to municipal council, has served on a number of community boards, and lives in the small village of Lakefield, Ontario.